Me All Over

James Kirkup

Me All Over

Memoirs of a Misfit

Peter Owen

London & Chester Springs PA

PETER OWEN PUBLISHERS
73 Kenway Road London SW5 0RE
Peter Owen books are distributed in the USA by
Dufour Editions Inc. Chester Springs PA 19425–0449

First published in Great Britain 1993
© James Kirkup 1993

ISBN 0–7206–0886–4

A catalogue record for this book is available from
the British Library

Printed and made in Great Britain

Contents

Acknowledgements

The author and publisher are grateful to the following authors, agents and publishers for their permission to reprint copyright material:

The selection from *In Defense of Ignorance* by Karl Shapiro is © 1960, 1987 Karl Shapiro, by arrangement with Wieser & Wieser, Inc., 118 East 25th St., New York, NY 10010. All rights reserved.

The extract from 'Night' by Ivan Bunin, from *The Gentleman from San Francisco and Other Stories*, translated by David Richards and Sophie Lund (Angel Books 1984, Penguin Books 1987), is © the Estate of Ivan Bunin and Agence Hoffman, Paris, 1984, 1987, translation © David Richards and Sophie Lund, 1984, 1987. Reproduced by permission of Penguin Books Ltd.

The selection from Robert Byron's *First Russia, Then Tibet* is © 1933 Robert Byron, by arrangement with Peters Fraser Dunlop, 503/4 The Chambers, Chelsea Harbour, London SW10 0XF.

Selections from *My Sister and Myself: the Diaries of J.R. Ackerley* (Francis King, ed., Hutchinson, 1982), and from the letters of Francis King are reproduced by kind permission of Francis King.

Part One
The East Is Extreme

. . . memories are at once not enough and too much

Ivy Compton-Burnett, *A Heritage and Its History*

Prelude
People Like Us

Lady Hoare and Joseph got up early to breakfast with us under the wistaria. The winter aspect of the Legation compound, resembling a Victorian asylum, was now almost hidden by blossom and young leaves. And as we drove away, I remembered with infinite gratitude the kindness I had found in those ugly little houses, and among the English community in general. Such kindness is easy to forget and impossible to repay: it needs a rich man to offer the same degree of hospitality in England as two clean sheets and a bath represent after a journey in Persia. Worse than that, he who writes is apt to repay it with injury, in the form of political indiscretion, which makes life for the residents more difficult than it is already. But this, I must admit, leaves me impenitent, regrettable as it is from the personal point of view. To asperse a sunset in these days is a political indiscretion; and equally so, to praise it, if there happens to be a cement factory in the foreground that ought to be praised instead. Somebody must trespass on the taboos of modern nationalism, in the interests of human reason. Business can't. Diplomacy won't. It has to be people like us.

Robert Byron, *First Russia, Then Tibet* (1933)

Bidding Adieu

And Joy, whose hand is ever at his lips
Bidding adieu . . .

Keats

'Are you a group?'
Greeted thus by the head waiter as with my customary nonchalance I
entered the breakfast-room on the stroke of 6 a.m., I cast my gaze
around the still-empty restaurant in a Swiss hotel, as if to reassure
myself that I was on my own before braving the fellow's inquisitorial
scowl. Had he unconsciously sensed that I am a multiple personality?
Or had he detected in me the presence of that contemporary fluke, the
loner, the solitary traveller now accepted only on sufferance wherever
he strays? More than ever I felt myself to be the Wandering Jew of
modern literature. But I realized just in time that he was asking if I
belonged to the large group of American tourists that had descended
upon the hotel the evening before. I felt hurt at being mistaken for an
American: I thought it was only the Japanese who believed every
foreigner they saw in their land must be from the United States.
So: 'Do I look like a group?' I said, smiling, only to be met with
stony incomprehension, then relegated to a dim corner table near the
door. It was one of those places where you have to help yourself to food
and drink at a groaning buffet table. The coffee, as usual, was not quite
hot enough. But, fortunately, there was no music. I had become weary
of foreign travel – something I should have thought impossible thirty
years ago. But now that almost everyone travels, and usually in vast
gabbling groups, I really prefer to stay at home. I had begun to feel like
Lady Parvula de Panzoust in Ronald Firbank's *Valmouth*, who complained: 'I go about, as other fools, in quest of pleasure, and I usually
find tedium.' I am sure that is the divine Ronald himself speaking.
Reading his brilliant novels, so often set in foreign lands or almost-
recognizable musical comedy kingdoms, one would never imagine him
suffering even a moment's boredom. I hope this book will provide a
similar sensation.

13

The fact is, it is travel itself that has become tiresome. It has become too fast, and too utilitarian, too much of a business. There are no more far-off romantic destinations: the whole world has become one enormous, crowded airport where the services are usually on strike. I used to travel in order to get away from the British, who have terrified me ever since I was a small child feeling absolutely at the mercy of those unpredictable grown-ups. In my youth, what bliss it was just to escape for a few weeks to Paris or Madrid, to Padua (not Venice) and Amsterdam! How the feeling of censorious persecution dropped away as soon as the ferry left port and I could turn my back on those gloomy grey cliffs of Dover! I still occasionally return to Britain for a day or two, just to try to recapture that sensation of instant liberation from prudery and hypocrisy and philistine ignorance as soon as one departs. And it still works. The magic is still there for a fleeting moment, until the crowds of one's fellow human beings impinge rudely upon one's spirits, which fall even lower when one sees the sort of food available in the self-service café.

Then I wish I had a home of my own, instead of spending most of my existence in cheap hotels and borrowed accommodation.

It had not always been so. There was a time, in the funless fifties, when travel meant all the world to me. I drank in strange lands and foreign faces as if I could never be satiated. I especially loved countries whose language I could not understand, where I could be totally alien, an outcast from society, an absolute loner. I have never enjoyed conversation. Not to be able to speak some foreign language absolved me from that wearisome duty. I utterly agreed with Roland Barthes (in *Digressions* – the very title is balm to the over-edited author), when he writes: 'If I had to create a new Robinson Crusoe, I should put him not on a desert island, but in a city of twelve million inhabitants, whose speech and writing he would be totally unable to understand: that, I believe, is the form the modern version of the myth should take.'

Unfortunately, the English language is now almost universally spoken in some form or other. I should have liked to live with some aboriginal jungle tribe of incomprehensible chatterers, were it not for the fact that as a Taurine I require a certain degree of comfort and even luxury in my life.

However, when I was invited, after two disastrous love affairs in Franco's Spain, to live and work in Japan, I thought this would be the ideal solution to my problems. I must again quote that fount of disabused wisdom, Lady Parvula de Panzoust: 'In the Happy East you live untrammelled by the ghouls of insular convention.' I was so sure she was right. Yet how wrong I was! But at the time, anything seemed better than life in dreary Bath, so after some initial hesitation, I accepted the invitation, hoping at the same time to leave myself and my past behind. I left the Old Continent in order, as old-fashioned romantic heroes used to say, 'to forget'.

But one can never escape from oneself, however multiple. I was like that old joke about the multiple personality who 'just wanted to be loved for himselves'. And for a writer, the past is always present: he cannot write without it. As for my broken heart, I resolved never to fall in love again, even with myselves. I knew I was oversexed to an abnormal, obsessional degree, so I decided to live in future for sex alone – for pure, anonymous sex with strangers who could not speak my language. That was before I had discovered Japanese English, for which I invented the word 'Janglish' (analogous with *franglais*). 'There were rumours, to be sure, he was above love,' writes Firbank, again in *Valmouth*. I intended to encourage such rumours about myself, and learnt by heart the hilariously bathetic lines 'by a Court Poet' from another of my favourite novels by Firbank, *The Artificial Princess*:

> I am disgusted with Love,
> I find it exceedingly disappointing.
> Mine is a Nature that craves for more
>   elusive things,
> Banal passions fail to stir me.
> I am disgusted with Love.

There's many a wise word spoken in jest, and again I think Firbank was hiding his own sad failures in human relationships. Certainly the lines applied to me. 'Mine is a Nature that craves for more elusive things. . . .' In the mysterious East, perhaps, I might find them.

But before I begin to reveal all, I think I should complete that Keats quotation from his 'Ode on Melancholy', lest it should be thought I approach life with too frivolous an attitude:

> . . . and aching Pleasure nigh,
> Turning to poison while the bee-mouth sips:
> Ay, in the very temple of Delight
> Veil'd Melancholy has her sovran shrine,
> Though seen of none save him whose strenuous tongue
> Can burst Joy's grape against his palate fine. . . .

Persona Very Non Grata

Advance Epitaph

To a bright prison, proud,
  Alone, without a name,
Tongueless, wild and ignorant
  Unwillingly I came.

In a dark prison, blind,
  Lustful, ill, afraid,
Careless and improvident
  Unwillingly I strayed.

From this black prison – small,
  Selfish, mad, impenitent,
Vain, and knowing nothing more,
  Willingly I went.

James Kirkup

Towards the end of 1958, after my separation from Dana in Bath, I was destitute, bankrupt spiritually, emotionally and financially. In order to make a little money, I had accepted the offer of Barley Alison at Weidenfeld's to start translating Simone de Beauvoir's interminable, terribly tedious and humourless autobiographies. I worked ten hours a day on the first, *Mémoires d'une jeune fille rangée*, trying to forget Dana and to make Madame B. presentable in English.

It was a thankless task. Her prose was so clotted and confused, so riddled with repetitions. Later, when I read her *Journal 1939–1941* and the letters she wrote to Sartre between 1930 and 1963, I realized that she was constantly repeating certain words like *plaisant* (also a favourite word in her first novel, *L'invitée*), *petit* and *fameux*. Her judgements of her contemporaries like Leiris, Cuny and Salacrou were spiteful and reeked of envy. Most memorably, she described the 'faecal odour' of the girls with whom she had sex. She never cracked a joke in her life, which is no doubt why she said I had missed all her 'wit' in my translation.

This particular odour was the first thing I noticed about *her* when I went to see her and Sartre in Paris. I had been in despair over this translation, and I couldn't think of a good title, so Barley gave me some cash to make a flying visit to Paris, where I confronted them in the Café de Flore. Madame was wearing one of her tight Stakhanovite turbans, worn to conceal her large ears – a wartime fashion that recalled images of 'Music while You Work.' She mentions all her new turbans in her wartime letters to Sartre. They made her look like a concierge. I think she also used the turbans to tighten the skin round her baggy eyes, pulling the corners up to give her a fake oriental look. She was like a shrill-voiced old Chinese laundrywoman, sitting with her mythomaniac frog prince Sartre on *lour coin* of the banquettes, drinking cheap red wine and eyeing the cakes under their glass dome. At first she seemed to like me. Then I made the mistake of asking her about her wartime activities, when I knew she had worked for the Nazi-controlled French radio. She was later an apologist for Stalin.* She compressed her roughly rouged lips. I was dismissed. And I was relieved of the painful task of translating her subsequent volumes. Galantière found my title: *Memoirs of a Dutiful Daughter*.

All that summer and autumn of 1958, my tears kept flowing. I wept so much, day after day, that the skin round my eyes became sore with wiping. I went to see my old friends Fred and Muriel in Castle Bolton, and Fred's earthiness and common sense helped me a lot. But it was Muriel who really understood the depths of my sadness. Sonia had told her of my appearance at the Royal College of Art accompanied by Joe and Dana, whom she had described as 'another James Dean'. Emotionally disturbed herself, Muriel could enter into my feelings as no other person could. For all the years of our loving friendship, I had accepted her just as she was, as I had accepted Dana. I did not, as most people did, tell her to 'snap out of it', or say that she should do some charitable work that 'will take you out of yourself'. It was the attitude I had adopted with my other disturbed woman friends, Veronica and Joe's catatonic sister Nancy West. They all sensed that they had something in common with me, and that was never more clear to Muriel and Nancy than in those long, dark months of emotional and mental agony.

My mother, of course, did more than sense my mental disarray: she

* For the wartime activities and self-promotion of Sartre and Beauvoir, see Gilbert Joseph, *Une si douce occupation* (Paris: Albin Michel, 1991).

knew I was ill, having what she later described as 'a nervous break-down'. But it was more than that, whatever that vague expression means: it was a complete collapse of self-confidence and self-respect, a perpetual confusion of the actual and the imaginary in which the only growing thing was my hatred of Dana and all he had done to me. I tried to overcome this hatred and get the anger out of my heart by writing poems that now shock me with their evil bitterness and vengeful tone – the poems in the last section of *The Prodigal Son* (1959). Yet I still believe that they are good poems: the quality of a work of art does not depend upon its subject-matter, but on the perfection of its means. I am shocked by those poems but not ashamed of them. And writing them helped to save my sanity.

I visited Joe and Nancy in London, and once or twice they came to Bath. Joe brought up again the question of my going to teach in Japan. When Spender had asked him to suggest a poet who might do so, Joe had loyally given my name above all others. So we went to lunch with Stephen Spender, who was as always his usual supercilious self, address-ing me with smug condescension, and acting as if he thought he was doing me the most wonderful favour in even deigning to see me with Joe. 'Such a pity you never appeared in *Encounter*' was one of the things he said, knowing full well that I had often sent him poems and articles, which he had rejected with the constant refrain: 'These I liked very much but alas we are full up with poetry, in fact overstocked until next year. . . .' He said almost the same thing on all his rejection slips, which I kept, intending to paper the lavatory with them. Cyril Connolly, who was also present at that lunch at the Criterion, was even more odiously smug and patronizing and had obviously invited himself out of idle curiosity to see what this poet creature might be like, whose poems and short stories he had rejected with so many insincere excuses – 'We don't have the space for longer poems' or 'You should try the Americans who have more paper than we do for this sort of extended thing.' Connolly reminded me of a cat that has been at the cream, brimming with self-importance and self-satisfaction, or like a bilious minor Buddhist figure, or a toad all paunch and panting petulancy, with sinisterly tiny hands, tiny feet.

Joe sat almost silently between Stephen and Cyril, facing me. He had the familiar look of baffled amusement on his face, as if he were trying to stop giggling. That ruefully twitching mouth and the heaving shoulders when something struck him as funny or he laughed at his own jokes are the things I remember best about that meeting. I was never so grateful as I was then to Joe for his friendship, because the occasional glances we discreetly exchanged comforted me with their complicity while Connolly burbled on mandarinly 'civilized' and Spender made what he obviously considered spitefully witty remarks, looking sideways at us for approving reactions and conspiratorial titters that never came. They were a right pair, as my father would have said, with their testy flippancy and mediocre chatter about who was sleeping with whom in London's dismally self-conscious and maliciously envious literary circles. They acted as if the whole world revolved around their dilettantish scribblings, like the sixth-form editors of a school magazine with their ears to the ground for a breakthrough into desiccated Bloomsbury or the pathetic Angry Young Men circles of cultural cronies. I was bored by their insularity and priggish provinciality: thinking themselves at the centre of excited comment, they were merely bourgeois drudges exchanging tips on who was paying how much for jumpy and banal diary extracts. It was in order to get out of this stultifying atmosphere of literary back-biting and jealous cliquishness that I finally decided to accept the post in Japan.

But it took an awfully long time to arrange matters. The Dean of the Faculty of Arts at Tohoku University, my official sponsor, had to obtain the approval of the Japanese Ministry of Education, known by the curiously cuddlesome, teddy-bearish name of Mombusho – an institution, I was later to discover, with a heart of flint. I had a kind letter from the Dean, dear Professor Atsuo Kobayashi, written in flawless English and in the elegant italic script with I believe had been introduced to Japan by Edmund Blunden. The Dean assured me of a hearty welcome in Sendai, and asked me to send all kinds of tiresome documents like my curriculum vitae, my degree certificate (which I had either lost or thrown out with the rubbish) and my birth certificate (which I falsified to take off my age the six years I had spent so uselessly in labour camps during the Second World War). Then he asked for some recent photographs and copies of all my published works, which cost a fortune to send air mail to Japan. Then there were requests for medical certificates and copies in quadruplicate of at least six references 'from persons of good character and academic distinction'. Who on earth could I ask for that kind of thing? Joe very kindly wrote a lengthy eulogy, and approached Morgan Forster, who said he would be delighted to recommend me, but I refused the offer, very foolishly, from a sense of honour, feeling he did not know me well enough. I would give anything now to have a recommendation from Morgan. I wrote to Professor Girdlestone (Girdle Scone) at

Newcastle, but he did not bother to answer my umpteenth request for a reference (he was probably gaga by then). I would have written to my German professor, Dr Duncan Mennie, but he had left Newcastle and I did not know where he was: he was one of the few people in that dump of academe who tried to help me.

All these delays began to seem suspicious to me. I soon found out why: the British Council were trying to block my appointment in favour of one of their own lickspittles. They even had the nerve to call me to their offices in London to 'vet' me, when in fact it was no business of theirs at all, as I had received a private invitation to teach in Japan. I spent a day in Davies Street undergoing a third-degree inquisition from a starchy bureaucrat who had switched on a tape-recorder hidden under his desk. I later wrote a full account of these humiliations in the chapter for a book commissioned in 1966 by a Japanese publisher, Eichosha of Tokyo, entitled *Sinking Old Empire, Britain*, which was also issued in a Japanese translation by Professor Fumiko Miura of Keio University, as *Shizumiyuku Rotaikoku** and became a best-seller – in fact it is still selling. Here is that chapter, entitled 'The James Kirkup Dossier', or 'Facts on Why I Am *Persona Non Grata* to the British Council':

Two recent events, small but significant, have prompted me, after years of thought and indecision, to set down my experiences with the British Council under the above heading.

A few years ago, one of my students in my seminar class for graduation theses at Japan Women's University came to me and asked me to do her a favour. I am always ready to help my students and colleagues, so I asked her what it was. She wished to join the British Council Library so that she could read books to help her in her scholarly studies of the Metaphysical Poets. Regretfully, I had to tell her that I could not put my signature to the British Council Library Membership Application Form which she had filled in and brought for me to sign as a guarantor.

'But why can't you sign it, *sensei*?' she asked in surprise.

(I should add here that the word *sensei* in Japanese is a title of deep respect for a beloved teacher, one much more significant than our meaningless 'professor' or paltry and disrespectful 'prof.'. I am proud to have the title of *sensei*, and have never cared tuppence about being

---

* In later editions, Eichosha was compelled to cut this chapter by the then representative of the British Council in Tokyo, an academic booby and total nonentity called Eric Walter Frederick Tomlin, CBE (1913–88).

called 'professor'.)

'Because I am *persona non grata* to the British Council,' I answered gravely.

'What on earth does *persona non grata* mean?' she gasped, a look of uncomprehending horror on her pretty face.

'It means,' I sighed, 'that I am not welcome in Japan, or indeed in any other foreign country, by the representative and staff of the British Council. They consider me to be an undesirable person – "not one of us", as the British say.'

'*You* – an undesirable person?' she said, laughing incredulously.

'In the eyes of the British Council, yes, I'm afraid so,' I replied. Therefore I am not allowed to enter British Council premises, and I am not permitted to use the British Council Library. Indeed, all my books have been removed from the shelves of British Council Libraries all over the world, under strict orders from Headquarters.'

'But you are a poet, and a writer, and a *sensei*! It seems to me very wrong that you should not be allowed to use the library, and that your books should be taken from the shelves and not made available to foreign readers who are passionately interested in your work.'

'I don't mind,' I assured her. 'Lots of other libraries stock my works, and in any case the British Council Libraries in Tokyo and Kyoto cannot be called adequate. They have only a small and badly chosen selection of books and boring out-of-date British periodicals, and it is very difficult to obtain membership, which requires a high fee. It would be much better for you to go to the splendid new American Cultural Center in Akasaka Mitsuke. There you will find a large and excellent selection of books, all the latest periodicals, and a kind welcome as well as sound advice from the highly qualified staff.'

Just recently there was a well-attended farewell party for a highly respected and deeply loved member of the teaching staff on her retirement. In replying to the congratulatory speech I made in her honour, this courageous lady spoke out boldly and spiritedly in my defence, attacking the absurdity of the British Council's attitude towards me, even though there was a representative of the Council sitting right next to her at the head table. She made particular reference to the fact that I was on the British Council 'black list' – a list which, I can assure my readers, contains the names of many distinguished British writers and teachers. Apparently she had been warned, when engaging me as a teacher in 1963, that the British Council would have nothing to do with me, giving as their excuse

that I am a 'bad teacher'. After three years' experience of my character, ability and teaching methods, she was in the best position to say
whether I was a good teacher or not, and she felt compelled to say
that I was indeed a wonderful teacher – indeed, the best foreign
teacher in Japan, and that Japan Women's University, one of the
most prestigious in the land, was lucky to have me.

Now on this occasion much amusement and laughter greeted her
reference to the 'black list' – a sinister Stalinist document which also,
by the way, includes the names of many Japanese teachers and
writers. But there were some people who were puzzled as to why I
should be called a 'bad teacher', a comment which is, after all, a libel
on my professional character. It then became clear to me that the
Japanese people, unlike the people of other foreign countries, live in
ignorance of the true nature of the British Council and their so-called
'cultural' activities. Therefore I feel it is my duty to speak out freely
and relate frankly the knowledge I have acquired of this deeply
reactionary institution through my contacts with the British Council
and their staff.

I first applied for a teaching post abroad through the British Council
round about 1947, after spending the war years as a conscientious
objector in various labour camps – an honourable fact that was always
held against me by the British. The post I applied for was one as teacher
at a school in Egypt. I sent my application forms in, and was invited to
an interview, where I sensed at once definite hostility towards me. All I
remember of that interview is some woman asking me, right out of the
blue: 'What do you think is the purpose of education?' This was
obviously a question meant to disconcert and baffle me, but with my
aplomb and fluency I was able to give her an answer, off the cuff, that
surprised me by its astuteness and perception. Even the woman inter-
viewer admitted that I had given her an extremely good answer. I had
said something to the effect that the duty of a good teacher is not just to
teach the bare outlines of his own subject, but in teaching that subject
to teach also about life and humanity and the purpose, if any, of our
existence here on earth. That is, he must arouse interest in his subject by
relating it to life and death, to the level of experience of his pupils, to
their human hopes and dreams in general. Only thus can a subject
become real and living for a student, through the realization of human
contact with the teacher, and with the rest of humanity, through the
sincere and imaginative teaching of that subject.

However, I did not get the job. I was probably considered an undesirable because of my pacifist record and because of my bisexual nature. Realizing that it was hopeless for me, as a social outcast, to expect any kind of appointment from a body hostile to me from the outset, however good my qualifications and ability, I decided never again to apply for a post through the British Council, and I have never done so.

About ten years later, in 1956, after spending three fairly happy and successful years as Visiting Poet at the Bath Academy of Art, where all my classes were given the highest mark, 'A', in a very rigorous inspection of the Academy's teaching facilities and staff by inspectors of the Ministry of Education, I decided I wanted a change. I was bored by Britain, and afraid of its police repression of homosexuals, and wanted to go abroad. I saw an advertisement (not inserted by the British Council) for a post as Travelling Lecturer for the Swedish Ministry of Education, applied for it, and obtained it without difficulty. The British Council, urged by the British government to cut down their expenses, had just closed their offices in Stockholm, but the library remained, headed by an ex-member of the British Council staff, who had some reputation as a clown in his teaching of English on Swedish television. Around this time the British Council were closing down offices in many countries because of the endless criticism about the way they squandered taxpayers' money abroad: these criticisms were voiced in the press and by prominent members of British political and cultural life. The same criticisms have been expressed more recently by the Conservative government of Thatcher the Job Snatcher.

Though the British Council had closed down in Stockholm, I met the same hostility and lack of help I had experienced in my first interview from those sacked Britishers left behind in Sweden. I was given no books, no periodicals or newspapers, and absolutely no information in the course of my year travelling around Swedish schools and colleges. Nevertheless, as the Swedish Ministry of Education admitted, I was a great success as a teacher, and I was given a pressing invitation by the head of the Ministry to stay on and teach for another year.

However, I had grown tired of Sweden, and disappointed by the callousness of the treatment I received at the hands of the British officials there. It was at that stage that I began to realize why they disliked me: I was an intruder into the sacred circle of British Council professional culture-mongers. Rivalry and competition for promotion and 'perks' are unbelievably intense in the Council's serried ranks. The professionals were all very concerned about my appearance on the scene, because they were afraid I would prevent their obtaining quick promotion. Any outsider is treated in this way, and this I believe is one of the reasons why the British Council reject many highly gifted writers and teachers, simply because these intruders might disrupt the hierarchy of advancement within the Council. Therefore, in making appointments abroad, the Council is very careful to select, not the best teachers, but mediocre ones who can be trusted not to jump the queue in the long march of official promotions. So brilliance and ability and imagination are at a discount. That is why the Council made it a new policy to appoint only officially accredited teachers, however uninspiring (and mostly language teachers), to Japan, instead of outstanding writers and poets like Hodgson, Blunden, Empson, Nichols, Quennell and Enright – all brilliant but unpredictable, 'unsafe' people of intelligence and imagination who have left their mark unforgettably on Japanese life and culture, and on the history of English teaching in Japan.

Stephen Spender visited Japan in 1958, and while he was in Sendai Professor Atsuo Kobayashi asked him to find some writer or poet in England who would be willing to spend at least two years in Sendai teaching English literature. The Japanese quite rightly believed that the best people to teach literature were those who practised it. Spender promised to find someone. But he could find no one courageous enough to abandon the academic and literary fleshpots of perfidious Albion for the unknown and low-paid remoteness of Sendai. In England in those post-war days, to be sent to Japan was equivalent to banishment to the salt-mines of Siberia.

Through Joe Ackerley and Morgan Forster, Spender dropped me a note asking if I would like to teach in Japan. I had already been invited to teach at Massachusetts Institute of Technology – a post I was eventually prevented from obtaining through the machinations of C.P. Snow. Nevertheless I felt that the proposal for me to go to Japan was a rare opportunity I should not miss. (One can always go to America.) My acceptance of Spender's offer was to be the beginning of a long and passionate love-hate affair with Japan.

My flight with BOAC was booked, and I was happily packing a few panties – I always travel light – when I suddenly received an urgent summons from the British Council in London. I was commanded to make my way to Davies Street and be interviewed by the Director of Recruitment.

I wondered what right the British Council had to interfere with my plans. It savoured horribly of our dread Secret Services, which find foreign embassies and official cultural organizations abroad convenient covers for spies and informers and all the skulduggery of industrial espionage.*

Nevertheless I obediently departed for my interview, and I shall never forget that harrowing experience. First of all, I was conducted by uniformed guards into a sort of reading-room where a number of foreign students, some of them Japanese, were crouched in terrified silence, religiously reading Anglo-Saxon primers or painstakingly copying, with trembling hands, page after page of *The Cambridge History of English Literature*, something they could have done equally well, and with less oppressiveness, at home in Japan or wherever they came from.

I was made to wait a long time. Then a pert, youngish female secretary came to me with a form and asked me to fill in my expenses. Now I knew perfectly well that I should be allowed only a second-class fare, and I had in fact travelled second class from Bath to London, as I always did in those days. But just to show my independence and my contempt for bureaucracy I put down the first-class return rail fare. I was also hoping to get something for nothing out of the notoriously skinflint organization. The pert female came back and told me, grinning widely, that I was allowed only second-class rail expenses. 'Poets should not travel first class,' she reprovingly informed me. I pitied her for her primness, bigotry and very plain face, but made no reply. I thought it better to let her have her little triumph.

Then, after another long wait, during which the uniformed guards at the door kept looking in on me, under the female secretary's instructions, to see that I was not damaging Council property, I was conducted to the Holy of Holies, the inner sanctum of the Director of Recruitment. I could see at once that he was the most dreadful militaristic bureaucrat. The first words he snapped at me were: 'Why do you give your year of birth as 1923 in *Who's Who*? We have here your previous application for a post in Cairo in 1947, and on it you give

* Those wishing to obtain more precise information on this fascinating subject are strongly recommended to read Margret Boveri's excellent work, *Treason in the Twentieth Century* (London: Macdonald, 1961). Originally published as *Der Verrat im XX Jahrhundert* (Hamburg: Rowohlt Taschenbuch Verlag, 1956), it also discusses the persecution of brilliant men like Ezra Pound, William Joyce, Knut Hamsun and Quisling.

your date of birth as 1918!' His voice was sharp and bad-tempered, but I refused to be drawn. What a stupid way to talk, I thought, and what a stupid question with which to start an interview! I am free to give the public whatever age I like: in some reference books I give my year of birth as 1900, in others 1927, and so on, as fancy takes me. I like to baffle literary historians and the dreary bureaucrats of our Welfare State. I am not beholden to tell the exact truth on those forms *Who's Who* and other publications keep sending me, so in exchange for the waste of time spent filling them up every year, I allow myself a few fantasies. (Actually, I bother to do it only because, for a person who is constantly on the move, such entries are invaluable.) But to the careerist culture-mongers of the British Council, such uses of the imagination are incomprehensible. I consider myself ageless, beyond mere time.

It soon became obvious to me that the Director of Recruitment was firmly determined not to allow me to go to Japan. I could see that the British Council, which D.J. Enright in *Figures of Speech* (1965), a most amusing work, contemptuously refers to as 'a cultural and educational agency', a sort of governmental Gabbitas-Thring, was trying to force me to reject the kind invitation I had received from Japan. I think that here I should point out to the innocent Japanese that the Council like to keep their claws on all appointments abroad. I would advise any Japanese university or organization desiring to acquire a teacher with literary ability from England to bypass the Council and to make their choice directly from England through personal recommendations. The Council, however, often bribe their way into Japanese and other foreign institutions by boosting salaries and hinting at the possibility of study years abroad for professors who bend themselves to their wishes.

To support this point, allow me to quote from a letter I received from a colleague of mine at the University of Malaysia in Kuala Lumpur. The writer is a distinguished British historian and authority on classical Chinese literature who had asked me to write a recommendation for him in his application for an appointment to the University of Hong Kong. I wrote back to him saying that I should be delighted to do so, but that if he was making his application through the British Council, it was useless to have a recommendation from me, as I was *persona non grata* with that body, and that indeed a recommendation from me would disqualify him for the post. He sent me the following reply. As will be readily understood, I have had to suppress the writer's name in order to shield him from reprisals:

My Dear Kirkup,

It was heartening to find that my efforts at coping with Chinese verse were so appreciated. Praise from a critic of your discernment is praise indeed. I was furious to hear how brutally the British Council has been treating you. Loathsome organization! I well remember that when I was desperately hunting for a job out East, two years ago, as a penniless graduate student, they turned me down for post after post, on the flimsiest of pretexts. This in spite of the fact that I was almost invariably the only candidate for the post with any knowledge at all of the language of the country in question, as well as a double-first in English. I learnt afterwards that I was not considered conformist enough

What is really distressing is the way their power has increased over the last ten years. At one time many universities abroad did their own recruiting; now the Council handles 90 per cent of these posts. Their advertisements are badly phrased and misleading: their insistence on London interviews means that no overseas candidate can hope to get a job: their application forms are an insult to the intelligence. To me they personify everything that is wrong with England today, a microcosm of the Establishment in all its senility.

I think you have done a public service in thus exposing them. I think you showed great courage in attacking them, though, for they are vicious and unscrupulous. . . .

Well, there I was at the British Council's new Court of the Inquisition at the heart of 'liberal', 'democratic' England, which once prided itself on 'fair play' and 'equal chances for all'. As Orwell so rightly said: ' . . . some are more equal than others'. But what on earth was I to do? How could I get round the sinister Director of Recruitment's stubborn refusal to let me depart for Japan? A flash of inspiration came to me, for after all I am a poet: such illuminations always come to me in my most difficult moments. So I said calmly to the Director of Recruitment, mastering my terror of his militaristic title: 'But I have already dispatched all my books, clothes and furniture to Sendai. My mother is already on her way there by ship.'

This was, of course, an unblinking lie, for I went to Japan with only a small bundle and the clothes I stood up in, while my mother, being aged and blind, was in any case unable to travel. But the Director of Recruitment was not to know that. So it was a good lie, for it turned the scales in my favour and I went to Japan without let or hindrance by the British Council, though without their special allowance for teachers abroad.

Before I left the offices in Davies Street, I was invited to meet a number of people who had been stationed at some time or other with the Council in Japan, and a dreary lot they were. They included one pop-eyed woman who could think of nothing better to say than: 'But how, Mr Kirkup, will you be able to mark all those *thousands* of examination papers? Do you really think you are qualified to do such important work?'

To this I simply replied with the gesture of brushing away a fly, and her jaw, which was of considerable size, dropped in shock and indignation. How to mark papers indeed! If I had my way, all exams would be abolished, and in Japan I managed more or less to do that, as I learnt to judge my students by their performances in class, not by some artificially devised and useless 'test'.

Then one of the British Council men told me a lot of childish scandal about foreign teachers in Japan, and in particular about the goings-on of my late predecessor, Burton Martin, an American dilettante (the most charitable way to describe that doyen of Japanese body-building) at Tohoku University, matters that had not an atom of interest for me. Another 'expert on Japan' told me: 'Of course, these Japanese are very, stuck-up. They'll never invite you into their homes.' I felt secretly rather relieved by that information, as I do not enjoy empty socializing and idle chat, but in fact I was to be invited into some Japanese homes, and enjoyed the experience, which is indeed a rather rare one for both Japanese and foreigners.

Another expert told me: 'And they'll be pestering you for English conversation practice, free of charge, at every hour of the day. They have no respect for the free time of others. They'll work you till you drop dead.' All that was rubbish, as I soon found out: I was able to keep my distance and my privacy at all times, for the Japanese are sensitive about intruding on others. And I had some interesting conversations with these English language fanatics, as well as some dismally boring ones that they conducted with great cheerfulness and with an aimlessness I found very relaxing after a hard day's intellectual labour.

Looking back now on that sinister interview, with my present knowledge of Japan and the Japanese, I realize that none of those 'experts on Japan' knew the first thing about real Japanese life and real Japanese people. They were talking about non-existent stereotypes. They certainly had no understanding of the true heart of the Japanese, and seemed as if they had no wish to understand it. The tedious 'thrillers' of a certain James Melville, a former British Council hit man, with their gross errors of fact and ignorance of Japanese body language and psychology, are typical products of British Council mentality. His Japanese detective and wife are all too British, their Agatha Christie relationship totally unreal in its English cosiness, and a source of great amusement to the Japanese who can read the dull style in which the heavy-handed plots are written. And like most British Council top bananas, Melville kowtows to anyone with a title, especially a Japanese imperial one, for in Japan, British snobbery knows no limits. And anyone who could praise the pretentious maunderings and fake intellectuality of modern Japanese non-novelists like Haruki Murakami and Yuko Tsushima, as Melville once did in *The Times Literary Supplement* (not to mention encomiums on the bland *japonaiserie* pastiches of dry-as-dust dead novelists by Kazuo Ishiguro) has no literary judgement whatsoever. He is on the same intellectual level as his incompetent Superintendent Otani of the Hyogo prefectural police. A thickhead.

I am known to only a handful of people – personally, I mean. Perhaps that is why I am 'caviare to the general'. My few friends, trying to defend me against official slanderers, ask them: 'Have you ever *met* him?' To which they are forced to answer 'No, but. . . .' It is the 'but' that betrays their infamy, and their lack of honest scholarship – to base a judgement upon hearsay from those who have heard it from someone else et cetera et cetera.

Even upon ocean-going liners and cargo boats, places chosen by dramatists and novelists at a loss for what to write about next, so that they can assemble the usual predictable bunch of characters, I never made friends with anyone. On Atlantic liners to New York I used to scan the passenger lists to see if there was anyone famous and therefore to be avoided: Alexander Trocchi and Rex Warner were among those I spotted; and though Trocchi made advances, I would have nothing to do with him – like the rest of the Beats, a bit of a fake. Frederick Ashton was the only one I ever spoke to, and it was he who made the first advance as he was returning from a somewhat unsuccessful season in New York with the Royal Ballet, where his new jazz ballet had been condemned – the Americans believe only they can handle jazz dance. At his request, I sent him my Noh play, *Cloak of Feathers*, as vehicle for the ageing Fonteyn, but nothing came of it.

There was another, more personal problem. In those days, travellers to Japan were required to have a valid smallpox vaccination certificate, and they had to carry a booklet registering those vaccinations they had received, as well as a whole slew of injections against cholera, yellow fever, tetanus – what doctors called a cocktail of immunizations against every kind of eventuality. My problem was that I had never been vaccinated against smallpox.

The reason for this was that my father, an ardent admirer of George Bernard Shaw, agreed with Shaw's progressive views on vaccination, saying that to inject disease into the body was a defilement of the spirit as well as of the body. Therefore, when I was about eight years old, and a law was passed by the British Government requiring all schoolchildren to be vaccinated against smallpox, my father adamantly refused to allow me to be immunized in this way. He was breaking the law, and this distressed both him and my mother; but he was determined that no evil germs should be artificially introduced into his son's body. Were we not known as 'The Holy Family' of Ada Street? Though my father had no strong religious convictions, he had a deep feeling for religion which he instilled into me as a kind of personal moral code, more Ancient Greek than Christian. So though we were in a sense pagans, we had what Schweitzer called 'reverence for life'. It was because of this reverence that my father refused to allow me to be vaccinated. Of course, at that age I did not properly understand what he meant, and indeed I pleaded with him to let me be vaccinated like all the other boys, because after vaccination they were given a bright-red ribbon to tie round their vaccinated arms, and I longed with all my heart to wear such a gorgeous badge. But my father kept me hidden at home all through the schools' vaccination period: we expected to be arrested by the police for breaking the law. It was an exciting time for me, watching from behind our front-room window curtains for a bobby coming to put us all in gaol; but in fact, nothing happened.

I went back to school carrying the excuse that I had had a severe cold. My father had won the day, and his principles were vindicated later when several children fell ill after the vaccinations. I believe there were some deaths. My father made me give a solemn promise that I would never allow myself to be vaccinated. I was impressed by the solemnity of the occasion, and never forgot that promise. My father had written a letter about it all to George Bernard Shaw, and to our immense surprise and pride, Shaw wrote back – *not* on a postcard, his usual means of postal communication, but in a sealed letter to preserve our secret – praising the stand my father had taken, along with quite a large number of other parents. Unfortunately, that precious letter was lost in the

Blitz: I carried it everywhere with me. One of my arguments when I was fighting with my father against conscription was that if I joined up I should have to be vaccinated. But by then, so strong was his desire to avoid the embarrassment of having a pacifist son, he was willing to break the pact we had made when I was a boy to refuse such defilement of the spirit. But I had made that solemn promise: I was not going to break it just for his convenience, or for the glory of serving King and Country.

So now, at the age of forty, if I wanted to go to Japan, I had to break that solemn vow and allow myself to be impregnated by disease. It was a hard decision to make, but in the end I persuaded my mother and myself that it was the only thing to do. I went to the doctor's at the bottom of Avondale Buildings. He warned me that at my age the after-effects of first and second vaccinations could be very distressing, especially when I also had to have injections against all those other tropical diseases. However, I submitted to the needle, the vaccinations being done with a three-week interval to allow the first to 'take'. It took all right. I developed a high fever and was in agony for weeks afterwards. I regarded all that pain and discomfort as a punishment for breaking my promise to my dead father.

Just before I left for Japan, I gave a poetry reading at the ICA in London, running a high fever and streaming with sweat. Those symptoms, with later bouts of malaria, contracted in Malaysia and Borneo, continue to discomfort me to this day. Was Japan worth all that physical and spiritual agony? I often wonder.

The last straw was when I could not get a visa for Japan in time for the flight that Professor Kobayashi had so kindly arranged for me. He made a useless journey from Sendai to Haneda Airport in Tokyo in order to meet the plane on which he expected me to arrive, only to find I was not on it: the British Council in Tokyo had not thought to inform him! It was obvious that the Council had again stepped in with their heavy authoritarian boots and were using their familiar disruptive and delaying tactics. I had to cancel my original flight. However, the Japanese Embassy in London (which has always treated me with the utmost courtesy and consideration) was not to be intimidated by the British Council. I had my official invitation to Japan sponsored by the Ministry of Education in Tokyo. I was entitled to a visa for three years, and eventually I got it. I finished off Madame Beauvoir the night before I left, and posted it to Barley with a shudder.

✳

Stephen Spender described his experiences in Sendai to me. After giving his lecture, he was taken out to dinner by the entire faculty, and enjoyed it very much. In particular he praised Professor Kobayashi, who was a perfect gentleman, speaking excellent English: he had studied Anglo-Saxon at Oxford. But unlike most Japanese professors of foreign languages, he could actually *speak* English as well as read it. I was soon to find out what a rare thing this is in Japan. There had never been any love lost between Spender and me, but I will say this for him — he was very frank about what he had seen in Sendai. My predecessor, Burton Martin (who a few years ago was discovered dead of a heart attack in the toilet of a Korean Airlines plane), invited Spender to dinner, which he prepared with the help of his Japanese friend, who lived with him at the house in Kozenji-dori that I was to occupy. Spender gave a malicious account of that awful meal, consisting mainly of half-cooked spaghetti and beer, and I shuddered at the thought of what I had missed.

Burton Martin and his friend regaled Spender with all the scandal about the English Department, which consisted of two rival factions, each fighting for domination. It was Professor Kobayashi's faction that had ousted Burton Martin with great difficulty from the post he had held since he was a GI, just after the war, when simply anyone who could speak English was welcomed by war-torn university faculties. I believe he had no academic qualifications at all, and he used to write weekly columns in execrable English style for *The Mainichi Daily News*, a paper not noted then for its high intellectual standards. Spender gave me a rather confused account of all the in-fighting going on in the department, and I could see already that I was going to have a difficult time with the representatives of the rival faction under Professor Muraoka, whom I discovered to be a most distinguished scholar of English literature. But I intended to ignore all these petty quarrels as much as possible: it was none of my business, so let them get on with it. I would do my job as best I could, and if they did not like it they could lump it.

The house, Spender assured me, had a garden, and was quite spacious by Japanese standards, with two floors of Japanese-style and Western-style rooms, and a large kitchen. Of course Spender never had to stay there, so his account was lacking in many of the details I longed to know. I had been reading books about Japan, and I was wondering if the house had a traditional Japanese toilet, such as is described by Tanizaki in his book of essays, *In Praise of Shadows*, and which I longed to experience. I had found a Spanish version, *En Elabanza de las sombras* in the literary magazine *Sur*. The more sordid aspects of the Japanese toilet were revealed in old travel books, describing how the night soil was removed by untouchables carrying big wooden buckets and scattered in the fields. Or in more modern times, it was pumped out by a 'honey-cart' on infrequent visits. It would be just like my childhood in South Shields and our outdoor netty, which was not replaced by a flush until the mid-thirties. Spender could give me no information about that sort of thing. But he did tell me something interesting: with a roguish and knowing smile, he confided: 'And the boys are willing and very nice.' I gave him *such a look* (my Picasso-like *mirada fuerte*), as reproving as my gentle features could make it. 'Really?' I replied in my best Lady Bracknell tone. 'Oh, yes,' he babbled on, 'they'll do anything for a little English conversation.'

I had no intention of acting as a 'sleeping dictionary' for ardent English scholars, as I do not like to lose my beauty sleep, always badly needed. Besides, I wondered what he meant by 'boys', If he meant schoolboys, that was of no interest at all to me: I always preferred robust, mature men. But just how robust were the Japanese? I was soon to find out.

First, I had to say goodbye to Britain. There could be no better way, I thought, than spending my last evening at the Turkish baths in the Harrow Road, before embarking next day on the long flight to Tokyo. Once more, I enjoyed the sense of danger: before ducking into the baths' modest entrance, I cast a brief glance up and down the road to see if I had been followed. All seemed to be clear.

After my bath came the ritual massage by a pale, skinny, elderly ex-Navy masseur. We were always naked for the massage by this man, whom I often suspected of being a police informer. Once, when his ministrations induced the beginnings of an involuntary erection, he slapped a wet towel over my midriff to cover this adventitious hard-on.

My left arm was still sore and inflamed from the vaccinations and inoculations, so I told him: 'Steady on, Tom – mind my arm', pointing to the band-aid.

'Gettin' posted overseas, are yer?' he said, hoping for a bigger tip. 'Shakin' the dust of the Old Country off yer feet? And not afore time, I should say, eh?'

I gave him a bigger, farewell tip, vowing never to return to that frightening police trap. And I never did.

Oriental Heresies

'Can you always tell whether a stranger is your friend?'
'Yes.'
'Then you are an Oriental.'

E.M. Forster, *A Passage to India*

The Japanese, who have a sense of beauty, have no sense of ugliness.

James Kirkup, *These Horned Islands: A Journal of Japan*

His oriental heresies
Exhilarate the bee
And filling all the earth and air
With gay apostasy. . . .

Recounting nectars he has known
And attars that have failed
And, honeys, if his life be spared
He hungers to attain.

Emily Dickinson

I have been set apart from many of my fellows. And although, all my life, I have been agonizingly aware of the weakness and inadequacy of all my faculties, I, in comparison with some, am truly no ordinary man. And thus, exactly for that reason (on the strength of a few peculiarities, on the strength of my belonging to a certain distinct category of human being), my perceptions of time and space and my own identity are particularly unsteady.

What is this category? Who are these human beings? Those we call poets and artists. Of what should they be possessed? Of the capacity to feel with a singular intensity not only their own epochs but other epochs, the past, not only their own lands and tribes but other lands and other tribes, not only their own identities but those of other people – the capacity, in other words, to recognize what is generally known as re-incarnation, coupled with an especially vivid and especially graphic sensory memory. And in order to be such a person it is necessary to be someone who has been travelling down the chain of his ancestors' existences for a very long time, someone who has suddenly uncovered within himself a perfect replica of his savage forebear, with all the immediacy of the latter's senses, all the pictorial vividness of his thoughts and all the

34

immensity of his subconscious mind, and at the same time has been immeasurably enriched by his journey and has managed to acquire an immense consciousness.

Is such a person a great martyr or one who has been greatly blessed? Both one and the other. The curse and good fortune of such a person is his especially strong sense of Self, his inordinate craving to have that Self affirmed, and at the same time (by virtue of past experience he has gained during his time in the vast chain of existence), an inordinate awareness of the vanity of such a craving and a sharpened sense of Oneness with the universe. And here you have Buddha, Solomon, Tolstoy. . . .

Gorillas, which in the days of their youth and maturity are terrifying in their physical might, immensely sensual in their approach to the world, merciless in their quest to satisfy their every lust and distinguished by their spontaneity, become, in old age, hesitant, thoughtful, melancholy and pitiful. A striking parallel with the Buddhas, Solomons and Tolstoys!

Ivan Bunin, 'Night', in *The Gentleman from San Francisco and Other Stories*
trans. Sophie Lund and David Richards (London: Angel Books, 1984).

I have described my thirty-six-hour flight from London to Tokyo in a BOAC jet-prop Britannia in my first book about Japan, *These Horned Islands* (1962). (It now takes just over eleven hours from Paris by Air France.) Most of the time I was in terror. I was still suffering from my break with Dana, and although I was scared stiff, at the same time I did not care what happened: if the plane was going to crash, that was a blessed release. My Aunt Lyallie, who had come to Bath to keep my mother company, had not improved matters by remarking, in her soft Scots accent: 'Ye wouldn't get me intay ane o' them things for a' the tea in China.' My mother was of the same opinion, and we took leave of one another as if we would never see each other again – an agonizing parting that was to be repeated time after time during the next fifteen years or so. That long flight – Zurich, Beirut, Bahrain, New Delhi, Rangoon, Bangkok, Hong Kong, Tokyo – made me feel as if I were being pulled through a hedge backwards, and between hops I never stirred from my seat, where I kept the window-shade drawn. The slightest sound and the lightest turbulence made my heart jump into my mouth, and by the time I reached Haneda I was horribly jet-lagged.

I was met by Professor Kobayashi, whom I liked immediately. By the time I arrived, he was on the verge of retirement from Tohoku University: he must have been about sixty, a charming, elegant, white-haired, scholarly gentleman of the old school, Meiji period. We took to one another at once. It was as if I could read his mind, and several times he expressed astonishment when I anticipated what he was about to say, so I had to learn to control my clairvoyance in his presence. I came to admire and venerate him. How different he was from the British Council's character assassins, literary hacks, status-seekers and contract reviewers! I at once had the impression of entering a cultural asylum.

Unfortunately, I was also met by some petty official of the British Council, a dour Scotsman, whose first words to me were: 'Is *that* all the luggage you've got?' And then: 'The last fellow who came out to Japan died of cancer soon after he arrived, just a few weeks ago.'

The large, luxurious British Council limousine conveyed us to the British Council offices, which were then in Nihonbashi, in the building occupied by the head branch of the Maruzen Bookstore, now more dedicated to the sale of expensive Burberry goods with their revolting 'club check' pattern that looks like beer, curry rice and pickles' vomit than to the sale of books. Even in those days, the choice of books available was dismal, the result, I was told, of a chronically costive distribution system.

Professor Kobayashi and I went up in the lift with the Scotsman and were ushered into the sacred presence of a certain Mr Phillips, who at that time was director of the British Council. As soon as I saw him, I thought: Here comes another BC phoney.

All I wanted was to go to bed and have a good sleep, but Phillips seemed to feel it was his duty to 'brief' me, giving me such useless advice as: 'It is better to learn Japanese from a woman, as their style is more refined and polite.' I could see that poor Professor Kobayashi, who had not said a word, was fretting with impatience and embarrassment. But Phillips went on to arrange, through laborious telephone conversations, a meeting with my predecessor, Burton Martin, a person who, after Spender's amusingly spiteful descriptions, I had no desire to meet. The British Council officials in London had already indicated that he was a trouble-maker. I could see that Professor Kobayashi also felt it was pointless to arrange such a meeting, which he refused to attend with me, although Phillips pressed him to do so.

When I did, most reluctantly, meet my predecessor for a few moments, he spent all his time retailing petty gossip about teachers in

Sendai and about 'grave dissensions' in the English Department there, where the leader of the rival faction, Professor Muraoka, wanted not a poet but a 'scholar' – that is, someone who could write the usual turgid literary essays heavily embellished with 'critical apparatus' of footnotes and fiddling glossaries that pass for 'scholarship' among Japanese academics. Burton Martin gossiped about the very agreeable German who was to be my neighbour, a scholarly bachelor living with an elderly maid and a student houseboy from the German Department. It was all extremely unpleasant and discourteous towards former colleagues, and I felt deeply embarrassed by these sly efforts to put the wind up me. But I am not the sort of man up whom the wind can be put, as Burton Martin was to find out when he tried to destroy my reputation in the coming years. In fact, I got on well with members of both the rival factions at the university: the Japanese were too polite to show a guest any kind of discourtesy; they were not Oxford boors. The only people I had any trouble with were those in the office, especially the ones concerned with the domestic affairs of foreign teachers. I have made, and kept, many true friends in Tohoku.

However, on this my first meeting with a British Council representative in Japan, I became aware of certain things. I discovered that the Council had no intention of helping me in any way whatsoever, and that the staff were not interested in culture or education, but rather in bureaucratic-diplomatic careers and ambitions. (The representative has diplomatic status, as they were all very careful to impress upon me.)

Behind each other's backs, members of the staff treated me to the most cruel and beastly remarks about their colleagues. Hatred, envy, jealousy and back-biting were rife, as I was to discover in my contacts with one of the staff, Cyril Eland, who did not have a good word for anyone, and whom everyone I met 'sent up' royally and pulled to pieces. Phillips was the first of the three representatives I was to meet, all of whom told me, with fatuous pride, of the large number of cocktail parties they had to attend each evening with other foreigners of the diplomatic and commercial 'set', Tokyo's terribly unsmart, materialistic, philistine foreign community, a lot of dowdy provincials aping high-society glitterati. One of the more fatuous aspects of life in Tokyo is the gossip-column descriptions of these inane events written by gushing American female amateurs in the inimitable style of small-town Yankee newspapers that are published in the English language press. (The Japanese press does not defile its pages with such dull rubbish.) These lady columnists always refer to women guests as 'gals', and their New

World matiness and vulgarity extend to first-name terms with diplomats and commercial travellers, including the British Council and staff, chummily referred to as 'Bill' or 'Ronnie' or 'Fred'. . . . It all reminded me irresistibly of the hilarious pastiches of gossip-column writing perpetrated by 'that ever-popular diarist Eva Schnerb' in Ronald Firbank's *The Flower beneath the Foot.*

The delights and discomforts of my first weeks in Sendai I have related in *These Horned Islands.* Academic years in Japan begin in April, and the Dean kindly allowed me to do no teaching, apart from an 'inaugural lecture', to give me time to settle down – a privilege that would never be granted today. It took some time to settle down in that house, where I arrived in the middle of winter to find no heating, and my bed unmade and unaired in the Western-style bedroom that had been occupied by Burton Martin and his friend. This was one of the ways the university office tried to make me feel unwelcome, in hopes of driving me away. It was so freezing cold in the house when Professor Kobayashi and I arrived with a delegation of professors that he asked us all to keep our overcoats on as we sat on the ice-cold *tatami* to drink green tea provided by the maid they had thoughtfully but quite unnecessarily engaged for me, without consulting me. She was a very kind and good woman, the sister of one of the professors, and she had been engaged at a very low salary – the most I could be expected to afford. What I was not told was that she had accepted such an ill-paid job on the understanding that she would receive free English lessons from me. She did not, of course, tell me this, assuming that the authorities who had engaged her had informed me of the arrangement. She came every morning to shop and clean and cook my lunch, after which she would spend the afternoon sitting downstairs at the kitchen table reading English textbooks. I even congratulated her on her knowledge of English, and on her assiduity in learning it, never dreaming that every afternoon she was expecting a couple of hours' free English teaching. Then she would prepare my dinner and heat the old-fashioned wooden bath or *o-furo* with kindling and charcoal, and she would leave for home about six. The 6,000 yen a month that was deducted from my salary was indeed a meagre wage for such an excellent person, who looked after me devotedly during my first months in Japan, sending washing to the laundry and ordering blocks of ice every day for the ice-box. (The university office never provided me with any new furniture like a proper refrigerator or a washing-machine or even an electric fan, at a time when every Japanese household was beginning to consider these essential appurtenances to daily life.) I was given a very antique radio which did not work, and in any case it could only have brought me the local NHK station with its programmes of unremitting dullness. I had no vacuum-cleaner, and of course no black-and-white TV set, and there was no heating except from a charcoal-burning brazier whose fumes were toxic, and an old-fashioned stove with a metal chimney angled through the wall in one room only. The other rooms were all as cold as ice, and full of mosquitoes.

But I remained cheerful and content in these rigorous conditions, which the Japanese pretended not to know about. (When *These Horned Islands* was translated into Japanese, the translator, Shozo Tokunaga, was asked to omit all passages that described the hardships I suffered, in order to 'save face' in the English Department and the university administration.) For months I was paid no salary, and when I went to the banks to change my small stock of Cook's travellers' cheques, they refused to accept them – they had never seen such things before. I had to borrow money from my German colleague. But one day when we were in town with Professor Muraoka, I had to borrow money from my German colleague to buy stamps for a letter to my mother, and I think the Professor was shocked by that, for at once he put things in motion with the Educational Affairs office, which so far had ignored my existence, and insisted on my salary being paid promptly and on time. I was always grateful to him for that, and for the charming indigo-blue cotton *yukata* or summer kimono, the very first I possessed, that Mrs Muraoka kindly made for me when the weather began to turn unpleasantly hot and humid in May.

Before I left for Japan, Stephen Spender had given me the names and addresses of several people he said would be willing to help me. One of them was an excellent young scholar, Shozo Tokunaga, who had acted as an interpreter for Spender, and who is one of the very few Japanese who really understand modern English and American poetry. We have collaborated on several books, and he has also translated some of my works very well. He came to see me on my very first morning in Tokyo, and had lunch with me and Professor Kobayashi. We have remained good friends and collaborators to this day, and it is a friendship I value for its rarity, in a land where personal friendships of the kind we know in the West are almost unheard of.

Another name Spender had given me was Cyril Eland's at the British Council, who once invited me to his house for dinner to show off his pictures and *japonaiseries*, but we did not hit it off, and I never returned his hospitality – something which I understand is considered unforgivable in certain circles of society. Spender also introduced me to someone at the American Embassy, a person who I think was in charge of either information or cultural activities, but who gave me no assistance, and I never met him.

The third person was a personable young man whom Spender writes about extensively in his diaries. Spender had tried to obtain a university post for him by using his influence as a famous poet, which goes for nothing in Japan when that kind of business is in question. Spender was simply ignorant of all the intrigue and log-rolling and old-boy networking that surround even the least significant appointments to companies and universities in Japan, and the person he was trying to help was taking advantage of his innocence. In the end, of course, the appointment was not made, and Spender was upset about the insult offered to his Japanese friend.

This friend was one of the first persons I met outside Japanese and British officialdom. He had written to me already in Bath, asking for my photograph so that he might be able to recognize me when we met in Tokyo – at least, that was his story. I sent him a snap of myself lying or half-recumbent on a bench at Wydale Hall, a picture that he said he found 'sexy'. (It is reproduced in *I of All People*, 1990.) We met at one of the stations on the Yamanote Line – Ochanomizu, I think, and he took me to a coffee-shop where he told me Spender had asked him to 'put me wise to' what he called 'the gay scene' in Japan. I shuddered at the use of that Americanism which was becoming popular in Europe at that time, and which I detest, because 'gay' life is usually far from gay – in my case, terribly un-gay most of the time.

All the same, I was curious to have someone 'dish the dirt' with me, and grateful for the advice of someone who was evidently an expert on the ins and outs of homo life in Tokyo. I find the particularities of such life of engrossing psychological and sociological interest, and I wondered what on earth the underground gaiety of Tokyo could be.

My informant soon instructed me. There were no real 'cottages' such as we have in Britain and Europe and the United States. A certain toilet at Tokyo Station and another on the subway line at Shinjuku Sanchome were sometimes 'active' but not to be recommended. (Indeed, at the latter, a foreigner was murdered a few years later.) But at least in Japanese toilets there were none of those female lavatory attendants who crouch like crabs behind their little tables on which stands a saucer for tips, such as I had found in Spain, Portugal and France. (The only one without a female attendant in Lisbon, in the Rossio Square, was very active until it was closed down during the revolution.) So where did one go to find whatever cocks were in town? There were certain baths in Shinjuku and Ikebukuro and Asakusa, and even in the Ginza, where contacts `and more could be made in darkened steam-rooms – something that aroused in me memories of the Turkish baths in Leeds and in the Harrow Road in London, both dens of danger where I nevertheless had many a fling, even under the noses of the Vice Squad, all too obvious in their skimpy bath-towels. (The attendants would give us the wink when the plain-clothes dicks were around, but alas, some of them were gays in the pay of the police, granted immunity from prosecution in exchange for tip-offs.) There was nothing of that in the Japanese steam-rooms, even in those not exclusively for homos, which were the ones I preferred, for quite a lot of Japanese men are willingly bisexual in the right situation.

My heart sank when I was also recommended to go to 'gay bars' and to 'sister bars'. In the latter, the boys dressed up as women, in either geisha style or in Western fashions. William MacAlpine at the British Council told me the hilarious tale of how he had escorted Arthur Koestler to a bar catering to *onnagata* or kabuki female impersonators. Koestler was already raging drunk by the time they entered the bar, and they had not long been seated at the counter before our leading Mitteleuropa intellectual without warning poured his glass of whisky over the expensive and complicated geisha wig and gorgeous costume of the man seated next to him. It was only with the greatest difficulty, as can be imagined, that William extracted his guest from that ugly situation: I believe Koestler refused to apologize and some kind of substantial money payment was made. After that, foreigners were never again allowed to enter the bar, which put up one of those frequent and depressing notices, *Japanese Only*. William MacAlpine and his gifted wife, an expert on Japanese dance, were my only good friends at the Council. In Bill MacAlpine I saw the man who had come to the poetry reading at the Ethical Church and given a superb imitation of Dylan Thomas, who was too drunk to attend as he had promised. And both the MacAlpines were shining examples of British people who knew how to relate to the Japanese without autocratic condescension. They were the only British Council people admired and trusted by the Japanese, and Bill was the personal friend of Professor Kobayashi, who had sounded him out about me and my poetry. Though he did not know me personally, Bill told Kobayashi *sensei* that he was very lucky to have such a good poet coming to Sendai, and the Dean never tired of repeating this judgement. It was a great tragedy that Bill and his wife did not become permanent residents at the Council, for at one point I thought Bill might be made representative. Unfortunately, however, they were moved to Rangoon, where I am sure they created the same legendary rapport with the Burmese as they had done with the Japanese.

I have never forgotten their kindnesses to me. For example, Professor Kobayashi wanted to rush me away to Sendai the very next morning after my arrival, without giving me a chance to see anything in Tokyo, but Bill tactfully suggested that I might want to see traditional Japanese theatre and visit some art galleries and museums. Kobayashi *sensei* compromised by staying an extra day in Tokyo, taking me on a bus tour of the city in the Hato bus. But on my very first visit to Tokyo from Sendai, Bill and his wife took me to kabuki to see *Chushingura*, an experience that was to colour the whole of my attitude towards Japan. Each time I went to Tokyo they would give me lunch or dinner at traditional restaurants or at their own luxurious house, where I was introduced to interesting Japanese artists, poets and professors. Or we would go to the Noh theatre or to the strip shows in Asakusa. I think the officials of the Council like Phillips must have disapproved of this friendship, because after a while I saw no more of the MacAlpines: presumably they had been warned by Phillips not to be seen with me.

In any case, I was finding my own way around Tokyo quite well, guided by Spender's boy-friend. I hate gay bars, but allowed myself to be taken to one by him. We spent all night there after the bar had closed, doing some heavy petting with the bar boys, and I staggered back to my hotel in a 60-yen taxi just as the wintry dawn was breaking over the River Sumida. But that was my one and only visit to a gay bar at that period.

I much preferred cheap working men's hang-outs, where one could get drunk in amiable company on beer and *shochu* and third-rate *sake*. And those unsophisticated workmen, many of them bachelors from remote country districts, were not averse, I discovered, to male group sex in their huts and dormitories and doss-houses to which they often conducted me when their drinking-dens closed. I much preferred those men, in the full vigour of carefree and drop-out youth, to the sissies of the gay bars. This was something the Japanese could never understand, because they have still the most ignorant and stereotyped ideas of what a male homosexual is like – seeing him either as an effeminate screaming

queen or as a transsexual like the delightful Carrousel Maki, star of TV
chat shows, or as boys dressed up as girls, often brilliantly successful
transvestite transformations. The perfectly ordinary and 'normal' married men of all ages who like to dress up in special bars as little girls,
nurses, Girl Guides, high-school misses and hilarious versions of Mar-
lene Dietrich or Sophia Loren are a case apart, and they are not
regarded as anything out of the ordinary, just as long as they do not
exhibit themselves in public.

There are also special haunts where respectable white-collar workers
can act out fantasies such as being little babies again, wearing nappies
which they have to soil satisfactorily before they can be changed by
ministering nursemaids (either men or girls), who proceed to smack
them on the bottom for being so naughty and filthy, then lovingly wash
and masturbate them before powdering them all over with Johnson's
Baby Powder (no other will do) and putting them into fresh pampers
and rompers for a session of highballs at the bar. The bartenders are
grumpily maternal middle-aged housewives doing this part-time job,
which involves scolding anyone who so much as spills a drop of liquid
on the bar, and making really bad boys stand or sit in a corner or in a
special bassinet. Then, when it's time to catch the last commuter train
and go obediently home to wife and kiddies, the men are dressed, with
many a fit of screaming rage as they are bundled back into their dreary
old business suits. There are always violent struggles to put on their
socks and underwear and to give their hair a final combing. Then they
trot home through the midnight streets like any other wage-slave after a
night out with the boys.

As I did not like the ghetto atmosphere of male gay bars, I sometimes
went to the small, discreet lesbian haunts in Shinjuku and Shibuya,
which in those prelapsarian times welcomed homosexual men and
ordinary salaried workers. It was so restful to sit at the bar in 'Sunshine'
or 'House of Ladies' or 'Murasaki' and not be pestered or importuned.
There was no feeling of strain or artificiality in the lesbian bars, and the
girls there were among the nicest I ever met in Japan – both the butch
and the bint – and the most unaffected. Today, there is no more of that
freedom: with the advent of Aids, all foreigners are outcasts, and the
Japanese Only notices have been supplemented by *No Foreigners Allowed*
outside bars and saunas.

When Spender's friend realized that I was not interested in gay bars,
his astonishment was great, for had he not taken Spender to several of
them? This had caused an almighty scandal when he let it be known to

the press what had happened, and the reverberations of that scandal were still rocking academic life in Sendai when I arrived. Burton Martin had had no scruples in spreading the gleeful news that Spender was gay and had visited gay bars. The Japanese are inveterate gossips, and there is nothing they like better than a fresh 'shock' to tattle about, to take their minds off their humdrum lives. When it was announced that I was 'a friend of Spender's' – not true, in fact, for we disliked each other – it was assumed by everyone that I was his lover, and Burton Martin and his friends did nothing to dissipate that false impression. So when I arrived in Sendai, I was met by would-be knowing looks and by titters of excitement. At the first 'welcome party' I attended, I remember so well the *goguenard* expressions on the faces of some of the students, and the hostility and fear and suspicion on the faces of others, who pointedly kept their distance and would not even speak one word of welcome to me as I sat exchanging *sake* cups (cupules the size of an eye-bath) as a token of amity with Kobayashi *sensei*, Hasegawa *sensei*, Muraoka *sensei* and some of the more courageous graduate and post-graduate students who acted as these professors' assistants, doing the donkey-work in their literary research, farming out chunks of the books they were translating into Japanese.

After the party had been going for about half an hour, there was the entrance of an extremely pretty boy student, who seemed about to die of embarrassment and shame as he was dragged in to greet me. He knelt on the *tatami* at a good distance from me, and bowed his head to the floor in a very graceful way. Now why couldn't they have given me someone like that as a houseboy, instead of my dutiful maid? I wondered. The young man was obviously the butt of the other students because of his markedly feminine appearance, and I so much wanted to speak to him, but he was whisked away before I could offer him my *sake* cup. To my sorrow, I never saw him again. He never turned up in any of my classes. I did not even know his name. But this unknown person was the one human being I felt attracted to at the time, and he was denied me. I have often wondered what happened to him. Perhaps he could no longer bear the opprobrium of being associated, even indirectly, with one of his own kind, and a foreigner, and had dropped out of the university altogether. If so, I am truly sorry to have been the unwitting cause of his defection. My heart ached for him. The fact that he was not 'my type' did not matter. What did infuriate me was the attitude of the other students towards him, and their ignorant assumption that I should want to be his lover when I just wanted to be friends and to show him my solidarity. That ignorance of the Japanese seems even today invincible, despite films like *Cruising* and *Prick Up Your Ears* and *The Naked Civil Servant*. The 'gay' stereotypes are ineradicably embedded in the Japanese consciousness.

But there was something Spender's friend opened my eyes to for the first time. That was the extraordinary sexual behaviour of the Japanese in their movie-houses. These were nearly always 'SRO', and when I say 'standing room' I mean that people were standing bumper to bumper in the aisles and at the back of the cinema. What on earth would happen if a fire were to break out, I shuddered to think, especially as many of the most popular theatres were in first, second and third basements, or at the top of tall office buildings with only one elevator. One had to push one's way in through the doors at the back or the sides, and at once found oneself in very intimate contact with one's neighbours. It was impossible to move, but somehow one often felt exploring hands creeping around, both men's and women's. These sexual *attouchements* were always very discreet, though sometimes one heard the serpentine hiss of a well-used zipper descending between expert fingers, or being hauled up as the lights went on. Today, Japanese movie-houses are no longer jam-packed and pitch-dark: audiences are sparse, and illumination, on orders of the police, is so bright that, what with the overhead lighting and the tiresomely bright green exit signs on either side of the stage, one can hardly see anything on the screen. But in certain cinemas one can still observe men moving from seat to seat in search of a willing accomplice: they are looking for girls and women, not men, and when I once or twice sat down next to one of these molesters, known as *chikan* (who are rampant in packed commuter trains also – try the first and last carriages on the Chuo Line in Tokyo), they gave me indignant looks, as if to say 'We know what *you* want, but you're not getting it from us', and moved away with scandalized expressions on their faces.

Spender's friend took me to some of the movie-houses in which homosexual gropings were notoriously easy. 'Just stand quietly at the back,' he instructed me, 'and someone will come beside you and start holding your hand and squeezing your fingers tenderly.' That was the first signal: after that, he said, it was up to me to decide if the contact should go any further. If I did not like the look of the man, I could simply move away and stand beside someone more attractive. At that period in Tokyo there were a number of such 'gay' cinemas in the Ginza, Asakusa, Ueno, Shinjuku and Shibuya. There was a particularly celebrated one in Ikebukuro.

They were not without their dangers. Beneath the constantly smiling and too easily laughing surface of the Japanese there are surging violences. Under the snow-capped cone of Fuji-san there is only temporarily dormant boiling lava. And ultimately the foreigner is always excluded from those groups of consensus-seekers, with their sagely nodding heads – the one totally distinguishing mark of the Japanese that sets them apart from all other orientals. Exclusion often means aggression or betrayal, suspicion and deceit. So at the baths I was sometimes shunned as a leper, sometimes given unamiable sidelong looks, sometimes reported to the management, especially if I were the only foreigner present. The inferiority complex of some Japanese makes them ever on the alert for falls from grace on the part of Westerners, especially if the Westerners are seen to be condemned by their own countrymen, and the Japanese, who are almost incapable of forming personal judgements of a highly critical kind, can attack with the assurance that they must be in the right. Then, from a position of inferiority or 'low profile', they can out-top everyone in righteous superiority, their consensual heads wagging up and down in tut-tutting agreement, followed by cold looks and hard words. The Japanese in defeat, someone has said, are at their best: when they are on the way up, watch out for cold-hearted cruelty.

I used to run all over Tokyo and Osaka and Kobe looking for cheap movie-houses, which was where sensualists gathered. The expensive 'road shows' had audiences that were too mixed, though often contacts could be made. Once in Asakusa, on the top floor of an ancient movie-palace – Spender's friend had told me always to go to the topmost balcony – I made the wrong sort of contacts with a couple of *chinpira* or petty hooligans who approached me as an easy prey in the stuffy darkness. I was the only foreigner and stood out even in the pitch-dark. After groping me, they signalled to accomplices and I knew I could be beaten up, so I dashed away down endless flights of slippery stone stairs, casting pocketfuls of small change in my wake, which the bad boys foolishly stopped to collect, thus allowing me to gain the street and comparative safety.

There were strip shows where hundreds of silent men gawped at the nudes on stage, and almost abstractedly fondled me. At one small basement place in Ueno, men performed sex acts – audience participation!

These were my dream palaces. They were the perfect settings for the release of my abnormally strong libido. The fact of my having survived both the affair with Dana and that long plane flight seemed to have intensified my sexual urges and exacerbated my erotomania. I was still mourning my father's death: sex relieved me. I used to spend hours in those close-packed Tokyo movie-houses, undergoing all kinds of initiations. The homo audience consisted of both active and passive players, of voyeurs who were a dreadful nuisance and exhibitionists who didn't matter. But there were also sometimes pious frauds who felt it their duty to look shocked and call a policeman or the manager when they thought things were going too far. I remember the cops, a couple of blue-uniformed young men, coming down the stairs into the darkened back of the cinema and keeping an eye on us. Their presence was enough to deflate the randiest erection, and gradually the scene would clear until even I had to give up and leave.

But on one occasion my persistence rewarded me, and in the empty darkness at the back of the movie-house a young brute of a policeman gave me a good time. There were occasionally plain-clothes' cops, too, and they also were not above taking advantage of the dark. Indeed, one of them once tipped me the hint that the person standing next to me was an undesirable, a *yakuza*. And another cop once gently shook his head when someone started making up to me – it was a 'business boy' or *chinpira*, a teenage hoodlum prostitute, and so highly dangerous. Often the police seemed to be there just to protect me from unwelcome attentions. But I realize now I was lucky never to be arrested or charged with affronts to public decency – whatever that may be. I never forced my attentions upon anyone, and never behaved any more outrageously than the Japanese around me, some of whom were quite shameless in their porno pantings and grotesque groanings. In those Tokyo movie-houses, I had found the paradises of my dreams. There were some Japanese who always refused to have anything to do with foreigners; but on the whole most men were willing and able. However, Sendai was not Tokyo, as I was to find out to my cost.

What were my first impressions of Japan? My most enduring memory is that at once I felt as if I had come home. There was a curious sense of *déjà vu*. This confirmed my belief in reincarnation: I was sure that 'I have been here before.' Yet Tokyo and Sendai were like Wild West towns.

But I must have been in a very different body. Beside the slim, elegantly proportioned, dark-haired Japanese, my European body felt too tall, gross and cumbersome. I envied them their grace and modesty, though at times I felt that their deference to foreigners verged on an almost imbecile servility. It seemed that a foreigner, particularly a fair-haired, blue-eyed male, could do no wrong, and I felt embarrassed to be accepted as a superior person everywhere I went.

I remember the constant ripples of laughter, the light-hearted titters and girlish giggles filling the streets: everyone was smiling broadly and laughing merrily, and the young girls in particular seemed always on the point of hysteria. This was not due just to my outlandish appearance: it went on when they could not see me at all, and I was behind a window curtain watching them, marvelling at the truth of Gilbert and Sullivan's song in *The Mikado*, 'Three Little Maids from School'. It was absolutely true!

The neon signs at night were a perpetual source of delight, and I soon learnt to prefer night-time views to the usually sombre and ugly daytime ones of Japanese towns and cities, often of an unspeakable drabness. The neon signs with their complex characters were things I could admire in the abstract, almost as works of art, and I had no desire to understand what they said. I felt thankful release from the tyranny of advertising. Unfortunately, from time to time English or pseudo-English words and phrases began to creep into the pure abstractions of Japanese and Chinese characters, and these I could not ignore. I came to be depressed and sickened by excruciatingly incorrect English spelling and grammar in advertising, by idiotic Janglish brand names that were exploited cynically to give Japanese, ignorant of their childish mistakes, an impression of high-class foreign cachet. As a writer, the unavoidable sight of such idiomatic perversions and linguistic intrusions filled me with despair. I could see from this uninhibited misuse of my native language that the Japanese did not take English seriously – an impression at once confirmed by my first classes. They did not even seem to take their own language seriously, otherwise why should they defile it with such crass and incorrect English – and French and German, too, sometimes? It looked to me as if these people, constantly seeking the best of everything in the way of expensive Western goods and status symbols, did not in fact know the value of anything, because they did not know the value of words. And as Pierre Emmanuel has written: 'Those who do not respect language do not respect life.' I sensed a horrible cheapness and violence beneath all these displays of useless English. W.H. Auden wrote somewhere: 'When words lose their meaning, physical force takes over.'

Was all this illiteracy a relic of pre-war authoritarianism and the *kempeitai*, the 'thought police'? Did this destruction of English represent a form of revenge for defeat in war? Was it a kind of linguistic colonialism? Even the *katakana* syllabary the Japanese use chiefly for transliterating foreign words and names began to seem to me a weapon to turn English into a Japanese vassal language, for as a guide to the correct pronunciation of English it is useless, and makes speakers of Japanese English quite incomprehensible. And native English speakers, pronouncing English names correctly, are often misunderstood, because they are not speaking with the anti-language *katakana* accent. This tendency to destroy true English at all costs has increased over the years, so that today we hear and see everywhere imbecile and illiterate slogans like 'I Feel Coke' and 'Speak Lark'.

The sweet trills of laughter I loved to hear have also degenerated into coarse, loud guffaws and screeches, partly imitated from rabid commercials on TV and radio. The sound is painful. The composer Toru Takemitsu has said: 'Japanese people laugh constantly but their laughter is empty and hollow.' I teach my students the English saying: 'A loud laugh betrays an empty mind.' That empty mind seems to me the result of the Japanese bastardization of language.

On that first grim night in my house in Kozenji-dori I lay for hours awake under icy blankets and *futon* that smelled musty and looked none too clean. I shivered with the intense cold, and also with fear, as I heard scamperings across the roofs. If these were caused by rats, they must be exceptionally big ones. The whole house felt unclean: there was dust on all the ledges, and I was to find out that such unswept, half-clean states were common in Japanese houses.

I had been provided with a long, padded kimono of the type known as *dotera*, but it was far too small for me. On top of this I was supposed to wear a padded jacket of the same dun, black-edged material called a *tanzen*, whose long, square sleeves kept getting caught in all the sliding doors. Neither of these garments could keep out the penetrating chill, and they also smelled musty, as if they had been worn often and never cleaned. On the lapels of both garments was inscribed *Property of Tohoku University*.

As I lay there in bed, I had a foreboding of doom and disaster. The house itself seemed to me unsafe as it rocked in minor earthquakes. Indeed, about eighteen months later, when I finally persuaded the authorities to repaint the interior, it was discovered that all the wiring was half rotten and could have sent the whole wooden structure up in flames at any moment. And when the painters moved the heavy wardrobe in the bedroom away from the wall, in order to paint it, they showed me an extraordinary accumulation of dirt, dust and trash behind it, which must have lain there since the house was built a hundred years ago. When I pointed this out to the authorities, they said it was impossible, that the whole house had been cleaned before my arrival: they simply would not admit the evidence of their eyes, for to have done so would have been to 'lose face'. This is a peculiar oriental attitude, for which I have neither understanding nor sympathy.

My little maid went round dusting, flapping at shelves and window-frames with a bunch of coloured rags tied to the end of a bamboo pole. One morning as I was descending the stairs to make a cup of tea in the kitchen, I was confronted by an enormous rat, which bared its teeth at me and refused to budge. I stamped on the shaky wooden stair, and it suddenly twitched and disappeared: for a moment, I thought it must have run up the leg of my pyjamas, which I always wore under that ill-fitting *dotera*. It was the first of many horrifying encounters with savage rats and hordes of impertinent mice. Cockroaches, too, swarmed in the half-clean kitchen, and there were huge spiders and hoary crickets in the bathroom among the bits of stick and lumps of charcoal used to heat the water. The whole place seemed to me spooky and creepy in the extreme.

The furniture was ancient and minimal. There was not even a hang-ing scroll or *kakemono* in the sacred *tokonoma* or alcove for flower arrangements and art objects that I had read about with such fascina-tion in my studies of Japanese traditional culture. My little maid was shocked by this bareness, and from her own home brought three charming, simple *kakemono* for me to choose from. I chose the plainest – a mere hint of a little boat and a fisherman drifting on reflections of mountains and pines. There was not even a vase or a bowl in which to arrange flowers, so we had to use an earthenware stew-pot or cheap Noritake china 'Made in Occupied Japan'. The garden was untended and empty, but there was a small tree at one end that suddenly burst into flower as if to greet my arrival: the delicate white blossoms were *ume*, a kind of green plum, so my maid told me.

I was given several assistants from the English Department. At once I could sense that this was an unpopular assignment, so I gave them as little trouble as possible: it was always the one at the bottom of the ladder who was given this unenviable job of looking after an unpredict-able foreigner, so it was associated with 'loss of face'. Nevertheless they all helped me whenever I asked for help. The last one I had, Seiji

Sekino, was an admirable assistant, personally concerned about my welfare, and he remains my good friend. He is now a respected professor: he came to visit me when I lived in Dublin and we are still in touch. He provided me with many pictures of Sendai.

As soon as I got to Sendai, I began to reconsider the famous bit of dialogue from Forster's *A Passage to India*. Surrounded by orientals, I could sense its sentimentality and unreality, for there were some whom I knew to be friends, but others I knew were not. So I was a true oriental in that respect. I had arrived in an atmosphere charged with hostility and agog with childish scandal.

On my very first morning in Kozenji-dori, before my maid had arrived to make me a cup of tea, the telephone rang around eight o'clock. I had never had my own telephone before, so at first it was something of a novelty for me: but I soon learnt to detest its intrusions at all hours of the day and night.

I picked up the phone and heard the formula I had learnt to expect when I studied some elementary Japanese grammar and vocabulary before leaving Bath: 'Moshi-moshi?' Then a voice spoke in Janglish: 'Good-morning, Professor Kirkup. I hope I do not disturb you so early, ha-ha. My name is Hiroshi Uno – Ooh No, spelt U-N-O, you know, like United Nations, ha-ha, my family name. How are you Professor Kirkup you don't know me I am a reporter of *The Mainichi Daily News* in Tokyo may I ask you a few questions? How are you getting along in Sendai? Do you find your house comfortable? Have you any problems? What are your first impressions of Japan . . .?' The questions went on and one without waiting for my answers. Later, I found out that Mr Uno was an old friend of Burton Martin, and he was just one of the many stringers for the English Japanese press who tried to trick me into saying something unfavourable about Japan, Sendai, my house, my colleagues, my students. This journalistic scandal-mongering is something peculiarly Japanese – though now it seems to have spread its despicable tentacles into British dailies. The press in Japan, encouraged by the British Council, was to give me a hard time, especially towards the end of my stay in Sendai, when I was practically driven out of Japan by scandal-mongering reporters and sensation-seekers. I must admit I gave them a good run for their money.

Most of the time I was left to my own devices. I had been engaged to give some extra classes at Tohoku Gakuen and at a girls' college, in order to supplement my university salary – even in those days, 60,000 yen a month, though more than that earned by my Japanese colleagues, did not go far – and I had only four classes a week at the university, so I had a lot of free time on my hands. I used it to study the basics of Japanese, extending my vocabulary and my knowledge of grammar, but totally ignoring the spoken word, which did not interest me. In this respect I could sympathize with some of the Japanese, who could read English in a passive way but were incapable of expressing themselves correctly in speech and writing. I also started doing some translations of modern Japanese poetry, with the help of students who transliterated the texts into *romaji*. And I wrote down everything in my journal every day, thus providing more than enough material later for *These Horned Islands*. I did not care much for the Japanese in the mass, but there was something about Japan itself that I always found strange and exciting, and I wrote many poems about my experiences. Even more important, egged on by Mark Bonham Carter, I wrote my first published novel, *The Love of Others* (1962), which is part autobiography.

Among the poems I wrote was one about the infernal nuisance of my telephone, called 'Wrong Number', which is in *The Prodigal Son* and in *Japan Physical* (1974), a collection of my Japanese poems with Japanese translations by Fumiko Miura which was published by Kenkyusha. The poem was printed in one of the university's magazines, *Musophilus*. It was perfectly straightforward: my German colleague Edmund had warned me that the Japanese do not understand irony, and indeed that is true, for they always confuse it with cynicism. It was about all the mysterious calls I kept receiving in the middle of the night, and begins:

> In the dead middle of the night,
> Like a bad alarm-clock
> The telephone shook me awake,
> And from a long dream I jumped
> Right out of my skin, afraid
> To hear sad news of you. . . .

(I later discovered that my number differed by only one digit from that of the 'Scotland Bar', which explained why I was always getting wrong-number calls from prostitutes, bar girls and drunken businessmen demanding the services of Yoko or Junko.) The poem goes on to describe the background noises of a bar, and the voice of a woman shouting unintelligibly until I gave an exasperated answer in English, something like: 'Get off the fucking line, you crummy old bag!'

> . . . Then she uttered a cry like a bird
> In a voice still pretty with surprise, and,
> As if I'd given her an electric shock, rang off. .
> The bar, the music and the voices vanished,
> And left me alone again. Returning to bed
> In the dead middle of the night
> I peeped out at my snowy garden,
> And was suddenly glad to be alone, and sober,
> At home, with no sad news of you.

The 'you' in the poem referred to my mother. I knew her blindness was getting worse, and that she was now all alone in our house, so I was expecting at any time to hear she was in hospital. But the poem, when read by my students, was interpreted in a quite different way. In their ignorance they thought I must be referring to some boy-friend, and so in class I had to put up with arch looks, mimed telephone conversations between two effeminate queens, and the usual knowing smiles. No one smiles more knowingly than a Japanese who thinks he knows something nobody else does.

A number of my writings, both in poetry and in prose, were misinterpreted in this way, as one of my students told me several years later, when he came to see me in Tokyo. I was invited to write a series of essays for the local newspaper, *Kahoku Shimpo*. In them I described with my legendary frankness my impressions of Japanese daily life. They were all absolutely true: I was not making anything up. But the citizens of Sendai were incensed by my observations of what they referred to as 'the dark side of life' and seemed to think I was damaging the town's reputation when I commented, for example, that the fruit shop in Kozenji-dori never sold me bad fruit, as sometimes happens in England. To the Japanese, just the suggestion of 'bad fruit' meant that I had indeed been sold bad fruit. And when I said that the shoe-cleaners charged me extra when I sat down at one of their little shoe-cleaning stands outside Sendai station, it was a little joke against myself, against my big feet, so much larger than those of Japanese, and so deserving to be charged more for cleaning.

This gentle little piece of irony escaped the shoe-cleaning fraternity and sorority, as Edmund had warned me it would, and ever afterwards, as I walked along the streets round the station, they would give me furious looks and shout insults at my feet. When I sat down to have my shoes cleaned, they refused to serve me. Incidents like that resulted in the cancellation of my contract with the *Kahoku Shimpo*, which for six weeks or so brought me in a welcome little extra money in my straitened circumstances, for I was sending half my salary home to my mother every month, despite the great difficulties I experienced at the banks in doing so. There was some currency regulation in force which I did not understand. In the end, I got so fed up with the banks, I just sent the banknotes to her with my letters every week, and she was able to cash them at her bank in Bath, though in those days the exchange rate for the yen was very low – something like 1,000 yen to the pound sterling. Luckily this subterfuge was never discovered by the Japanese authorities, or I could have been imprisoned for breaking the currency regulations.

I had repeated troubles with the university department in charge of housing. Sendai in summer is an inferno of humidity, almost as bad as Kyoto. I pleaded with the office to give me an electric fan, as I could not afford to buy one myself, and in any case did not see why I should do so. The reaction of the office was to say that 'revolving electric fans' did not exist in Japan. Then to soothe me they invited me out to dinner in a Japanese restaurant, and there, standing in each corner of the *tatami* room, were four standard fans, which revolved from side to side in a measured, stately way, like royalty acknowledging the loyal applause of, subjects. The office men lost face: in fact, their faces were red, and not just with *sake*. But I still did not get my fan. In cold weather, Professor Kobayashi provided me with an electric heater I could carry from room to room, paid for out of his own pocket. And always there were those strange telephone calls. When it was a blackmailer, saying simply 'Money, money' in English, I devised the trick of whispering, as if to someone standing next to me, and that frightened them off for a while.

Sometimes, one of my colleagues would invite me out to a bar or a restaurant. Around ten o'clock he would be ready to go home, and fully expected me to go home too, sharing his taxi which would drop me off on the way. But sometimes I was not ready to go home so early. So I would refuse the offer of a lift and say I wanted to visit a few more bars, and this caused great offence. But after an evening of desultory chit-chat about Graham Greene (Grim Grin) or Somerset Maugham (Sunset Mum) I wanted to relax on my own, to unwind from the strain of having to talk about authors who were of little interest to me, but who at that time were considered to belong to the top flight of British literary genius, as was evidenced by the depressing row upon row of their books in Maruzen.

On such evenings I would go on a bar-crawl, trying to visit a new bar every night. In this way I discovered some interesting places, like the bar called 'Mon', which played French *chansons* records, or the little *sake* snack-bar run by an enchantingly pretty ex-geisha, who addressed me as 'Kup-san'.

But some of the more sleazy bars round the station were the places I really preferred. Here there were railway passengers spending an hour or so between trains, and as non-residents they were more willing to talk to a foreigner or, if I found them amiable enough, to spend the night with me before going on to Aomori or Hokkaido in the north, Hiroshima or Osaka in the south. In this way I made some good friends who did not belong to Sendai, and who welcomed me on my visits to their 'native places'. There were also prostitutes in these bars, both male and female, and they always interested me. But the male pros reserved themselves exclusively for women, and were known as 'Adonis boys', though most of them did not deserve that sacred name. I got friendly with a cheerful pimp who agreed to sleep with me once or twice, in exchange for lending one of my downstairs rooms for 'special assignations' between male and female clients. Thus it was that I met a sailor with a butterfly tattooed on his glans penis. But I had to stop this 'side business' because of all the unwelcome telephone calls it necessitated, and besides, I think the police had their eyes on my house.

During my two years in Sendai, I was to receive many such mysterious telephone calls. Sometimes they were wrong numbers, and around midnight I often got calls for 'Scotland Bar', a place at the bottom of Ichibancho whose number as I have said was almost the same as mine. Out of curiosity, I once visited the bar, and found it deserted, attended by a solitary bar boy. A few years later, when David Kidd, a Kyoto exquisite, along with Francis King and his gay friends took me to a gay bar in Kyoto, 'C'est Bon', it was ostensibly to be confronted by that very bar boy, whom I did not recognize, but when I was told he had worked in Scotland Bar of course I remembered the name that had disturbed so many of my nights. 'It was a gay bar, wasn't it?' asked a prominent homo member of the Kyoto *gaijin* (foreign) community. 'No, I don't think so,' I answered. 'It did not give me that impression.' They all seemed rather disappointed by this admission, and the boy was covered in confusion, for he had been lying.

I got a lot of calls from strangers, from students wanting to practise a little English conversation, always stereotyped and limited phrase-book stuff that bored me to distraction. Occasionally there were crank calls from rightists or from naïve blackmailers: they did not seem to realize that my openness about my sexual preferences made me immune to blackmail. I got so fed up with that telephone I tried to rip it out, but it was firmly installed, and so I buried it under layers of blankets to stifle its persistent ringing.

Everyone I met in Japanese academic life seemed so respectable and holier-than-thou. It was the Christian missionary influence. Everyone seemed so *comme il faut* and regular, leading blameless family lives or preparing to enter the Marine Fire and Life Insurance Company or Hitachi or Sony, as if these were the most desirable places on earth in which to spend the whole of one's existence. I just could not relate to all that, and in Japan my difference made me feel more different than ever. The unbridgeable chasms between poetry and teaching, between my carefree lawlessness and bourgeois propriety and between all the ambivalent selves and non-selves in my life never appeared more profound and dizzyingly without support. In poetry I believe in taking chances, and in one's personal life, too – never go on writing the same thing, poem after poem, never keep on doing the same thing again and again and again. I hate being cooped up like a chicken, 'happy where your shit falls'.

I was reading St Augustine: 'So a man becomes more and more shrouded in darkness so long as he pursues willingly what he finds in his weakness is more easy to receive.' So I wanted to do exactly as I pleased, and to hell with reputation and convention. But I also wanted everyone to accept me as I wished to be, and if they did not accept me, I felt they could not be the sort of people I wanted to know anyhow. I was full of this necessary intellectual and spiritual arrogance: I could not live in any other way. It was no wonder I was born lonely. And in Sendai I found myself becoming lonelier and lonelier. Yet: 'Love, and do what you will' – St Augustine's symbol is *two* arrows piercing a heart. . . . In the *Confessions* St Augustine says: 'To Carthage I came, where there sang all around my ears a cauldron of unholy loves.' Sendai was my Carthage. 'Give me chastity and continency, but not yet. . . .'

On my first night in Sendai I encountered something that shocked me to the core. The professors and I were all talking in English for the first ten minutes or so. But then they all suddenly switched to Japanese, and I felt so excluded I could have wept for rage at their impoliteness in treating a stranger thus. I suppose they were discussing the inadequacies of my reception, and wondering what could be done, so they were not likely to want me to know what they were saying. But this custom of ignoring the foreigner after the first few minutes was repeated again and again. I had already studied basic Japanese grammar and had a working vocabulary, but I could not follow that they were saying. At that moment in my icy house, I made the proud decision that I would never learn to speak Japanese: if they wanted to exclude *me*, then I would exclude *them*. During the first few days, what English conversation I did have with the Japanese seemed to me so utterly trivial and formulaic, lacking in all interest and individuality, that I was reinforced in my decision not to communicate with them in their own tongue. This had the merit of preserving the privacy that is so hard to find and hold on to in that crowded land: I could just switch off contact whenever I liked

And I was spared the horrors of having to read all the millions of neon signs, advertising everything under the sun, which looked so beautiful at night – I was content to admire their strange shapes of jewelled, Klee-like patterns as they winked on and off or rippled and scattered and re-formed in dazzling pyrotechnical displays on the darkness that mercifully shrouded the dismal ugliness of cities. The Japanese seemed unaware of the hideous nature of their towns and cities. The countryside, too, was scarred by cheap advertising and gruesome blocks of concrete apartments and offices and factories. Even the renowned beauty spots and the famous gardens and temples were tainted with this crass commercialism, but the Japanese ignored it and concentrated on a passion for the cute, the quaint, the kitsch and the uncomplicated. I felt I could never have anything in common with these people, and I was thankful for that. I had never enjoyed idle chatter or any form of conversation in any language, even my own. But Japanese conversation seemed to me the ultimate in banality and bathos, so I have never regretted missing it. There are only about three Japanese with whom I have had a sustained and interesting conversation: the rest was just talk for the sake of talking, a chattering of monkeys in a house of cards.

I began to spend much of my time alone. One afternoon I came into the kitchen to find my maid in tears. I still did not know why on earth she worked for me on such a poor salary. I could not bear to see her cry, for I liked and respected her. So I asked Professor Kobayashi to release her from my employment. He did so at once, and I remember the radiant happiness on her face when I gave her a glowing reference. It allowed her to obtain a much better position in Tokyo, and we remained in touch by correspondence. I learnt that she was very happy working in the American family that had had the good luck to find her.

But some cads in the university offices put about a rumour that she had fallen in love with me, and that that was the reason why she had left. Of all the vicious, malicious and heartless gossip – gossip, like talk, just for the sake of gossip, to fill an idle hour in lives where nothing ever happened – that was what hurt me most, because it affected the reputation of an innocent person.

They could gossip as much as they liked about me, because some of their gossip was based on the truth, which I never tried to hide. I am accustomed to feeling lonely, but in Sendai I suffered agonies of loneliness. After the first novelty of my presence and appearance had worn off, I was left to myself. I was never invited to anyone's house. People would not even walk down the street with me. It was like being in Stalinist Russia, where to be seen with a foreigner could attract unwelcome questionings. The old spirit of the *kempeitai*, the thought police, that had driven George Barker out of Sendai, was still alive in that city, controlling the thoughts and actions of its citizens as if the war had never ended.

I remember only three excursions that I did not make alone. The first was with Professor Kobayashi, one spring Sunday, to Shiogama and Matsushima. The second was with a large group of professors and students to a rather dull beach called Nobiru. There is a group picture taken on that occasion, and on my face is an expression of total boredom. One of my former students (who rarely attended a lecture), Professor Takeshi Obata, wrote to me recently about that excursion:

> I have several vivid memories of you when I was one of your students at Sendai: a calm and profound tone of your voice in a gloomy auditorium; a figure of proud loneliness in a coffeehouse, 'Silver Star' where you often came to listen to classical music and so on. Among these memories, the most impressive one that I remember well is that of a picnic to Nobiru seashore in spring. I just dipped my foot into seawater, when you came to me and simply said: 'Too cold to bathe', looking over the sea far away. It was your first words spoken to me, but I remember I could not find any words to speak to you.

It was Professor Obata who kindly lent me the photograph taken on that occasion. Fortunately, many years later, in 1972, when I was living in Dublin, he suddenly visited me, and we were able to exchange more than a few words as my Japanese friend and I escorted him around Dublin and the Wicklow Mountains.

The third excursion was an afternoon's outing to Aobayama, the hill overlooking Sendai, to eat strawberries, but I have been unable to find any photographs of this outing, and remember nothing but the delicious taste of the strawberries eaten under a leafy arbour. All my other trips were made alone, and in a way I was glad of that, because it intensified for me the already intense impressions I was receiving and which are recorded in detail in *These Horned Islands* and *Japan behind the Fan* (1970).

There were no gay bars in Sendai at that time. Towards the end of my second year, my German colleague told me that one had opened, but when he told me that the boys were dressed as geishas, I did not bother to visit it. There were no amusing saunas or Turkish baths. But after a few weeks I discovered a small basement movie-house near the station called the Hinode, which means 'Sunrise'. There I found 'the place' – that special place which I always try to find in a strange town, where there is a gathering of like minds. But the homosexuals who haunted this dingy little movie-house, standing crowded at the back, where it was nice and dark, were very cagey. The presence of a tall, blond foreigner was something so unusual, they were as if frozen with fear. Nevertheless I did make one or two contacts, one of which turned out to be a plain-clothes' cop, another a scandal-mongering newspaperman, another a petty crook. If I made a score, I would whisk him off to Kozenji-dori in a taxi. If I did not, sometimes the taxi-drivers in those days would leave the meter running outside my door and have a quick fling with me in bed. In those days taxi-drivers were like amiable bandits, not the stodgy businessmen they are today. Before I learnt that there was no gay bar in Sendai, I once asked a taxi-driver to take me to one, thinking he would know if one existed. 'Are you sure, gay bar?' he asked, looking puzzled yet willing. 'Yes, yes, take me to gay bar!' I answered eagerly. I was completely drunk at the time – an increasingly frequent state brought on by a combination of boredom and despair in Sendai. We set off to find the gay bar, and drove on and on, out into the country, for miles and miles, until we reached a tiny village on the coast, the next stop to Matsushima. 'This is Geba,' the taxi-driver said, turning to me with a smile of triumph. 'What address, exactly?' I told him to drive back to Sendai.

On another occasion I came out of the Hinode alone at the end of the evening show. Summer was beginning, and the warm streets were filled with lively, strolling couples, children and drunken salarymen. I could feel something in the air as I gazed up at the great racks of brilliant neons tumbling, exploding and reassembling on the night sky. As I was strolling along, regretting that I had been unable to pick up anyone in the movie-house, a Japanese youth passed me and our eyes met. With the sixth sense homos have, I realized that he was available, and paused at the edge of the pavement, under a sighing willow tree. He soon joined me there. He was quite small, but had a charming face and figure. He was a truck-driver and his name was Goro. He invited me to get into his truck, which was parked in a side-street, and I followed him, trusting him implicitly. I thought he would take us to some deserted spot where we could make love in peace, like the thousands of young couples known as 'avec' who go in cars to remote sites and open a vacuum flask of hot water to steam their windows up in order to protect them from the prying eyes of the ever-present peeping Toms. The truck was not very big. Goro asked if we could go to my house, so I agreed, and he parked outside in the narrow lane where the house still stands. We went to bed at once, and I was amazed by his amorous skill and passion. He was my first real lover in Japan, and I have never forgotten his enthusiasm. I had been told that it was customary to give one's lovers 'car fare' or 'taxi fare' when they left. But Goro refused my offer of a modest sum. After all, he had his truck in which to get back to the workmen's dormitory where he lived.

I saw him once or twice again. He was from Hokkaido, I remember. Then one morning my maid came to tell me that someone was asking for me at the front door. 'He is not a good man,' she told me. I went downstairs and found Goro on the doorstep, looking ugly. He wanted money. I did not invite him inside, but gave him what he wanted, and he left. I never saw him again. My maid looked shocked and frightened. Later, I realized that he must have been some small-time hoodlum. In those early days, all young men looked alike to me, and I was willing to be friends with anyone who expressed the desire to be with me. But alas, they were not all real friends. I found, to my mortification, that I could not always tell when a stranger was my friend, and this often landed me in hot water.

It was in the autumn of my second year in Sendai, 1960, that I began to sense that ominous approach of doom I had so often experienced in Britain. It was something almost indefinable, impressions gathered from a word, a look, an inexplicable small event. My classes were unbearably boring; though I tried to make English literature as interesting as possible, I could not interest the students in it. They were lazy and careless and indifferent. One of those students told me in later years: 'We all thought you were quite mad.' Perhaps I was. In Japan, I was always in a class by myself: there was no precedent for me, and no one with whom I could compare myself. I was always a stranger, and I think this is what gave me intimations of disaster.

The new British Council representative in Tokyo was a poet, Ronald Bottrall. He invited himself and his wife to Sendai to give a lecture: they were greedy for all the perks they could get. I found Ronald a very sweet and amiable old poet, though I could not imagine why the Sitwells had taken him up at one time as their golden boy. He was a huge, powerful man. He once invited me to lunch at his house in Tokyo. It was curry. I was in a very bad state of nerves: I knew something unknown was going on behind my back in Sendai, some awful humiliation getting ready to devastate me. But Ronald's lunch restored my confidence a little. However, I was deeply shocked by the cavalier way he ordered his terrified servants around, shouting at them and yelling for more curry when I said I'd like a second helping – nerves and worry had prevented me from eating for days. Ronald recommended vitamin pills. 'You can't exist in this country without them, the food's so lacking in vitality', I remember him saying or rather roaring. His wife was an amusing, intelligent woman, with a sort of New York growl in her voice which turned out to be caused by nodules in her throat: she wrote me a long letter describing the successful operation to remove them. She was a great letter-writer.

I had been studying Yeats with my more advanced students in the post-graduate seminar, one of my more satisfying classes. So when Ronald asked what he should lecture to them on, I suggested Yeats, with particular stress on 'Prayer for My Daughter', a poem we had studied exhaustively. For some reason, no one in authority at the university would associate himself with this visit, so I had to arrange everything myself. when Ronald stood up to speak, he towered over all those shrinking students, and when at last he came to 'Prayer for My Daughter', they hung on every word, because I had made them learn it by heart. Ronald in full spate had a curious tic: from time to time he would use his free hand to give a reassuring twitch to his balls in their capacious trousers. At first I could not believe my eyes. But he did it again and again right under the noses of those young ladies and gentlemen, who sat with lowered eyes trying to keep a straight face, as we listened intently to the poem. However, Ronald stopped before the end. His secretary had typed out the poem for him, and in copying from the book must have assumed that it was long enough and had not realized there were two more verses on the next page. Ronald did not realize it, either, and sat down to polite applause after finishing an incomplete poem. 'Any questions?' he bellowed, looking around him. I held my breath. Japanese students never ask questions. In this case, I wondered if some daring spirit would mention that he had omitted the last two verses of Yeats's poem. But oriental tact prevailed. After the students had taken their leave, we three repaired to the hotel bar for a drink. After Ronald had had his first whisky and soda, I asked him why he had omitted the last two verses. 'That damned bitch of a secretary!' he roared. 'I'll kill her when we get back.' His wife calmed him down: 'Now then, Ronnie.' Almost at once his tone changed, and his face gave a great beam, and he broke into roars of laughter at the mishap. Yes, I liked Ronald Bottrall and his wife – they were no phonies.

On the day next day, Professor Muraoka invited us all to Matsushima, in a university limousine, to have lunch at the one and only Western-style hotel there at the time. After taking a boat trip round the islands, we all went to the hotel bar for an aperitif. 'What are you having, James?' Ronald asked. 'I'll have a pink gin, I think.' This drink fascinated me because it was popular with naval officers. But the Japanese bartender had never heard of pink gins, so Ronald took over. He spotted a dusky little bottle of Angostura bitters on a shelf, and made the bartender bring it to the bar. On opening the bottle, Ronald found it was completely blocked up, so that it was impossible to shake a few drops into my glass. 'Give me a toothpick!' Ronald roared at the terrified bartender. Ronald started digging at the blocked bottle with a small wooden toothpick until he had unclogged it. 'Now,' he said to the bartender, 'you shake it into the glass, like this.' He demonstrated, and the liquid, suddenly released from its year-long neglect, spurted out in unexpectedly large dollops all over the counter and the bartender. But he had got the idea, and, with Ronald's help, proudly presented me with a perfect pink gin, the first ever drunk in Matsushima.

All this time, dear Professor Muraoka was looking on from behind his glasses with an expression of the utmost bewilderment in his gentle, scholarly eyes. He was so impressed by the pink gin that when a year or so later he escorted Dr Muriel Bradbrook round Matsushima during her lecture tour of Japan, he is said to have offered her a pink gin for lunch at that delightful old-fashioned Taisho period hotel, now, sadly, vanished before the faceless and characterless hostelries of modern times.

Ronald was always on my side against the bureaucrats, both Japanese and British, and he knew how to squeeze every penny of expenses out of them when lecturing in various places in Japan. Francis King had arrived in 1960 to take over the running of the British Council in Kyoto, which he did with extreme efficiency for four years or so, after which he resigned, as so many people did who were hired by the Council. Their employees were not supposed to publish books, for some strange reason, and I think this is one of the reasons Francis threw in the sponge. He had a large and luxuriously appointed house and a large garden in the best part of Kyoto, and Ronald was always inviting himself to give lectures there. Francis used to give amusing imitations of people like Cyril Eland and Ronald Bottrall and some of the Japanese students and professors he so often had to deal with and so wittily satirized in his novel about Japan, *The Custom House* (1961). He described how Ronald would bargain with him to get invited to Kyoto so that he could milk the Council for every expense he could think of, in exchange for Francis's being invited to Tokyo for the sake of similar perks. The fact that they would justify their travels by giving a lecture or two at universities was purely incidental. After I returned *sub rosa* to Japan from Malaysia in 1961, Francis kindly invited me to his house in Kyoto, where I was looking in vain for a job of any kind. There was a party at which some gays and many Japanese professors were present, and I gathered that I had been invited because one of them wanted to explore the possibilities of writing a doctoral thesis about J.R. Ackerley, and intended to pick my brains. I'm afraid he did not get much out of me. I had just had a letter from Joe after I had written to him asking if he would inquire about the possibility of my getting a post in Nagoya, and he had written back saying: 'Cyril Eland tells me it is useless for Kirkup to apply for the post in Nagoya, as he is considered *persona non grata* by the British Council.' The news filled me with a strange delight: I accepted it as a compliment.

But to return to autumn, 1960 and Sendai. I got a letter from Joe, now retired from *The Listener*, suddenly informing me that he was coming to see me. Then I knew that something must be wrong. Joe always used to rush to my side whenever I got into trouble.

There was a persimmon tree in my garden, just beside the fence. In the garden of my neighbour, whom I never met, there was a fig tree. When my fruit were ripe, the ones hanging over the other side of the fence were unobtainable. One day the teenage son next door was taking fruit from my tree, something I did not mind at all, as I could not reach the persimmons myself. But when I went out of the back door to my kitchen to give him a hand, he ran back into his house as if I were a leper. That saddened me. I did not try to take his figs on my side of the fence; but if I had done so and he had caught me in the act, I would not have run away.

The local bath a little way up Kozenji-dori had a charming, naïve mural of Mount Fuji, and I liked to go and soak in the hot water and gaze up at the sacred mountain. But if there were other men and boys already in the bath, as soon as I got in they would all climb out. Running away from me again, as if I might rape them in public. It was rather hard to take.

Then the nice-looking boy who used to come twice a week to take my laundry to the cleaners showed a different reaction. Although I had always kept my hands off him, I used to give him little presents, like a bottle of Asti Spumante for Christmas or an exotic box of Black Magic for O-Bon. But now when he came into the house to collect the laundry he seemed ready to make himself at home, and when I made him a cup of green tea he blushed and gave me a meaningful look. This put me off. Why was he suddenly so friendly? Had he heard that I liked young men? The boys who used to bring the restaurant meals I telephoned for stayed to watch me eat, then washed up the dishes. The workmen who came to repair and paint the house used to push their girlish young apprentices into my arms and indicate that they, too, were available. Instead of exciting me, these insinuations froze my blood: it was all too true to be good. Yet these workmen broke my loneliness. 'When once they're gone she'll almost regret her workmen's blue sleeves' was a quote I found in Firbank's *Vainglory*. I just regretted their smiles.

When I visited a low bar where I had never set foot before, the raunchy old madame gave me a nudge and a wink and groped me, obviously thinking it was one great joke. I could see that I had become a 'character' for them. But this new friendliness rather frightened me. On the other hand, the ice-man would now rush in with his dripping block of ice on one shoulder, shove it into the top of the ancient ice-box and hurry out again without a word, when before he had sometimes stopped for a chat and a 'Hope' cigarette.

My German neighbour Edmund, who had been a good friend, started avoiding me. At the university, my classes were decimated.

When I asked why so many students were absent, I was told that they had 'taken a purge' and so could not attend: it was not the usual skipping of classes, which they called by the Janglish term 'sabotage'.

In the darkness at the back of the Sendai movie-houses I would sometimes see one of my colleagues, or one or two of my students. Once I saw one of my very prim-and-proper girl students there, staring apparently at the screen but actually spying on me out of the corners of her eyes – because of the shape of their eyes, I was told by one Japanese, they can see both hands at once if they are raised to shoulder level on either side: she was 'cornering' me.

I fell head over heels in love with the great jazz singer Anita O'Day when she sang 'Tea for Two' in the movie *Jazz on a Summer's Day*, and I went to see it nearly every day of its run in Sendai, in a large movie-house near the Hinode. The girl at the ticket window nearly had kittens every time I came in, and once or twice a couple of uniformed cops followed me in and stood at the back while I, for once, was in a seat up front, my short-sighted eyes glued to the screen.

The crowds of men who used to stand at the back of movie-houses seemed to be thinning out. Was it simply the hot summer weather? Or was there a witch-hunt? I really felt as if I had become too well known, and for the wrong reasons. But it was at this nightmare period that I was picked up by a young man who came and made an obvious pass at me: he became a faithful friend, and he still is. His presence saved my sanity when everything seemed to be collapsing around me. When the summer vacation arrived, I felt a change of scene would be helpful, so I went to Hokkaido, leaving the key of my house with my friend, so that he could collect my letters. I was hoping that Hokkaido would be cooler, and give me some relief from the 37-degree humid heat, unbearable without a cooler or a fan. In fact it is a myth that Hokkaido is cooler than Honshu in summer: the temperature might have been a little lower, but it was still horribly hot and damp, and Sapporo was full of flies. I stuck it for a week, because Ronald Bottrall had asked me to take part in a summer school run by the Council in a small town in Hokkaido – I forget the name.

When I arrived on the stated date, all the students and the other lecturers were already there. After dinner that first evening we retired to the teachers' staff-room, where Ronald produced several bottles of beer and asked who would like a drink. We all had a glass of beer except Ronald, who produced a bottle of the then very rare Johnny Walker Scotch – another of his Council perks, I suppose. He proceeded to drink it without offering any to the rest of us, so I just put my beer aside and helped myself, while Ronald tut-tutted and fussed. I hate the taste of Scotch, but from his expression one would have thought he already classed me as an alcoholic.

The knowing looks of Ronald and his wife were too much for me, like the horrid taste of the Scotch, so I set off for a walk down to the village, which was in almost complete darkness, hoping to find a friend, or at least a friendly *sake* shop. But everything was closed and there were no vending-machines. The village seemed deserted, but suddenly in the distance I saw a gigantic figure which I knew could not be Japanese: it was Ronald prowling around, presumably sent out by his wife to check on my movements. Taking a route along a back lane, I managed to get back to the school without meeting him.

Next morning the atmosphere was grim. Ronald had no idea at all how to run a summer school for foreign students of English, and he had begged me to come up with some ideas. I suggested the students might dramatize a Maugham short story as if for radio, with appropriate sound-effects, and suggested 'Rain', adding: 'I do hope we get some Sadie Thompson types.' Ronald thought that a great joke. But the plan was thrown out, and the students, teachers belonging to some militant trade union, seemed to be in an aggressive mood. Ronald's booming Oxford accent and colonialist manner did nothing to appease them, and I was so ashamed of being British that at the end of the first unhappy class I just packed my bags and walked out. One of the female British lecturers, Dorothy Brittan, cried: 'He's doing a Kirkup!' But I did not even look back. I went straight to the station, disdaining to ask for the staff car, which would probably have been refused me, lugging those heavy bags full of Ainu souvenirs of carved wooden salmon and bears.

When I got back to Sendai, my friend came as usual for the evening, and as I made him dinner, I asked him if the house had been all right during my absence: I was afraid there might have been some unwelcome visitors, or more dread telephone calls. To my surprise, he told me that there had been men patrolling the lane while I was away, and when he had attempted to enter the front gate they had asked him who he was and what he was doing and would not allow him to enter. 'I was frightened,' he told me. 'They were bad men, Jim.'

It was all very odd, and I was frightened myself. So it was good news that Joe was coming. But also it was bad news: if Joe was coming all the way to Japan to see me, things must be really bad. What was it all about? I was completely in the dark: nobody ventured to explain anything to me, not even my friend. I was in the grip of panic, but I preserved a perfectly calm outward demeanour, never missing a single class.

September came, but the heat hardly abated. I sweltered, drank pints of Kirin beer, tried to keep cool by sitting in air-conditioned pachinko halls, half deafened by the raucous recordings of military bands. I fell sick with an ear infection and had to attend hospital. I was given a blood segmentation test: normal. There was nothing really wrong with me, yet I felt I was dying. My appetite departed: the thought of food made me ill, and when I tried to swallow an aspirin I nearly choked. I gagged every time I brushed my teeth. This was partly the emotional aftermath of my affair with Dana, the death of my father, my mother's blindness. I had brought my heart-sickness, my soul-sickness with me from Europe, and I felt I would never be well again. At this period I happened to pick up a copy of Housman's poems, which I had not read for many years, and I was once more overwhelmed by all their stoic heartbreak. Under their influence, I wrote a series of short poems in the Housman manner: they were little more than exercises, yet the problems of language and structure they presented soothed my mind for a while. I have never printed them, but here is one that expresses very well my psychological confusion at that time:

Time's Antitheses

In years when I was young and free
    And felt my courage high,
I trod the ground with certainty,
    And yet I wished to die.

Now I am older, and the slave
    Of all the fears in hell,
With every breath I dig my grave,
    And wish I could be young, and well.

'Now I am older. . . .' That autumn, I was in the middle of my forty-second year, and thus approaching that period of a man's life when the Japanese believe untold misfortunes and even death are in his destiny. It is called 'the turbulent year' and falls in the forty-fourth year of a man's life. But it begins before that, and continues for two or three years afterwards . . .

I tried to assuage my terrors by visiting the local temples and attempting to pray. There was a temple not far from my house, where I used to go early in the morning, around five o'clock, when there was still a little coolness in the air, and I would pray to the Buddha in the garden until the level-crossing bell nearby – one of the most characteristic Japanese sounds – began to jangle, signalling the passage of the first train. Sometimes I stayed on until the young priest who lived there alone came out to sweep the paths. We could not talk much, but he was a good, simple man, and his mere presence brought me brief peace of mind as we sat sipping green tea on the veranda. He was one of my true friends in Sendai, among all the riff-raff, the tramps, the drunks, the drop-outs, the prostitutes I frequented. They seemed to me the only genuine human beings in a too-conformist society whose moral and social strictures I found infinitely tedious, as tedious as the tea ceremony with its stultified rules and regulations. And that awful, frothy green tea always gave me stomach-ache.

But as soon as I left my priest friend and started walking back to my house, the ominous anguish of my days and nights would overtake me, and by the time I got home in the already hot sun I would be sweating with terror at the prospect of what the day might bring me. All I could do was lock myself in my house and wait for darkness to descend around seven, as it always did in Japan, for there was no daylight-saving time, as in my childhood. I felt some relief when darkness fell – *ami du criminel*. And I would go prowling round the bars, the parks and the movie-houses, looking for I hardly knew what – perhaps just the consolation of a human touch. When I became desperate for the touch of a hand, I would go to the barber-shop and submit myself to the cool ministrations, hour-long, of the calm, gentle boys and girls, their fairy touch like balm upon my soul. I wished my hair would grow faster, so that I might go every day: but I went at least once a week, for a haircut in those days was cheap, and it was almost a spiritual experience – the massage at the end of the shampoo and trim was alone worth the money.

I used to have an 'at home' day for students every Wednesday, and a small group would come for tea and conversation in the afternoons. They were usually boys, as the young ladies seemed to think it improper to visit a bachelor's home. But suddenly the girls started to come in groups, bearing cakes and cookies they had baked themselves. I felt that someone must have instructed them to visit me: perhaps the neighbours had got the wrong ideas when they saw males exclusively visiting me. Yet those afternoons were times of simple companionship, of tea and sympathy, of readings and music and laughter. I would never lay a hand on one of my students. But I did meet a very nice one in the movies, who became a dear friend and we met often. He was not a literature but a medical student, and he lived in Kumamoto, where I visited him once or twice in later years. He had a rather plain face, but under his dreary uniform he had a beautiful body, passionate and strong. He was worried about his homosexuality, because he knew that according to the inflexible Japanese custom all males are forced to marry, usually a marriage arranged by parents or teachers or employers. This was one of the depressing facts of life in Japan for me, and for many men who nevertheless dared not go against tradition. I felt that Japan would always be a medieval land when such customs persisted in the modern world where freedom of choice was our Western ideal. The only unmarried men and women in Japan were foreigners, and they were looked upon as very peculiar indeed.

From behind my shuttered windows, with the *shoji* or paper windows slid shut against the broiling sun, I could observe the daily life of the lane. I could also watch for unwelcome visitors. One of these was Burton Martin's Japanese friend, whom I could sometimes see looking up at my closed windows. Once or twice he came to the front door and rang the bell, but I did not give any sign of life: I had no wish to meet him. I believe he was some kind of tea ceremony teacher, and anything connected with the tea ceremony filled me with ennui. Besides, he would be in touch with Burton Martin, Hiroshi Uno and various others in the Japanese journalistic field, and I had no wish to provide them with further fuel for their poison pens.

It was into this atmosphere that Joe came from England. I went to Tokyo to greet him, and I remember that somehow I was able to obtain admission to the tarmac at Haneda so that I could meet him as he was coming down the gangway of the plane – Air France, which in his letters to me he had glumly called 'Air Chance'. He had a horror of flying, and I knew that his doctor had given him various tranquillizing drugs in order to prepare him for the flight. He mentioned this to me in a letter and it was the first time I heard of Joe taking drugs. I cannot find any of his letters from the period when I was in Sendai, and suspect I must have destroyed them, along with other inculpatory papers and notebooks, in my panic packing when I suddenly decided to leave Japan in February 1962. Like my parents, he kept almost none of my letters.

It was lovely to see Joe coming down the ramp from the plane, looking pretty exhausted but smiling as he swept me into a passionate embrace. He was at his most handsome, sinister and grave, not unlike dear old Ferdy Maine in Roman Polanski's *The Fearless Vampire Killers*.

Cyril Eland had booked him into the San Bancho Hotel, which overlooks the moat of the Imperial Palace. At that period, when Japanese youths had a lot more initiative than they have now, it was said to be a good place for attentive room-boys. I believe Joe was supplied with a compliant young man by a student doing part-time work as a go-between. We took a taxi to the hotel, and I remember offering Joe a 'Hope' cigarette. They were the smallest and cheapest, and must have tasted foul. Only when poor Joe made a face and stubbed it out immediately did I realize how my taste had become Japanized, even in the matter of cigarettes, though I smoked only about ten a day. 'Dear Jim. How are you, darling?' he said, taking my hand and giving me a kiss, to the astonishment of the driver. 'Oh, Joe, I feel like death' was what I wanted to reply, but I put on a bright face and assured him that all was well. He gave me a suspicious sidelong look, with that hint of a cruel, witty smile. That finally convince me something was wrong. I asked after Morgan, who was again in poor health. Joe must have expressed his worries about me to Forster, because it was Forster who gave him the money to go to Japan. Joe, having retired from *The Listener*, was living in reduced circumstances, having to provide not just for himself but also for 'my women' – Nancy, Bunny (his aunt) and Queenie. I believe there were other calls upon his purse by various individuals whom I would rather not mention. 'And how is Bottrall?' he went on, cautiously. The Hokkaido incident had caused a complete break in my relations with Ronald, but I had liked him in spite of his bullying colonialism, and he had done his best to be kind to me. But he was hated by the British Council staff, who took him at face value only and so thought he was a boor. In fact, he was a deeply sensitive man who put on a mask of bluster and braggadocio to hide his real feelings. After all, he was a poet, and a good one whose work I had often admired. I felt in sympathy with him, and was sorry that my behaviour had finally been too much for him. It was the members of his staff who were the true boors.

When we got to the hotel, Cyril Eland was waiting to receive Joe and whisk him off at once to a British Council dinner. I had been hoping to have dinner with my old friend, and Joe had been hoping to spend a quiet evening with me. But Eland had been given firm instructions to take Joe straight to the dinner: the Council wanted to give him their own version before he could get mine. So he was swept away as soon as he had showered and changed and been introduced by Eland to his room-boy. I, of course, was not invited to the British Council dinner.

Next morning, when I met Joe after breakfast (I was staying at the Dai-Ichi), he gave me a hilarious account of that ghastly dinner. Eland had warned him: 'Don't mention Kirkup to Bottrall.' So I do not know how much Joe had learnt of the situation in Sendai, but probably Eland gave him the dirt, exaggerating as usual, and taking care to show me in a bad light, something that is always so easy to do. One of my foremost pleasures in life is affording idiots opportunities to prove their stupidity by revelling in the easy triumph of denigrating me or mocking what they take to be self-betrayal.

I had to return to Sendai to give my classes, so I left Joe in Tokyo to the tender mercies of Eland and Bottrall. Heaven knows what lies they told him. Joe hated Tokyo. After a few days, he was put on the train to Sendai from Ueno Station. The British Council tried to dissuade him from coming to stay with me, warning him that he would be living in squalor, discomfort and perhaps personal danger. But Joe was loyal to me. I met him one afternoon when his train arrived at Sendai Station. He was looking distressed and tired, so I took him straight home in a taxi. I had to give him my bedroom, as there was only one Western-style bed in the house, and Joe adamantly refused to sleep on the floor. I slept downstairs in a *tatami* room next to the kitchen.

One of the first things Joe asked me was: 'Does Professor Kobayashi come to visit you?'

'No. I would not expect him to.'

'Do your colleagues come?'

'No.'

'Don't you think Morgan Forster would come to see you if he was in the Dean's position?'

A pause. 'No, I don't think so.' This unexpected reply seemed to upset Joe, so I changed the subject. 'I've put a little present beside your bed,' I told him, smiling.

Joe never used make-up. But on his creaky little bamboo bedside stand I had placed one of those little Shiseido Sachets of *papier poudré*, in my favourite *rachel* shade, which I thought might suit his fair complexion as well as it did mine. I also placed there a lace-trimmed handkerchief imprinted with a black-and-white photograph of a young Japanese singer. On the wash-basin downstairs (there was none up-stairs) I laid a small 'hostess' cake of Cow Brand soap that had been presented to me, rather suggestively I thought, by a taxi-driver when I

paid my fare. When he washed his face and hands, Joe happened to
comment that the towel smelt of fresh semen, which was a ridiculous
charge, as I had only just rubbed it through and hung it out in the sun
to bleach. He later told Francis King, in the spiteful way he sometimes
had, that everything in my house smelt of boys' come, like the abode of
some vampire monster who needed, in order to stay alive, to milk
youths of their vital fluids each night. The truth is, that that particular
smell was caused by the industrial detergent I used to wash my smalls
and my hand-towels on a day-to-day basis – I could not afford the more
expensive blue-rinse kinds. But I have to admit that it did make the
towels smell of teenage ejaculations, which in young Japanese are
particularly rich and creamy.

I made some tea and we sat sipping it in the kitchen as we exchanged
our latest news. Poor Queenie was getting old, like her master, and Joe
hated having to leave her in Nancy's charge – both of his 'women' had
objected strongly to his visit to Japan. I told him that Hardy and his
wife were both 'owned' by an obstreperous dog that bit the guests and
snatched food off the table. 'Snatch food off the table!' Joe exclaimed
indignantly. 'When have you ever seen Queenie do that? Of course,' he
added, tittering, 'she does from time to time give Morgan Forster a
nip – she's so possessive, you know, and she can't bear it when I fuss
over the old dear.'

Joe hated uncircumcised boys, whereas I disliked the circumcised, not
for any racial or religious reason, of course, but simply that I preferred to
consort with those who like myself had not been 'cut'. They were practically non-existent in Japan, where I can remember meeting only two or
three cases in all the years I lived there, so I told Joe he was going to enjoy
himself. A few years later, I was reading an entertaining biography of
Lytton Strachey, in which there is an account of him (the 'funny little
creature') as a boy at Abbotsholme: 'He was circumcised,' an old
Abbotsholmian remembered, 'but quite unconscious of the fact that he
did not look like all the other boys in the dormitory.' This is thought
rather extraordinary, even for the enlightened twenties, before the
American rage for sexual mutilation broke out. The Japanese condition
is supposedly genetic, not artificially produced, which perhaps explains
certain unpleasant aspects of the Japanese character. If the Japanese *are*
born circumcised, as are the Chinese and other Asians – or at least born
with easily retractable foreskins that parents train in the way they
should go by constantly pulling them back – I do not think this
circumcised state is yet another proof that the Japanese belong to the

lost tribes of Israel, though the Jews and the Japanese have some common character traits. The Japanese are fascinated by the Jews, but in an ignorant, superficial way.

In a book on Tu Fu by Florence Ayscough, whose *A Chinese Mirror* (dedicated to Amy Lowell) I much admire, I found this interesting passage:

> In ancient China, one's bones were supposed to be a heritage from one's father, while one's flesh was a heritage from one's mother. So one is responsible to one's parents for one's body. It is laid down in the *Book of Rites* that a body shall be delivered to the World of Shade in the same condition that it is received from one's parents, which is the principal reason why the Chinese object so strongly to amputation or any mutilation.

I believe there is a similar reverence for the body in Jewish law, and among certain native American tribes.

I told Joe that I felt my own precarious situation in Sendai made me identify with the dispossessed and persecuted Jews of Hitler's time. In the streets of Sendai, I had had pointed out to me by a Japanese professor, always eager to be the first to convey trivial information, that a certain harried-looking old gentleman tottering towards us had been the Japanese translator of *Mein Kampf*. During Hitler's rise to power, he had been looked upon in Sendai as one of the beacons of Japanese intellect, but as soon as the war ended and the Yanks arrived, he was treated as a pariah. I felt a strange sympathy for the old man, and one day when we passed him in Ichibancho I pointed him out to Joe, with the words: 'There, but for the grace of Buddha, go I.' Indeed, I felt I was in something of the same situation as that sad old man, a fellow-hack in the ill-paid world of translation, who had just been trying to turn an honest penny in the stirring times of the Berlin-Rome-Tokyo Axis. Joe said he reminded him of Morgan Forster or Wyndham Lewis. I was recently surprised to find that the Japanese *Mein Kampf* is still on sale in a translation by Hirano Ichiro and Takayanagi Shigeru, published by Reimei-Shobo in 1960.

Joe had brought with him a few bottles of his favourite Gordon's gin, and as he did not care much for the taste of my tea (cat's piss), we had a few glasses as I told him how I had been investigated by two 'professors' from the University of Maryland who were probably FBI men. It had happened shortly after my arrival, and the interview took place in

Professor Kobayashi's study at the university. The dear Dean was obviously embarrassed at having to submit me to this ordeal, which I went through with my customary nonchalance. They were a very unpleasant-looking couple in Homburgs and long grey raincoats, like insurance salesmen from Philadelphia. 'Don't let them bother you,' Professor Kobayashi rather mysteriously said after they departed. A year or so ago, it was finally revealed that American universities were sending representatives to Japan to vet the political reliability of Japanese and foreign academics.

By the time Joe arrived, the superconductivity of my social and poetic antennae had reached a high level of sensitivity. I told him how I had gone to a bar the night before where the only other customers were a young couple. I was far gone in drink, and I tried to engage them in conversation. We got on quite well until the young man demanded to know who I was, so I handed him my *meishi*. As soon as he read my name and address (in Japanese on the reverse side of this 'business card'), he tore it up, with grave deliberation. This action reduced me to tears of despair – the first time I had ever wept in public. The young girl was so shocked, she remonstrated with her boy-friend. He remained grimly silent. It was a speaking silence. I paid my bill and left, feeling even more of an outcast than usual. If this was the price I had to pay for being true to my own nature, it seemed rather hard on me, as I never did anyone any harm: the only person harmed, if at all, was myself. It all appeared very unreasonable and unjust to me, to be thus discriminated against for behaving as God had made me – though the existence of a loving God was a myth I had long since abandoned, for how could any god be so stupid? At forty-two, I was still young and foolish. Would I ever learn?

Like me, Joe had little interest in gay ghettos, but as there was no gay bar in Sendai, I took him to the Hinode movie-house and to another, larger cinema that was usually crowded with men and boys standing at the back or sitting waiting for contacts on the sofas in the lobby. But that night everywhere was curiously empty. This too filled me with forebodings. We went on to a few bars where I was well known, and there were no untoward incidents. But I felt increasingly uneasy. What had happened? Joe seemed very guarded, as if he knew something, but I did not ask him to enlighten me. What had he been told at the British Council? I felt that his silence was a protective one: he did not want me to be hurt.

During the next few days, I took Joe to Shiogama and Matsushima.

Then I had to give classes, so he started going around on his own. It was on his second visit to Matsushima that Joe visited the local zoo and was appalled by what he saw. Three years later, he was to write for me – I was then literary editor of the Tokyo magazine *Orient/West* – one of his best short prose pieces, entitled 'I Am a Beast'. It starts in a characteristic Ackerleian fashion:

> I dislike children. I didn't mean to begin with that remark. I'm afraid it may pain the Japanese, who are fond of them, or at any rate compassionate towards them, but it slipped out. Shall I modify it and say that Japanese children are the best in the world – well anyway the prettiest? Yes, I will allow that. English children are seldom pretty and often odious, and as for American children the less said about them the better. . . .

But the real subject of the essay is the tigress with which Joe struck up a strange relationship at the dismal Matsushima Zoo. We both detested zoos, so I had avoided the place when I first went to Matsushima with Joe. But he had stumbled upon it, and upon this wretched tigress in her joyless little cage:

> . . . She was on exhibition, if only at the moment to me. No retreat for her if she wished to exchange the boredom of being gaped at for the boredom of a lonely lair. Besides, we paid to see her, how could she be allowed to hide herself away? We should not then get our money's worth. The children would be disappointed, and children must never be disappointed.
>
> . . . An elephant somewhere was squealing and trumpeting his head off.
>
> I found him in a closed wooden shed lined and fenced about with wire netting; he could just be glimpsed through a dusty window. Short chains attached to two of his legs hobbled him to a concrete floor; where he could reach with his trunk the wire netting inside he had torn it down. I had had enough of Matsushima Zoo and made for the exit. Then I glanced back. The tigress was standing motionless, her face fixed upon me. When she saw me returning to her she crouched again. 'Goodbye, pretty lady,' I said. 'I wish I had not seen you and I shall never see you more.' That was three years ago and she has paced up and down my heart as, if she is still alive, I suppose she has paced up and down her cage ever since.

Matsushima Bay had lost its charm. With its trashy tourist junk shops and the damp litter left lying about its accessible islands. . . .

I remember the evening when Joe returned home after that excursion. He seemed unutterably sad, so I made him a gin and tonic as he recounted his afternoon to me. I recognized in his description all the ghastly zoos of Japan – at Tennoji in Osaka, at Okazaki Park in Kyoto – and all over the civilized world. I myself felt caged in Sendai, but I was no beautiful tigress.

Joe's view of Japanese children was rosier than mine, for I found them insufferably rude, spoilt and noisy. In the quarter of a century that has passed since Joe's visit, they have become even more hateful, because standardized and brainwashed by a nationalistic system of education. And the zoos are no better: there are more of them, and they are detestable dens of misery, concentration camps for the wild.

I tried to keep Joe entertained during the week or so that he stayed with me, but Sendai then had little to offer in the way of entertainment for a sophisticated, elderly, Western intellectual. It was while Joe was staying with me that I fully realized the cultural barrenness of Sendai, its small-town mentality, its provincial smugness, its rigid hierarchies in academic life and in the traditional arts. I was bored to distraction, and if I had not had my books and my writing to fall back on every day, I should have died of inanition and despair. Most of the youths who picked me up were good for an hour or so in bed; but after that, they had nothing at all to offer me in the way of companionship or intelligent conversation. However, there were a few exceptions, and one or two are still my friends. I suppose that is the most anyone can hope for, whatever country one lives in. I was reading a lot of American literature at the time, as most students seemed to prefer it to English literature, in the mistaken notion that anything American must be 'easy', and in *The Education of Henry Adams*, a book that opened my eyes to that neglected author, I found: 'Friendship needs a certain parallelism of life, a community of thought, a rivalry of aim.' None of these things did I discover in the Japanese, with whom I felt increasingly that I had nothing in common. Adams also wrote something that reminded me of Auden's 'our love for five friends': 'One friend in a lifetime is much; two are many; three are hardly possible.' And in Mark Twain's notebooks I found: 'The proper office of a friend is to side with you when you are in the wrong. Nearly anybody will side with you when you are in the right.'

Joe was one of the very few who sided with me whenever I was in the wrong – or what the world regarded as wrong. So I shared my Japanese friends with him. There was a dear, sweet, simple country boy who worked on his father's rice-paddies somewhere on the way to Shioga-ma. Sunday was his only day off, and he used to spend it in Sendai, where I first met him at the Hinode movie-house. After our first meeting, when I took him home to bed and to lunch, I thought I should not see him again. But the next Sunday morning he was on my doorstep, waiting for me as I returned from my shopping. He used to come every Sunday morning after that. When I asked him if he would kindly go to bed with Joe, he looked shocked and sad, but he agreed for my sake. It was Joe who showed reluctance to take my friend away from me, but I bundled them both into bed upstairs while I made lunch, listening with approval to Joe's gasps and sighs and groans of bliss.

After lunch, Joe asked if he might go for a walk with the young man, who, like most Japanese in Sendai, was cautious about being seen with a foreigner. I gave them instructions about how to find Aobayama, and off they went while I had a bath and a siesta. When Joe returned he said he thought he had fallen in love with my friend. But he was infinitely sad, because he would be leaving for Kyoto next day, and there was no chance of his ever seeing him again. I, too, never saw the boy again. I do not know what Joe had said to him or done to him, but he never came back to wait for me on my doorstep on Sunday mornings.

Then there was the delightful young man in tight-fitting jeans who had called on me one evening shortly after my arrival in Sendai. He spoke no English, and I did not dare believe that he might want what I wanted, so I asked my German colleague Edmund, who as noted lived next door, to send over his student assistant as an interpreter. I could not make out what my visitor wanted, but I guessed he must have been one of Burton Martin's boy-friends. After a while, he left.

But next evening, after I had finished dinner and my maid had gone home, my front-door bell rang, and there he was again, with his well-knit figure in jeans that showed a promising bump, a charming smile on his attractive face with its monkey-like fringe of hair. He was standing directly under the porch light, and at first I though it must be snowing, because his thick black hair was shining all over with points of silver. Quite a number of young Japanese men have these streaks of silvery white among their midnight locks, but on the head only.

This time I did not call an interpreter, but asked him in, and after a few cups of hot *sake* we went to bed for a couple of hours or so. I found it utterly delightful, and I know he did too, because he would often come back to see me, sometimes bringing an interested friend anxious for one of those 'first time' experiences the Japanese are always seeking. He liked Joe, but though ready to oblige, did not show much enthusiasm for going to bed with him, and Joe, always the gentleman, did not insist.

Then there was my medical student from Kumamoto, highly intelligent, fond of good wine and music, a great reader and a karate black belt, with whom for about a year I had one of my more sustained relationships. He had a large wart on his penis which I begged him not to have removed, telling him that when he got a girl-friend ('No! Never! Sendai girls too ugly!') she would bless him for it. I had already met a seaman who had had three cultured pearls surgically implanted in his *membrum virile* to provide extra excitement for his partners of either sex – like tattooing of the glans and the shaft, a fairly common practice among the lower classes and the *yakuza*. My Kumamoto friend, being a medical student, was expert in technical matters, but not in any cold-blooded scientific way, for did he not come from Kyushu, noted for its homoerotic passions, a relic of ancient samurai love among comrades-in-arms? He used to come to see me after dark, dressed in a fine indigo-blue kimono and over-jacket (*haori*), wearing only a breechclout (*fundoshi*) underneath. He was a delightful friend, but when he returned to Kumamoto and settled down to marriage and a successful practice, we saw less and less of one another, to my deep regret.

I had no intention of offering this pearl to Joe, who considerately went out for a walk when he telephoned to say he would be visiting me. But one evening he was still there when Joe returned, and I was able to introduce them. My friend was deeply shocked when Joe gave him a friendly hug and a peck on the cheek as he was leaving. 'I just couldn't resist him in his kimono when he bowed to me like that,' said Joe. 'I loved his cropped, stiff black hair and wanted to lick it.'

We had no luck in the bars or in the movies. I think the sight of two foreigners together must have put the boys off. Even my pimp friend would not acknowledge me in the street. Or had he been warned off me by the cops? However, when Joe returned to Tokyo, where he was to stay at the Kanda YMCA, in those unsanitized sexy days a perfect hotbed of international sex exchanges, I arranged to have a good friend in Tokyo stay there at the same time. He contacted Joe through the front desk soon after his arrival, took him out to dinner and then came to his Spartan little cubicle and gave him a good time. Alas, again Joe fell in love! He wrote to me telling me all about it, and seemed to be really in pain at having to leave the young man and go on to Francis King in Kyoto. That friend still remembers Joe. He is now a successful businessman, married with two children but now divorced, and thus free to indulge his real sexual inclinations. On his first business trip to Europe, he went to London and gazed up at Joe's balcony at the top of the Star and Garter mansions: but by that time Joe and Nancy were dead.

Joe attended one of my Wednesday afternoon 'at homes'. About seven male students were there, all wearing their stiff-collared Germanic student uniforms, which Joe found off-putting, not realizing what wonders are to be found underneath those drab exteriors, once the eyeglasses are removed. The students were fascinated by Joe's voice, with its gentle James Mason Cambridge drawl, affected by Enright and that lot, but with none of the art displayed by Joe, who had used it to full effect as an announcer for the BBC, or a presenter of interview programmes.

After the students had taken their leave, we settled down to gin and tonics, and discussed their salient features. 'What plain-looking boys!' Joe exclaimed. 'How can you bear to face them in class?' I told him that in fact they were not as plain as he thought: many of them, if provoked, would blush charmingly and flash brilliant smiles from their perfect teeth. In class, I took care not to look directly at them, but somewhere above their heads, though if there happened to be one especially attractive student, I would venture to gaze upon his beauty from time to time, rationing my glances so as not to awaken suspicions in the rest of the class. I always gave top marks to good-looking students, but I was merciful also to the lazy, the incompetent, the sad and the ugly, so that in my courses no student has ever failed his final examination: I just couldn't have the heart to fail anybody, for I knew how much their future lives depended upon passing.

Some of the students came with me to see Joe off at Sendai Station. There were tears in my eyes as I said goodbye to him. As the train was drawing out and all the students were bowing farewell, he shouted to me 'Be happy!' Advice which I have never forgotten, for I have been happy ever since, despite everything.

The heat of Tohoku in summer extended to the autumn. Day after day, the sun blazed inanely in a blank blue sky. I was in a constant fever alternating with shivering fits, the effects of malaria and the persistent reactions from those middle-life inoculations for smallpox I had received in Bath. I described my agonies in the following poem. It was the last ever to be published (by the then literary editor, Anthony Thwaite, whom Joe described to me in a letter as 'the new char at the Corporation'). Joe had by this time been put out to grass, very unhappily, and *The Listener* had begun its gradual degeneration into unreadable and badly edited tedium. After Joe left, it became obvious that he was irreplaceable, and the 'paper' as he called it was never the same again.

Fever

The clinical thermometer, a small
Dagger of glass at the armpit,
Dangerously near the heart.

The mercury's persistent splinter
Works deeper than the crystal blade:
Bad blood in a poisoned vein.

Beyond the mosquito net's dry tent
Whose blue shower drenches me with sweat,
My wet shadow battles with the wall.

Admiring my brown and healthy hand,
I restore the mean thermometer to
Its red glass of water, furred with pearls.

There it leans its neat illusion, sick
As a snapped stalk, pickled
In the rosy heart of light.

Nothing, at last, makes sense.
I know I shall die, and feel
Only indifference.

(*The Listener*, 14 Jan. 1960)

To my surprise, it was broadcast on what I called 'The Turd Programme' by that comical pair of Oxford literary brokers' men, little Anthony Thwaite and pathetic George MacBeth. There was a red cut-crystal glass on my bedside table in Sendai, standard equipment at that time, a relic from the Meiji era. And the blue mosquito-net, hanging over my bed like a cobweb from 'The Sleeping Beauty', had been a present from one of my non-academic Sendai friends, Takuro.

Many times I regretted having gone against my father's wishes and convictions: I dreamed of him and George Bernard Shaw gazing accusingly and pityingly at me. Professor Kobayashi called a doctor, who could find nothing wrong with me. 'Segmentation rate normal,' he pronounced in German, the 'secret language' of Japanese doctors, not knowing I could understand it. But winter eventually came, and I wandered for days, lost in the mountains:

> A land of long mountains and level lakes of light.
> The dark plateau is bare,
> The houses hidden caverns deep
> In waves of snow.
>
> Far in the lonely mountains
> Where black pines are clouds of rime,
> I wander all alone, and lost, a ghost of ice,
> A shadow pale as mist, my breath a dream. . . .
>
> (from 'Paper Windows')

After Joe left, I had a surprise visit from Raymond Mortimer, who was making a tour of the Far East. Joe had asked him to call on me. I was rather nervous about meeting Raymond, whose writing I knew but whom I had never met. (He had given my first autobiography, *The Only Child*, a great review.) How could I accommodate in my sparsely furnished old house this Bloomsbury exquisite who had been the intimate of Lady Ottoline Morrell and all the other Garsington gang? It was beginning to get cold again, but I now had two electric fires as well as the stove and the brazier. Raymond announced that he would like to stay with me for a week or so, and seemed to think I was available to conduct him round all the famous places in Tohoku.

He was flying from Tokyo to Sendai, so on the morning of his arrival I took a taxi to the airport, but it was so far out of town that after an hour or so I realized I should never get there on time, and asked the driver to turn back. When I reached Kozenji-dori, Raymond was sitting on my doorstep surrounded by luggage.

All my doubts vanished as soon as I met him. He was a wonderfully entertaining man, full of funny anecdotes about his past and about present-day writers like his reviewing colleague on *The Sunday Times*, the urbane Cyril Connolly. He declared himself completely comfortable in the bed Joe had had, while I again slept on the floor downstairs.

He had known one of my literary heroes, Ronald Firbank, but he rather disappointed me by saying that Ronald was a malicious, self-destructive egotist with a strong streak of narcissism, and was totally unreliable, as he was drunk nearly all the time. I secretly thought he sounded just like me. Raymond also knew Ivy Compton-Burnett, and I remember asking him how she managed her strange, wiggy-looking hair-style, which never altered. Raymond knew Joe, of course, but said he was 'a sad case' of ruined talent, and another self-destructive neurotic who had damaged his life irreparably, as well as that of many of his friends. This was a new view of Joe for me: I did not feel at all damaged by him, and he had shown me nothing but kindness. Raymond, I suspected, was rather damaged himself. Once, when he caught me wandering round the house naked, eating some grapes, he seemed to think I was extending an invitation to him, for he started throwing off his own clothes. I hurriedly donned my *yukata* and gave him some grapes. He was always going on about bathing naked in lakes and streams, seeming to think that was the utmost in felicity – providing there were native boys available at the same time. I think this fad must have been a hangover from the twenties. I had no intention of taking him bathing with native boys, for I hated the sun and public exposure of a body no longer in the first freshness of youth, though still in quite good trim. Joe had even called me 'brawny'. Raymond said I was an Adonis, which reflected badly upon his knowledge of Greek antiquities, so I said, teasingly: 'Oh, Raymond, you flatterer! I'm just well proportioned.' 'And well hung,' he countered lasciviously.

But he was a generous man. He took me out to several expensive traditional restaurants, and we took a limousine, not the local train, to Matsushima, where I made him laugh by relating how Ronald Bottrall had been completely stumped when asked by the priests of Zuiganji Temple to write a 'memorial haiku' on the piece of white cardboard trimmed with gold that is employed for such poetic gems. Knowing that Professor Muraoka would inform the priests that we were 'famous poets', I had come well provided with pre-composed haiku for the occasion, which I proceeded to inscribe fluently on card after card, after appearing to take deep thought, while Ronald and his wife gazed on admiringly. This time, I had provided a haiku for Raymond as well as for myself.

Raymond showed a pettish old-maidishness only once, when we were going from Sendai by train to Hiraizumi and there were no reserved seats. He got into a state verging on panic, until he saw that in fact there were plenty of unreserved seats available in the first class. On the whole, I greatly enjoyed his visit, though nobody at the university had ever heard of him or Lady Ottoline. No student wanted to write about him. Joe was also refused as a subject for a literary thesis – 'because he's not dead yet', a professor blurted out to his face.

Raymond was a wonderful letter-writer, and for several years until his death he wrote me many amusing accounts of his daily life at Long Crichel House and his *garçonnière* at 5 Canonbury Place, crammed with blue-and-white China. I have mislaid the letter of thanks he sent me after his departure from Sendai, in which I was delighted to read that one evening when I had been out on the prowl alone he had returned to Kozenji-dori in a taxi whose handsome driver he had seduced and brought to my bed. Ah, those *kamikaze* taxi-drivers of the fifties – they were a lovely, lawless lot, like bandits in a Far West frontier movie, good-tempered, enterprising and ready for anything! Both Joe and Raymond made passes at them, but if Joe succeeded, he never told me, so I suspect he didn't.

After I left Japan, Raymond remained unfailingly kind, and when I approached him for a letter of recommendation for the post I was applying for at the University of Malaysia in Kuala Lumpur, he at once obliged with a letter that was so full of my praises – and from a Chevalier de la Légion d'honneur at that – the interviewers in London (kindly academics, not the British Council boors) unhesitatingly gave me the job. Raymond also urged me to get a recommendation from Morgan Forster, but again I declined, for I knew he was ill and I felt it would be dishonourable, as we had met only a few times.

Raymond also gave me introductions to people, most of whom I avoided when they came to Japan, but one of them, Desmond Shawe-Taylor, became a friend: we had a common passion for opera and *zarzuelas*. A gramophone record freak, he had written to me about one of my poems in *The New Yorker* in which I described the delights of listening to a batch of ancient recordings by nineteenth-century opera stars that I had unearthed at Corsham. He took me out to dinner in London, and laughed when I mimed Japanese exchanging 'name-cards', bowing, examining the fine print like jewellers evaluating dubious trinkets. This always reminded me of Frenchmen exchanging name-cards prior to a duel – like Edward Everett Horton and Maurice Chevalier in *The Merry Widow* (Lubitsch, not Stroheim) with a scrumptiously camp Jeannette MacDonald shrieking her silly head off as she ogled every man in sight.

Declining West

We were young, we were merry, we were very, very wise,
And the door stood open at our feast,
When there passed us a woman with the West in her eyes,
And a man with his back to the East.

Mary Coleridge, 'Unwelcome'

Where can we find two better hemispheres
Without sharp North, without declining West?

John Donne, 'The Good-Morrow'

What happened after Joe left me to stay with Francis King in Kyoto can be read in Neville Braybrooke's edition of Joe's letters. They contain some amusingly malicious remarks about me as 'the fairy of the north', or some such camp silliness which always makes me laugh when I read it, because it conveys so exactly the tone of Joe's voice when putting down his friends. It was not really spitefulness, but rather a deep pleasure he took, especially after his retirement, in exercising his wit at the expense of people he admired and loved. I could understand that only too well, and never thought of forgiving Joe for anything, as no offence had been taken and there was nothing to forgive.

After Joe left, things went from bad to worse in Sendai. It was all my own fault, of course, but I could not help it. It was the beginning of my fatal 'turbulent year' – that dread period of bad luck and tragedy which Japanese males call *yakudoshi*. Everything did indeed seem to be going wrong with my life. I kept falling sick with vague aches and pains. Rubbing my smalls through with industrial detergent had raised an ugly sore on my right forefinger. When it became infected I had to go to the university clinic and have it lanced. When he saw the state of my finger, the young doctor grinned and pointed to his crotch inquiringly: yes, I said, it hurt there too. Apparently the finger and the crotch were connected by some important nerve. A pretty nurse held me down forcibly on the couch while he gave me an injection and then sliced open my finger. I tottered home with some pain-relieving tablets and spent the next two days in bed.

I finished my novel, *The Love of Others*, and sent it off to Mark Bonham Carter at Collins, only to be told by him that they wanted first to publish my book on Japan, *These Horned Islands*, which was still incomplete, the material scattered through dozens of notebooks. Christmas in Japan is a very depressing experience, with thousands of amateur choirs screeching out Beethoven's 'Ode to Joy' in Japanese, Janglish or even Gerpanese, and I began fortifying myself with bottles of Hermes semi-sweet champagne, which was quite horrible but had the power to render me insensible. Seiji Sekino had to clear away scores of empty bottles from my back porch when I left.

Even worse than Christmas is Japanese New Year. All my friends and students had left to spend the season with their relatives in their home towns, and I was left more than ever alone for days on end surrounded by people dressed up in kimonos making family visits to shrines and temples and eating special New Year dishes, which I tried at the one Western-style hotel then open, beside Sendai Station. I found them sickeningly sweet and sticky, glutinous and bland, and the spiced rice wine, *o-toso*, was for me undrinkable pap. The bars and restaurants were full of revellers who had nothing to do with me. And the movie-houses were practically deserted by available men.

I retreated from the agonies of boredom to my house, with Proust and Walser, Nabokov and Gongora. I thanked god for these writers, about whom no one had ever heard in Sendai. I read a lot of Simenon, too, attracted by the many tales of *fuite* and *fugue*, and in the end decided that I, too, must make my escape, fly away for ever from that heart-breaking city.

My contract was for three years. I was now approaching the end of my second year, and I felt I could not possibly stay another year. Professor Kobayashi had dropped out of my life: he had walked straight past me without a word when I saw him in Fujisaki department store in Ichibancho, the main shopping street. That shocked me so deeply, I knew I had to leave. But how?

I went to Tokyo for a few days. There, I sent a telegram to James MacGibbon, who at that time was handling my work at Curtis Brown's agency. I asked him to send me an urgent telegram demanding my return to England. It must have seemed a puzzling request, but James did as I asked: when I got back to Sendai, the telegram was waiting for me. Professor Muraoka, who had taken Professor Kobayashi's place as head of the English Department, came to see me that very afternoon. He must have suspected something, for he said: 'Please stay. Everyone wants you to stay here. So please do not go away.' Then I showed him the telegram requesting my urgent return to England. I told Professor Muraoka the truth, that I was worried about my mother's state of health, that she was going blind and that I could not leave her alone until I had taken her to another specialist, to see if an operation was possible, and found someone to take care of her while I was away. I wanted no farewell party. But before I left Sendai, Professor Kobayashi invited me to dinner at the Sendai Hotel. He was as kind and friendly as ever, and I realized that he simply had not seen me in that department store. He told me: 'Come back in a year's time, when this has all blown over.'

Professor Muraoka took the trouble to travel with me to Tokyo, and came to see me off at Haneda, saying rather touchingly: 'I like to see the planes taking off.' As my SAS plane took off I felt an immense lightening of the spirit, a sense of such profound and utter relief that I overcame any sense of nostalgic regret which had been haunting me ever since I left Sendai. My heart ached for that lost land, but at the same time I was thankful to be leaving. For the first time, I flew across the North Pole, a route I was to take so many times in the future. Today, the experience is so familiar, I never bother to look out of the plane window. But on that first occasion I was spellbound by the beauty of the polar regions, and by the Arctic I had fallen in love with in Sweden. I wrote a poem about it on the plane, a poem that was printed first in *Orient/West* (to which I had contributed a poem about a gay bar, totally imaginary, that had caused a terrific uproar by people who assumed it was a real place, in which I was a regular habitué). The poem about the polar flight appeared in *These Horned Islands* and *Paper Windows*. The 'scandalous' poem 'Gay Boys' was reprinted in *Refusal to Conform* (1963) and can now be found in *The Penguin Book of Homosexual Verse*. When I read it now, I wonder why the Japanese made such an ignorant fuss about such a beautiful and harmless poem. The truth is, they love to be shocked, to have something to chatter about in lives that are often sadly humdrum, and in which any incitation to gossip or scandal-mongering is welcomed by minds long starved of the material for excited comment.

I often return to Sendai, now utterly changed, Matsushima, Hiraizumi – yet I try to remain incognito.

*

I found my mother in a sad state in Bath. Aunt Lyallie had had to return to Woodbridge to take care of her own cottage. My mother's sight had deteriorated, and she hated living alone in the house where my father had died. I took her to several specialists, but they all said the same thing: the arteries were hardening, reducing the flow of blood to the eyes, and at her age there was nothing they could do about it.

She was in deep depression. So I looked for another place to live, somewhere brighter and more comfortable, removed from the sad memories of my father's last days. I found Hill House in Sion Road, where there was a large, airy, sunny ground-floor flat with enormous rooms and tall bow-windows. It had a pleasant garden and wonderful views of Bath. And it was near the grave of my hero, William Beckford. Apart from a flight of six stone steps at the front door, everything was on the same level. My mother and I moved in and she was delighted with the place. As she cheered up, her sight seemed to improve. We moved in as spring was bringing fresh leaves and flowers in the garden. I had a telephone installed for her, and engaged a maid to come each day to clean and cook. This was Agnes, a dear old soul, who soon became devoted to my mother. I wished I had made the move before going to Japan.

My mother took part in numerous activities connected with the Blind Club, which had several dedicated helpers upon whom my mother grew to depend and to love. They would come and collect her in a taxi or a minibus and bring her back in time for tea, which I prepared for her. I shall always remember my mother's happy face as she returned from these activities, full of news about what she had learnt that afternoon and about the new friends she had made. 'And it's so lovely to come home and find you here,' she would add.

These words made me feel very guilty, because I knew I could never stay there with her always, as she wished. I tried to hide my depression and my nervous weakness. The memories of Salamanca and Sendai had built up a solid accumulation of regret and sorrow in my heart. I tried to work, but could do nothing much. When my mother went away for her annual Blind Club vacation, I took a trip round Europe, spending most of my time in Vienna. I got a small inexpensive room in a boarding-house. Just to be out of England and Bath sent my spirits soaring, though I did not really care much for Vienna.

But on my way there, I stopped off in London for a very important event. It took all my courage to face it, but face it I did, for Joe's sake.

To my great delight, Joe had won a substantial prize of £1,000 –

quite a large sum in those days – for his novel *We Think the World of You*. It came out in 1960, shortly after I had returned to Bath from Sendai. It was the W.H. Smith prize, and the only one of its kind then, so the award was very much more prestigious than all those vulgarly competing book bangs that proliferate today, mere publicity gimmicks to sell books that might otherwise go almost unnoticed, and which are usually forgotten as soon as the prize is awarded and greedily commented on by the press.

Joe was to be given the cheque at a grand reception in the Dorchester Hotel, to which hundreds of writers and celebrities had been invited, among them all Joe's personal friends. I had not received an invitation: for some reason, W.H. Smith refused to stock my books. Joe had to make a great fuss with Smith's in order to obtain an invitation for me. I hate such affairs, but as this one was in Joe's honour I accepted the invitation he had been to so much trouble to obtain for me. My mother and I jointly sent him a greetings telegram of congratulation from Bath, and flowers by Interflora for Nancy.

The reception was awful, though Joe was excited and happy to be with all his friends. I kept myself in the background as much as possible, but Joe kept coming up to me to embrace me and say a few words, bringing his friends to talk to me. Morgan Forster came running up like a little boy or a furry animal, his spectacles flashing delightedly, gazing up at me shyly and taking my hand, holding it for a long time as we chatted about Joe and his books. It was then that Morgan invited me to stay in Cambridge, an invitation I was foolish enough not to accept. I was still in a state of infernal nerves after my experiences in Japan, and could not face the company even of that kindly and generous-hearted old writer. Jack Sprott, William Plomer, Geoffrey Gorer, Stephen Spender, Elizabeth Bowen, Raymond Mortimer, Rose Macaulay and so many others who either loved or admired Joe were there, as well as a lot of literary hangers-on like John Weightman and Anthony Thwaite. But it was Joe's day, and he only wished Queenie had been there to share it. 'Well, Joe, every dog has its day,' I told him, for Queenie, the Evie of the novel, was its undoubted heroine.

One of the great events of my life occurred just after I had returned to England from Sendai. I met Bertrand Russell. This is how it happened.

Trafalgar Square, in the centre of London, is the traditional place for demonstrations and protest meetings. Another is Hyde Park. But the police forbid the use of microphones in the park. In Trafalgar Square they are allowed. During the sixties, Trafalgar Square was the scene of many anti-nuclear demonstrations by the Campaign for Nuclear Disarmament, whose leader was Bertrand Russell. In 1950, he was awarded the Nobel Prize for Literature, for his very original book *Marriage and Morals*. I feel that he should really have been given the Nobel Peace Prize, because he was one of the world's greatest pacifists.

I am also a pacifist, and one of the founder members of CND and Amnesty International. During the Second World War I registered as a conscientious objector. I was given two trials, and condemned to spend the six years of the war in various British labour camps, where pacifists, anarchists, nihilists and all anti-war individualists were confined. It was during this period that I began to read Bertrand Russell's essays: *What I Believe, The Conquest of Happiness, Education and the Social Order* and *Which Way to Peace*.

Naturally, I approved of the aims of the Campaign for Nuclear Disarmament. Bertrand Russell, in a series of eloquent speeches, some of them delivered in Trafalgar Square, kept warning the world's governments of the dangers of nuclear proliferation, and of the immorality of war itself. His speeches and his personality filled me with admiration for his independence of mind, his forthrightness, and his great physical and spiritual courage. He was several times arrested and imprisoned for his views by a reactionary British government. The last time he was imprisoned was at the age of eighty-nine, when he was very sick and frail.

Russell was tried and imprisoned after speaking at an important anti-nuclear demonstration in Trafalgar Square in February 1961. I took part in the demonstration, whose participants marched up Whitehall to Trafalgar Square in freezing rain mixed with sleet and snow. Over twenty thousand people gathered in the Square to hear Russell speak. Then about five thousand of us marched to the Ministry of Defence and staged a sit-down outside the entrance. Russell and other leaders of the CND had prepared a notice of protest against the US Polaris base in Scotland, where American nuclear-powered submarines were to be harboured. The notice was fixed to the Ministry door. On that freezingly cold day, the Government ordered the Fire Department to use their hoses to disperse us, but to their credit the Fire Department refused to obey orders. Russell and other leaders were arrested, tried and imprisoned.

When the First World War broke out in August 1914, Russell, a pacifist, joined the No Conscription Fellowship. One day in Oxford Street, he met T.S. Eliot, who was then living in London. He asked

Eliot if he was a pacifist. Eliot cautiously replied: 'I only know that I am *not* a pacifist.' Russell was filled with contempt for this mealy-mouthed reply, and he writes: 'That is to say, Eliot considered any excuse good enough for homicide.' Indeed, all true pacifists regard war simply as legalized murder; and all too often, it does not have the artificial seal of legality upon it. When Russell was sent to gaol – the first of his several prison sentences – he wrote the popular *Introduction to Mathematical Philosophy*.

The war was a great turning-point in Russell's life:

The War of 1914–1918 changed everything for me. I ceased to be an academic and took to writing a new kind of book. I changed my whole conception of human nature. I became for the first time deeply convinced that Puritanism does not make for human happiness. Through the spectacle of death I acquired a new love for what is living. It was a change that was to affect also many of the brave men who had fought in the trenches and at sea and in the air.

Russell had spoken to me kindly when I introduced myself to him that February day at the Ministry of Defence. I had been going to make a short speech at the demonstration, but as usual when about to speak in public I had stage fright. I confessed to Russell that I was feeling very nervous about speaking before such a large crowd. He just smiled at me and said: 'I always feel the same. But I tell myself "Bertie, your speech may not be very good, but at least you will do your best." Don't worry. You will do your best.'

He shook my hand, and I remember how dry, small, thin and brittle his hand felt in mine: it was like a withered bird's claw. In the end, I did not have to make my speech, as darkness was falling and we had to stop the demonstration. But I have always remembered Bertrand Russell's words. I still get stage fright whenever I have to give a poetry reading or a lecture. But his kindly, wise words help me to overcome my fears.

Nine years later, back in Tokyo, on another cold, snowy afternoon in February, I heard the news that Bertrand Russell was dead. I was at the Yaesuguchi entrance to Tokyo Station, among hurrying crowds, and I felt so overcome by sadness that the tears poured down my cheeks. I was sad, not so much at the news of Russell's death – as a rationalist, he had always looked upon death with indifference – as at the thought that his brilliant speeches and courageous thoughts had been useless. For the world was closer to nuclear war than ever. In Tokyo, in the falling snow, I was also weeping at the memory of his kindness to me on that dreadful day in London. He was one of those who had 'watched over me. . . .'

At the end of his Prologue to his *Autobiography*, Russell writes: 'This has been my life. I have found it worth living, and would gladly live it again if the chance were offered me.' On the day of his death, 3 February 1970, I wept for him in the snowy streets of Tokyo: and I wrote this elegy for him, which was immediately printed in Japanese magazines and newspapers, and later published in my book of poems, *The Body Servant: Poems of Exile* (1972):

In Memoriam: Bertrand Russell

In another February, on a Sunday afternoon nine years ago
I wept for you, and for a world that could reject your voice.

You were so frail, so ancient: yet stronger than us all.
You stood beside me on a platform in Trafalgar Square
among the toothless lions of a tyrannous imperial pride,
under the shadow of Nelson strutting in the falling snow.

Your head was bare, and your wild white hair
blazed like your mind in the wind of whirling flakes.
Your face, the mask of a tragic hawk,
was sad and bitter as you cried your warnings and defiance
at the armed forces of error, the police of Britain,
the criminal politicians, the priests of power, the insane
manufacturers of arms and poison gas and atom bombs,
inhuman profiteers all, sucking the blood of human misery.

You stood alone before the gathered heads of microphones,
tilted intelligently, raised like vipers, cobras about to strike.
– But like a saint, or like Apollo, god of poetry and music,
you charmed them into peace. You won their love with love,
with the fearless beauty of your mind, your noble voice.

Dear man, I remember your friendship for the lost and helpless,
and the grasp of your withered hand in mine that February day,
delicate but strong. I remember the wise humour of your smile,
twisted yet pure; the sparkle in your hooded, sombre eyes;
the deep lines in your cheeks; the nose like a mountain peak.
– And O, that great and simple brow – so vast, so calm, so full!

Most of all, I remember how you taught me to have courage
to defy the world in solitude; how to disarm
the dangerous stupidity of man, using weapons not of this world –
intellect with love; wit with pity; candour with compassion.

Now, in a foreign snow, my tears are falling for you,
and for the world, that did not heed your warning cries.

Russell was a man who loved love in a passionate, physical way that
was also spiritual. The fact that he had many love affairs has drawn
spiteful criticism from self-righteous and loveless hypocrites. A man's
love life is his own affair. It does not reduce Russell's greatness in the
slightest. Lesser human beings always try to attack their betters with
envious, petty moralizing. Why can't they mind their own business?
Because their foolish minds are so empty, so narrow, so unenlightened
by the visions love brings. He taught me about love as well as peace. He
was one of my father-figures.

Around this time, I was lucky to find another father-figure, another
'someone to watch over me' in the person of E.M. Forster, to whom I
had been introduced by Joe Ackerley in 1948. At our first meeting, in
Joe's flat, I saw Morgan admiring my sun-tanned ankles showing above
the white socks I then affected – as every Japanese student does now. I
sensed he had an almost irresistible desire to stroke them, so I took his
dry old hand and laid it on their burnished tinsel down. He gave a big
sigh, and laughed, giving my whole foot an affectionate squeeze. Both
Joe and Nancy noticed this manoeuvre, Joe with amusement, Nancy
with one of her charming jealous pouts.

I had long been a devotee of Forster's work, and during the war my
friend from King's College in Newcastle upon Tyne, David Paul, wrote
him a letter of admiration, to which I added some lines. I cannot
remember what he replied to David, but I wrote him another long
letter on my own. I sent him my long (unpublished) autobiographical
poem, 'The Sound of Fountains', which I had started writing before the
war in France. To my delight, Forster replied, in a letter dated 6 May
1942, when I was trying to 'do my bit' as a lumberjack at East Witton,
Wensleydale, wearing a beaded muff and consequently narrowly escaping a chopped-off toe on several occasions. Forster's letter opens with
an appreciation of this poem, which certainly (as does my other long
poem, 'The Drowned Sailor') shows some influence of the early Eliot,
and particularly of 'The Waste Land':

Dear Mr Kirkup,

Please forgive me for not answering your letter before. I can't pretend I hadn't the time – it was rather a question of 'settling down'. I was glad to get it, and your poem. I liked many of the images in the poem, e.g. the fountains with shoulders – and the dreadful thin red cold meat hands – and some of its actions or rather inactions, e.g. the bungled second meeting at 8.0. It also struck me as true, though I can't myself be so interested in frustration, or in the failure to poeticize experience, to float it off the ground and away from the dust and flux, which is – I suppose – the poem's main theme. Technically it is too much Eliot, I thought: so it is well you have pushed him, for whatsoever reason, from his pedestal! – Yes that Kipling essay (by Eliot) was pretty bad; and worse, since still more timorous, was his tribute to Virginia Woolf. I lose all patience with him when he starts guarding himself.

I'm sorry your job is so uncongenial; it's certainly valuable and necessary. I was more or less a conchie myself in the last war, but this time, owing to my age, I haven't had to face up to the problem; also I feel to understand this Germany better than the last one, and am more certain that it is wrong. What's really wrong though is the age – the gap between scientific achievement and human adaptability. – I don't know if you ever see *Horizon* – I had an article in the December number in which I tried to express this 'New Order' nonsense. Nor could I if I wanted to, for there are no more chairs. – Thank you very much for your sympathetic remarks about my work. I shall be very pleased to have a copy of your poem when it comes out. With best wishes:

[Yours sincerely]

[E.M. Forster]

The poem, which Kay Dick had accepted for Staples, never came out. She offered the excuse that there was a paper shortage, but I think that even so liberal and fair-minded a person as Kay had possibly been overruled by someone higher up in the firm, because the poem was sexually and poetically well in advance of its time. I treasured Morgan's letter for its sensible ideas and friendly tone, and for the sudden humorous remark about the chairs at the end – a typical Forsterian quirkish twist. I received several more letters from Forster, but they were destroyed in the Blitz. On that first meeting at Joe's, he presented me with a very rare, unrationed, fresh egg, wrapped in a page from the *New Statesman*. I never ate it, but carried it with me from one lodging to another, until eventually it broke, releasing, not an awful stink, but a curiously sweet aroma.

Gay Vienna

> Each minute would be complete in itself, like a room with four walls in which one can stand, sit, move about. Each day would be like a complete city shining in the sun, with its streets, parks, crowds. And the years would be whole countries to roam in. . . . It seems to me that if one could accept existence as it is, partake of it fully, the world could be magical.
>
> Paul Bowles, 'If I Should Open My Mouth'

In gay Vienna, stepping backwards, at the intersection of Stiftgasse and Mariahilferstrasse, to admire a green and gold pumpkin-and-onion-domed steeple, I sent sprawling a large, whey-faced nun who furiously resisted all my attempts to pick her up and brush her down. She had sensed my concern was only on the surface, and that my labouring hands were in fact beating her, slapping her breasts and backside, throttling her and taking certain other secret liberties with her person.

Once, I did not like to see old people out late at night. I felt that, like children, they should have long since been in bed. But now, looking at the modest, unassuming face of an old lady sitting up straight and composed in the last tram from the Ringstrasse, well after midnight, I am beginning to change my mind. She sits there opposite me with lowered eyes, in her unpretentious straw hat, neat and well-polished old-fashioned strapped shoes, calmly folded gloved hands, giving a reassuring impression of general decency and mildness, like a quiet, well-behaved little girl, so simple, lonely and undemanding. I am touched in an indescribable way. She reminds me of my mother, in her black straw hat, as she sat beside me in the tour bus bringing us back from Weymouth, shortly after my father's death, as she gazed quietly at the passing countryside in a pose that Renoir could have painted – the 'lost profile' of her cheek. This Viennese old lady is so quiet and good, and I can feel for her only affection and concern: she seems so careful not to draw attention to the fact that she is still alive, as if, in her old age, simply being alive were privilege enough. As she raises her head now and looks without insistence at all that is going on round her, she is like a well-mannered young girl at her first, formal ball at the Opera, and she is moving to the point of heart-break. In the noisy, dirty old tram that painfully machines the tracks up the neon-lit street fatigued with so much day and now only just beginning to repose from the weight of so many feet, she sits looking at everything as if she were seeing it for the first time, or the last time. I wish I could tell her how glad I am that she is here, and that we are less than she deserves.

In the dim recesses of the Business Efficiency Centre, a girl with a head like a deserted beehive talks into the mouthpiece of an ultra-modern white telephone that resembles a bleached bone. Or is it a big nourishing sandwich or a greenish melon slice out of which a large bite has already been gulped? Therefore, she is not really talking, she is masticating; and when she falls silent, she is not listening, but swallowing politely.

Conversation between two people observing a 'war criminal' trial:

A: You have lovely hair.
B: That's not hair. It's my hat.
A: You have a lovely hat.
B: That's not my hat. It's a wig.

Outside the eighteenth-century stables of the chandelier-hung Spanish Riding School in gay Vienna, I was gazing at a display of old riding-breeches and marvelling at their wrinkles and sweat-stains and suggestively rubbed inner-thigh areas. Dreamily, I turned to go, stepping back on a stout housewife's big toe. I did not apologize, as that would have made it all seem accidental, and in any case I no longer care to apologize for anything in this city of pseudo-elegant *küss-die-Hand* mannerisms. The housewife, though I had trampled very lightly on her toe, let out howls of despair and fury, shot malevolent and plaintive looks at me, and limped and shouted fastidious remarks like 'Why don't you look where you're going, Bigfoot?' As I moved quietly away from her, I smiled, then laughed and laughed, throwing back my head like Garbo. That shut her up.

Rushing out of a publisher's office with only one thought in mind – to get to a chiromancer's just off Graben as quickly as possible – I knocked over a very old lady. Her grey lisle stockings were torn, showing bits of dirty white knee with blood oozing out like rosewater. I set her on her feet, and she was all apologies – 'I should look where I'm going', and that sort of thing. So *that* was all right. It takes all sorts to make a world.

While its sluttish mother was in a tapestry-ware shop matching some silks, I made, in passing, a ferocious face at a big bland baby sitting up attentively in its luxurious perambulator with a fringed awning. No reaction. But it will not be able to say what happened, and its mother will sense that something has come over it. Years later, it will remember, and think: 'Surely he was a bit odd?'

When I ride on an omnibus, and any people get on, I am always the last person any individual will sit next to. In a restaurant, no one ever shares my table: indeed, people come from neighbouring tables and take away all the other chairs at my table, always asking politely, of course, 'Is this seat taken?' Sometimes they do not even bother to ask that, so evident is it that I am a chronic loner. Whenever I sit next to anyone in the subway, the seat, it transpires, is vacant only because it is next to a drunk making a scene, happening to be temporarily quiet when I get on, while all the other passengers are rigid with delight and interest, waiting for me to walk into the trap. Then the train starts and the drunk starts shouting at me, showering me with spit that stinks of beer, and I have to pretend not to notice until the next stop. Or else I sit down where a little girl has vomited. Yes, I am a person who finds it all too easy to make contact with others, but for the wrong reasons.

I get up to offer my seat to a frail old lady in a tram. She seizes on it like a white-haired vulture, with a smile of triumph that seems to say 'More fool you'. On another occasion, I offer my seat to a smartly dressed, pretty young woman. She remains standing, giving me a hard look that says 'Don't worry, buster, you're getting no change out of me.' I can't very well sit down again, so pretend I have to get off at the next stop, which is miles from 'home'. I can feel her steely eyes following me as I leave the train with slightly hunched shoulders.

A woman got up to leave the train, and as I was the only person standing, I gratefully sank into her seat, but immediately wished I hadn't, it was so unnaturally warm, a warmth impregnated with sinister fervour, an ardent warmth quite different from my own more modest glow, and one that my own body could not assimilate and pass through the transformer of my bottom to a more equable temperature. Indeed, the seat seemed to be getting hotter by the minute. She must have been harbouring some secret flame, cooking up something; or it was as if she had been hatching some monstrous egg, or getting ready to lay one. It was an unclean warmth, and I couldn't bear it, so I got off at the next stop and sat for a while on a wet park bench, with a feeling of intense relief, as if I were dousing a conflagration.

There are often mornings when I must be invisible. On the tram, the conductor does not approach me to sell a ticket. In shops, I stand there unattended at counters where customers arriving long after I did are served to their complete satisfaction and have protracted conversations with the shop assistants who always seem to be old friends whom they have not met for a while. In the coffee-shop, hoping a good strong black coffee will give my transparencies some pigmentation, no one comes to take my order. Unobtrusively, I cast a fleeting glance at my face in the mirror I carry inside the crown of my hat. The face, a trifle frail and ethereal, is still there. I pass a luminous hand like an X-ray photograph across my eyes, feeling the translucent lids flutter like trapped moths. I'm there, all right. But am I *all* there? Some mornings, I wonder.

Living day after day utterly alone in this foreign city, sometimes I go for weeks without speaking more than a few words, and my voice seems to be dying on me. When I speak to someone, no sound comes, and the other person passes by me on the busy Kärntnerstrasse, faintly surprised to have seen my lips moving soundlessly. When I call out to the waiter in a restaurant to bring me the bill of fare, my voice seems to carry no further than my front teeth, with their innocent-looking gap between the top two that makes me look like a silent film comedian, Buster Keaton or darling Harry Langdon. If I wave my hand at a waitress, she sees the movement but does not connect it with me, does not react at all, as if my gesture had no meaning, so I have to assert its meaning by pretending that I was actually just waving away a wreath of cigarette-smoke. When I ask for the bill, the waiter's pencil is lost or it breaks and he has to go and ask the chef to sharpen it with a chopping-knife. The bill is covered in blood. I smile to show that it doesn't matter one whit, and the waiter takes offence: 'Who d'you think you're laughing at?' 'I'm not laughing, only smiling,' I manage to say – a long sentence for me these days. But he doesn't seem to hear – neither do I, for that matter – because he then says something quite irrelevant.

Some days, in a half-dream of personal absence, I forget my money and when I want to pay for my tram ticket, I have to say to the lady conductor, a stout Viennese with bleached hair and an unbleached moustache: 'I'm awfully sorry, I've come out without any money.' She makes me descend at the next stop, remarking to the other passengers, as she tugs, rather too violently, I think, the starting-bell: 'Some people think they can get away with murder.' Some people do, too.

My umbrella is one of those collapsible affairs. Stopping to inquire the way of a depraved-looking policeman in the pelting rain of a Vienna square full of helplessly writhing statuary, my umbrella collapses over my head, obscuring my vision for a moment. By the time I get it up again, the policeman has changed into a bronze bust of Brahms, heavy and dripping wet, and I'm still lost.

Sometimes I find in my capacious navel a little nest of downy fluff. I wonder if I am alone in this respect?

Visiting the gloomy, grandiose Museum of Natural History in Vienna on a rainy Monday morning, I found I was the only visitor. It was awfully dark inside, and the high, immense dome made me feel quite sick. I looked up, and my head swam. Ten feet above me, the skeleton head of a colossal diplodocus was peeping coyly at me round a more than rococo pillar. I wandered slowly through dim, glassy halls of cabinets and showcases crammed with rocks and lumps of crystal, some of them in the most excruciatingly vulgar colours. As soon as I started, from time to time, to walk a little faster, an attendant's peaked cap and wondering Teutonic moon-face with its Hapsburg lip would rise from behind a section of rock-layers, to see what all the hurry was about, just faintly concerned lest I might be an over-zealous Minister of Education or somebody on a lightning tour of inspection. With averted eyes I passed a special exhibit of brains. Then there was a vast, rain-dashed window entirely filled, and darkened, by the skeleton of a dusty mammoth. Dazed, I staggered out into the formal rotunda; another window, cut in formal parterres, held the colossal statue of Maria Theresa, black, wet and touched with slimy green. She was the only person, apart from myself, in the garden, and her ponderous mass begloomed the entire dull window of the glum May heavens. On one of the rigid paths, so scrupulously tidy, I found a trouser button, and momentarily felt, with a twinge of relief and despair, that I remained in the land of the living. I staggered on, feeling I was still dragging behind me the virulent malachite green of one of the rock exhibits, like a stony shadow.

Always alone, I have begun to feel as if I no longer belong to the human race. I am utterly apart, utterly solitary. The sight of my fellows humiliates me. But when by chance I am brought into contact with people it is as if I am humiliating *them*, such accesses of trembling Franz Josef rage do I produce. Then I smile, and utter kind words, and am thereby placed even further apart. Total alienation. Sometimes I think I am still in Japan, and give courtly bows when receiving a museum ticket or an ice-cream cone, thus enraging people who think I am taking the micky out of them. A shop assistant almost throws an unwrapped purchase at me when I bow, holding out both hands to receive it, in the elegant Japanese manner.

How can people bear to live in constant suspicion and bad temper? That is what life is like in Vienna, where I move like a saint and a martyr, with all my imperfections, through frowning crowds in streets stinking with the most putrid-smelling petrol fumes, which have their own special smell in every city I visit. I see myself as a light in the darkness of barbarous Viennese civility, so close to vile authoritarian stiffness – but nobody else does. A prophet without honour even in a land that is not his own, a land where even the children have dark-ringed eyes and sharp, long noses and thin, compressed lips, and are always talking about money and the price of things. They obviously never had to be taught 'the value of money', as the saying goes. Blessed are those who never thought it had much anyhow.

The deserted Burggarten café, with its arched glass roof and luxuriant forests of palms, is a fit setting for me. The rain drums on the glazed vaulting, and I am so conscious of sitting under a drenching shower that I feel uneasy about the stillness of the palms, that no drop twitches, no breeze blows.

The ground is covered with a deep, pale-brown, crystalline gravel. From the remote distance of the engraved glass service door, a waitress observes me, far away at the end of this aquarium-greenhouse, as I sit in a faded basket chair alone at a white-enamelled metal table whose clawed feet are sunk in the gravel and on whose top reposes a shallow tin ashtray, light as a dead leaf. I'm so glad there's none of the eternal Mozart, nor any music at all. The utter bliss of silence in this music-demented city.

She finally bestirs herself to come and take my order. Her high-booted feet – she is wearing what appear to be the orthopaedic boots favoured by all Austrian and German waitresses – come trudging through the glittering gravel with a sound like waves falling on shingle, growing ever louder, step by step. My order given in a hushed voice, she trudges away, with rustling footfalls that grow fainter and fainter, until, entering the distant service-chamber, with its firm wooden floor, her footsteps stop, and, just before the glass door closes behind her, I hear her coarse voice giving my order, like the desperate cry of a castaway.

There is an umber pool with a few red-gold fish suspended in its murk. Sparrows fly through the door wide-open on the formal garden where the grimy *putti* pin stone roses on each other with broken fingers. The sparrows are of a wary tameness, and bounce and hop round my feet soundlessly, tilting their beaks, getting a sharper look at my unpredictable enormousness, hoping for crumbs I haven't got. Their grey fluff and brown feathers look ragged and dusty, and they cheep discontentedly, disconsolately, making brief flights from chair to table, their wings sounding of lightning zip fasteners by YKK. All I have to offer them is a burnt-out match, which they won't even bother to investigate. They see I have nothing to give and fly away down the long conservatory and out into the rain, where I hear them shouting and barking and frisking – real city birds. The red-gold fish, slim and cool as a Klee watercolour, nibble the surface of the pool.

I sit under my giant glass umbrella, shivering a little despite the warmth, while the white-fronted waitress trudges back along the shore towards me, bearing a green frosted bottle of pale amber liquid and one glass rimmed and streaked with white light. Her approach is like being overwhelmed by a gathering storm whose climax is silence followed by the loud pop of the opened bottle of *Apfelsaft* and '*Bitte höflichst, mein Herr*'. A faint tinkle of white, weightless coins, and the surging waves of her footsteps withdraw, leaving me again in silence, in utter isolation, where I refrain from moving except to pour the chilled, frothing apple juice that mists the cold, clear lights of the glass. How happy I am! I suddenly discover that I have been singing to myself silently all the time I thought I was miserable. The realization that I am secretly enjoying my aloneness is like a shaft of sunshine. How happy I am! There are two or three people in the world I should like to share this moment with. But only for a moment. Let me have it all to myself, for once!

Here, in this vast Viennese ante-room to life, at last, I have found a place where I am in my element, alone, washed by the waters of silence. Whisper, quietly, '*Prosit*', and remove my dark protective glasses, which I hear are the distinguishing mark of the very few members of the 'gay ' community in Tientsin. How glad I am not to be there – though there is precious little gay life in gay Vienna, whose vice squads are persistently on the watch, as a chap in that Turkish bath off the Kärntnerstrasse warned me. He looked terrified. But here in the Burggarten café, oh the stillness . . . the sense of security. I sit between two everlastingly cascading palms, suspended waves of glittering green in the metal and glass framework of my happiness.

It's difficult to say this without seeming smug and self-satisfied, when, despite my outward appearance of self-possession, I am no more self-possessed than most, and indeed even much less so, since I am tugged this way and that by so many conflicting identities and masks. Though it may at first reading sound self-centred and vain and – as Dana once told me – inhuman, I have no hesitation in confessing that I am by nature silent and solitary, an eternal alien, and that I enjoy my own company better than anyone else's, my own thoughts and impressions, my own silent conversations with myself better than shared views, exchanged opinions about nothing in particular, and those tiresome reciprocated emotions that always demand instant reactions. I am always surprised to find that other people feel the need to talk and move and do things, importantly displacing the air around them, making waves, making arrangements to meet people and actually meeting them, eating with them, telephoning right and left all day and night, visiting places and meeting other people in them in an endless chain reaction of man-made events and actions that have no purpose whatsoever. My only contact with people is when I happen to bump into them in a crowded street, or even in an uncrowded country lane, and that is quite enough, in fact already too much for my peace of mind. So my whole life is a search for silence, one of today's greatest luxuries, silence that lets me alone, happy and willing to be the only one with myself, a constant source of wonder and entertainment and refreshment. I talk to so few people (sometimes for days on end I am dumb) that when I have to speak, to buy a ticket or order a meal, my voice comes like a ghost's, and a few words exhaust my strength. While the inner voice never falters or weakens, but talks or is silent as I wish.

Perhaps you think this is a selfish way to live? I don't think so. It is the people who insist on talking to others who are the selfish ones, demanding constant attention and regulated reactions. One doesn't have to listen, of course; and one's own replies, if one tries to make any, are not really listened to. That is how I gradually fell silent, by having to listen to so much talk from so many mouths, and how I began to prefer my own company in a solitude that makes no demands, and hopes for nothing better than my own thoughts, the quiet observations of my eyes, ears, nostrils, mouth and hands.

Each man is an island, complete and self-sustaining, if only he will have confidence to be alone and silent, and to live in himself as in an impregnable stronghold. That is why I write, rather than talk, am an unsuccessful poet rather than a successful TV personality, hack reviewer, provincial lecturer or domestic novelist. I am totally undomesticated. Oh, the virtues of unsuccess! One requires then so little. Success means having things – personal relationships, for example, that un-necessary indulgence which I find so draining. Give up everything, and you lose nothing. This rainy morning in Vienna, how far away Sendai and all its folly seem! How remote, even remoter than Japan, are Britain, Bath. . . . As I left the Burggarten café, the wind at my trouser-leg ran sniffing like a stray dog. Then, at my side, ran leaping and pushing like a wild beast, my shadow, my only companion. Well, I'm not a nice person, *peu recevable*, like Genet, so. . . .

One day, I was feeling so desperate that I did the unbelievable – I went to the British Council, ostensibly to borrow a book. But the bureaucratic red tape of the British had been augmented by Austrian-Prussian manic thoroughness and in the face of such insuperable dif-ficulties I gave up. But someone had seen my application card. He was a slim, gentle, bespectacled English poet, Bernard Spencer, one of the sad relics of the Auden–Grigson 'New Verse' days – what a doleful ring their names have now! – Kenneth Allott, Bernard Gutteridge, Day Lewis, Louis MacNeice, George Barker. . . . Spencer's quiet, restrained style is one which endures beyond all the common man contortions and political posturings of the others. Not long after that, I heard that he had committed suicide in Vienna.

I suddenly felt suffocated by Vienna, and made a dash for Salzburg, which was no better, then to Munich, to visit the Alte Pinakothek and Hitler's grandiose art museum, the Englischer Garten, where I tracked down the park bench on which Unity Mitford (of whom my former German teacher, delightful Miss Robinson, had been a great fan) had bungled her suicide attempt.

But I found Germany as oppressive as Austria, and fled on to Italy, to Rome, to see the portrait by my ancestor the 'Barone' Seymour Kirkup in the Keats-Shelley Memorial House, and to sleep in the room where Firbank died at the Hotel Quirinal, after visiting his neglected grave in the Campo Verano. As usual, I stayed in Padua to avoid the crowds and the noise in Venice, which is only a short train ride away, and possesses exquisite Giottos. Trieste, too, with its memories of Svevo, Joyce and Saba, can be reached in a few hours by way of Venice, as can the graves of Pasolini and his mother at Casarsa, where the main street is named after Pier Paolo's brother, killed by fascists during the Italian Resistance.

Then to Florence, to see more of my ancestor's work in the Bargello, where I had a sudden revelation as I gazed at the beautiful marble bust of Lucrezia Donati by the fifteenth-century artist Andrea del Verroc-chio. Her grave, noble head with its slight, mysterious smile, and especially that gesture of her rather large hands, which immediately attract the eye, the left hand clasping a bunch of what seem to be lilies of the valley to her breast: what did it remind me of? As I was taking breakfast next morning at the rambling old hotel near the station, I suddenly remembered Eliot's poem, a delicious little thing, always neglected by anthologists set on reprinting the *whole* of the laboured *Four Quartets* or 'The Love Song of J. Alfred Prufrock', which a certain kind of fake intellectual can always recite in its entirety: 'La Figlia Che Piange' is the perfect title for that sorrowful smile. It must have inspired the poem.

A few days in Zurich, my favourite European city after Paris, so neat, so clean, yet so unexpectedly sexy, its homosexual rendezvous as open as the park resorts of drug addicts shooting up in public. But Switzerland, for its size, has the highest proportion of Aids victims in the world.

Vienna, Not the Viennese
or The Tourist as Spy

A man's thinking goes on within the consciousness in a seclusion in comparison with which any physical seclusion is an exhibition to public view.

The human body is the best picture of the human soul.

Ludwig Wittgenstein, *Philosophical Investigations*

For an unvarnished view of people and places, travel alone. If you put yourself in the hands of 'introductions' and misguided tours, the natives tend to show off. But try the un-rosy light of everyday, lit by the odd truth that only complete aloneness can give. The existentialist 'tourist-spy' can see a lot which the ordinary tourist always knows he is missing. That is how I saw Vienna, where I recently spent several weeks.

I look passably Teutonic and speak German, so I could meet the Viennese as one of themselves, particularly as I never carried a guide-book or a camera. I had memorized the street-plan and the tram and bus routes as well as I could, so I did not betray myself by using a map or gaping up at the names of streets. I wore what I considered to be unremarkable clothes, with just a touch of colour, the first essential for successful spying, and succeeded in passing myself off as a native. Of course, as I am so very un-British, this was not all that difficult.

My first impressions were so grim, I wanted to run away. It was like the recurrent nightmare of being back at school or at the university or in some dire military academy full of unfriendly pupils and cruel masters and mistresses – Westoe Secondary School to a T. Put one foot wrong in gay Vienna and at once a flood of protest is unleashed. The severe lady lecturers in museums and palaces address you like a naughty boy if you try to escape by falling behind the strictly regimented class. The policeman on point duty whistles imperiously and bawls you out in public if you try crossing the road without his permission; the conductor gives you a severe dressing-down if you get on the wrong tram or don't know the name of the stop you want. The women attendants in the public conveniences scream abuse if you don't tip them. The taxi-drivers are in a constant state of indignation; their taxis are the slowest, largest, oldest and most expensive in the world, and if you don't give them an enormous gratuity, a public scene ensues.

Once, dreaming along in the street, I discarded a tram ticket I should have dropped into a trash-basket. An old dame stopped dead in her tracks and pursued me with agonized cries and reproachful grimaces until I found refuge in a shop. There too I was greeted very coldly, and when I went out without buying anything there was a silence of rigid disapproval that could not have been cut by any knife.

Everywhere there were forbidding notices, which everyone obeyed to the letter, in a maddeningly organized way that often provoked me to do just the opposite. Curiously, in the parks there are no *Keep off the Grass* notices such as you find everywhere in Germany: they are quite unnecessary here, because no self-respecting Austrian would ever dream of leaving the gravel paths, they are so deeply indoctrinated. The only person who ever spoke to me before being spoken to, apart from scores of people asking me the way, was a man with a large stick in the grounds of Schönbrunn, and unfortunately he was a lunatic. I had taken one step on a very rough piece of grass under a beech tree to watch more closely the antics of a brown squirrel. The poor man started haranguing me in a loud voice, ordering me to get off the grass and calling me a 'West German', apparently the vilest term of abuse he could think of. An interested crowd of Viennese gathered round to watch the free show: the interesting thing was that they were all on the madman's side, for *he* wasn't walking on the grass. This was, of course, the country that produced Adolf Hitler: it still hasn't recovered from the shock.

During the first two weeks, my general impression was that the Viennese are the glummest and most bad-tempered people in Europe, and my presence seemed sometimes to rouse them to inexplicable fits of trembling fury: highly efficient and with everything under control, they cannot tolerate a Disorganization Man in their midst. In this capital once renowned for gaiety you never see a smiling face; everywhere sour and suspicious expressions lurk under the mean brims of Tyrolean trilbies, and cold hearts beat under those long green overcoats of loden with the capacious pleat at the back, which look like maternity garments, even on the men. The Viennese don't give anything away free: if you want smiles and *Gemütlichkeit*, you have to pay for them. Kindness is at a premium, and so one sees businesses advertising themselves as 'The Shop with Heart' or 'The Bookseller who really *tries* to help'. But all that artificial goodwill goes on the bill.

The Viennese are obsessed by money, by the importance of having it, of having more and more, and of taking it away from others. Stuck up all over Vienna are large lottery posters showing a clutch of banknotes, and bearing the legend *Hast du was, dann bist du was* (Only if you have money can you be somebody). This might stand as the motto for today's Vienna, where everyone wants to have his cake and eat it.

Surely leather plus-fours are the most unbecoming garments ever invented? I saw them being worn, for the first – and fortunately the only – time, in Vienna. But in a curious way this grotesque sight cheered me up, and I started to enjoy the city.

By now, most Viennese utterly loathe *The Third Man* and the zither theme tune. And they are right to do so, for they represent a dingy, depressing, immediately post-war Vienna, and the Vienna of Hitler, which no longer exists – at least, not on the surface, which is all that matters to a Viennese.

Vienna is one of the loveliest cities in Europe, and it is particularly enchanting in spring and autumn, the two seasons when I visited it. With its broad rings of tree-lined boulevards circling the centre, its parks full of pelicans and energetic statuary, its thousands of commemorative busts embowered in leafy squares (Now who will this be? . . . Oh yes, Brahms – fancy that.), its lakes and ornamental fountains, its green domes and cupolas and crocketed belfrics. St Stephanskirche is like a great stranded schooner of a cathedral, nearly all glass. There is a grandiose opera-house, where one can visit backstage, and there are unnumbered theatres, palaces, museums and expensive boutiques, full of dazzlingly worked gold and jewels. It is a fairy-like, Firbankian city.

One of its greatest attractions is the Spanish Riding School, so called from the fact that from its very beginning only Spanish horses or horses bred from them, the so-called Lippizza horses, have been on display there. The name Lippizza is taken from a village near which, in 1580, the breeding of the former imperial stud began with Spanish horses.

The beginnings of the school can be traced to the year 1565, when performing horses were exhibited in a specially fenced-in riding-track, on what is today the Josefsplatz. In later years, between 1729 and 1735, the Emperor Charles VI commanded Josef Emmanuel Fischer von Erlach to undertake the construction of the splendid Riding Hall which has provided a magnificent setting for classical equestrianism to this day.

I went there one sunny spring morning, when the brilliant light was streaming through the high-arched eighteenth-century windows and making the massive, five-tiered crystal chandeliers throw off rainbow sparkles. The long Riding Hall in the proportion of three cubes (like the triple cube drawing-room at Corsham Court), a favourite classical basis for architectural design, was pillared and balconied and balustraded. There was a red plush and gilt Royal Box at one end. The ceiling was coffered and decorated with plaster mouldings; the three crystal and silver-gilt chandeliers hung from it on crimson velvet sashes.

The exercising and riding space was covered with deep, dark-brown sand which had been raked into small furrows, like those of a Japanese rock-garden, with almost mathematical precision. In the centre of this space stood two wooden posts, on the outsides of which were fixed, neatly furled, the Austrian flags.

The recorded music for the Intrada or Opening Ride began. This festive tune reminded me of the bullring in its brash, theatrical panache. But here there was no gore, no tortured bull: the lovely horses, greys, whites and chestnuts, trotted quietly round the hall, bearing their finely seated riders, clad in eighteenth-century riding dress and tricorns, in a long, noble frieze of accurately controlled movement that was so beautiful to watch, it brought tears to my eyes. Centuries-old tradition and devotion to any art always move us so; in this case, apart from the physical beauty of horses and riders, it was the sense of complete unity and understanding between horse and rider and between all the individual members of the team that was so moving.

Then came the entry of the greys. Some of these were most charmingly dappled, and their long, full, sweeping tails were wonderfully graceful. They were put through their paces with quiet authority: they walked, galloped and trotted round the hall and described figures of eight by going through and round the posts. Then the long procession moved slowly off down the centre of the hall, through the beflagged posts, across the broken sand, in a stately exit.

Next came an exhibition of some of the *haute école* movements. These are all based on the animal's natural abilities and therefore most pleasing to watch, because there is nothing artificial or circus-like about them. The riders remove their tricorns. Their four white horses wear glittering, silver-ornamented leather harness and scarlet and gold saddle-cloths. It was a delight to see the tossings and swishings of those plumy white tails and manes, to hear the dignified snorts from pale-pink nostrils in heads gravely lowered. Their glamorous eyes seemed rimmed with kohl, their heads powdered.

Then came a *pas de trois*, danced on supple hoofs to Mozart's Symphony No. 40, followed by a work-out during which the greys, wearing black and gold saddles, gave spectacular jumps, with curiously delayed back-kicks which, when they did now come off, had the exhilaration of successful sneezes as the whips lightly whistled.

On the long rein, there were demonstrations of side-stepping, prancing, curvetting: then *levages*, *courbettes* and *caprioles* performed to Strauss waltzes. The trainer walks very undemonstratively beside the performing horse, holding lightly the long crimson reins. There is a savage force in the kicks of these ordered paces, and in the weight of the heavy crupper as the horses lift their pretty forelocks in perfect balance.

At the end of the show, the audience was allowed to visit the nearby stalls to see the horses being groomed and watered. I felt both proud and humbled after witnessing this great art, which restored my faith in the dignity of man and in his worthiness to live with noble creatures like the Lippizaner horses.

Ever since I read *Gulliver's Travels* in my childhood, I have loved horses, and when I went to the Far East I was delighted to know that, according to the Chinese zodiac, I had been born in a Year of the Horse.

The ponderously ornate baroque and rococo churches of Vienna are perhaps a little too overwhelming for English tastes, but the small country churches in the hills around Vienna, like the one on the Kahlenberg with its dusky Madonna and Child tanned by a blaze of gold leaf are serenely simple.

Schönbrunn Palace, though perfect in its classical way, is also of monumental dullness. The Viennese have not the gift for massive art; though they are good at small, pretty things, grandeur is something they cannot encompass. Schönbrunn's rigid, monotonous alleys are nice for gossiping nursemaids and mothers, children and old people. But there is not a quiet corner to be found there on a fine day, unless you go early, at 6 a.m., when the gates open. And alas, as in all Austrian and German parks, you must keep off the grass. But I used to enjoy evenings of Mozart opera in the charming little theatre.

However, there is plenty of grass, and music too, in the Vienna Woods and in villages like Grinzing and Gumpoldskirchen, Heiligenkreuz and Hinterbrühl, all of which have associations with Beethoven, Schubert, Strauss and Hugo Wolff, a song-writer whose life was flawed and tragic. At Hinterbrühl I went to the SOS Children's Village, where you can meet at work and at play in their own houses orphan children who have the happiest faces in Austria. In these country retreats it is still possible to enjoy cool glasses of new wine supplied by the growers themselves in their own *Heuriger* taverns. We drink under leafy arbours to the dubious *Schrammelmusik* supplied by a squeaky violin and a melodeon. At Klosterneuburg, I worshipped at Nikolaus von Verdun's twelfth-century altar of exquisitely fashioned enamel-work, a master-piece of religious art. But I was even more impressed by a Cena, about which I wrote a poem which was published by Veronica Wedgwood in *Time and Tide*, and which I later included in my volume *Paper Windows* (1968):

> A crowded Last
> Supper, thirteen heads,
> Twenty-six hands, some
> Under the table's
> Long linenfold skirts,
> Elbows getting in the way,
> Feet in sandals kicked
> Under the stout trestles,
> Fingers dipped in dishes,
> Breaking bread, carafe
> Decanting acid wine,
> Dark, muddy, poor stuff,
> John, James, Judas,
> Even the betrayer
> His face tanned by a golden halo
> Turned in profile
> And the thirteen auras
> All at different heights
> Bob and jostle above
> The tablecloth's white Jordan
> Like balloons, buoys, mooring lights.
>
> In mid-channel
> One full face
> In solitude.

Years later. I found a similar Last Supper in Nagasaki, Japan's most Christian city.

If you want to listen to Strauss waltzes, you must visit the plush-and-chandeliered restaurants of Vienna: you pay through the nose for the music and the sometimes very chichi décor, and a 10 per cent tax is added to the price of your bottle of hock, but once in a while it's worth it.

Viennese cakes are, of course, fabulously rich and pretty, if you like that sort of thing, and most Viennese do. To go with the cakes they drink excellent but expensive cups of coffee which you can order in every conceivable shade of brown. A Viennese café is like a public reading-room. There is usually little or no conversation; each customer sits alone at a little table in a little booth and reads through innumerable newspapers and magazines – German, Swiss, French, English, Italian, Spanish – supplied to him by the waiter. The newspapers are fixed to long wooden sticks so that the pages can be held upright in one hand while you drink coffee or eat cakes with the other. You can stay there for hours over one small cup of mokka, putting off to the last minute the tricky business of paying and tipping. Generally 10 per cent to 15 per cent is added automatically to your bill, but you are also expected to give the waiter something extra even when he has not performed any particularly noticeable extra service for you. As always in Vienna, money talks.

Wine-cellars, like the Augustiner Keller underneath the Albertina Collection of prints, are bearable only if you are with a crowd; sitting alone at a table surrounded by parties of convivial wine-bibbers is not, I found, the best way to enjoy wine.

The real joy of Vienna is the feeling that it gives you of being at the heart of a solid, truly European culture, in an historical and artistic meeting-place of all styles and periods, a great deal of it still untouched by the New World. There is an atmosphere of the Orient, too, from Turkey and Hungary, and an excursion to Budapest by boat on the Danube or by tour bus makes one realize just what Austria owes to these two countries. Perhaps it is no longer the legendary capital of wine, women and song, but on occasions like the vast May Day parades, an evening at the Opera or the Burgtheater, or in a concert or a wine tavern, you see that the gaiety has never been altogether lost.

Before I left Vienna, I struck up a friendship with an old man on a park bench. His face was hideously scarred: he had been in the British fire-bomb raids on Dresden. It was an appalling face, as frightening at first as the worn, featureless visage of an eroded statue. But the eyes

were blue still, and lively with intelligence. He was the nicest person I
met in Vienna.

Reading my favourite women's magazine, *She*, I always admired those
articles instructing travellers how to make the best of hotel life. I, too,
decided I would wear nylon or drip-dry garments, and take a little
packet of 'Jazz' with me so that I could do my own laundry. I, too,
would take a small electric coffee-percolator and a miniature Primus
stove in a picnic basket stocked with plate, cup, saucer, spoon, knife and
fork, and do my own cooking, to save expense. I intended to stay in a
modest hotel on my first three nights, before looking for a furnished
room. The first thing I noticed on entering the hotel room was a
grubby notice saying that the washing of clothes and the cooking of
food was prohibited in the establishment. Never mind, I thought, I'll
do it so unobtrusively and cunningly, no one will ever know.

Even before going out to look at the city up to that palpitating
moment when the spring sky darkens and the neon signs take on an
astringent vivacity, I washed the shirt and underclothes in which I had
travelled, and hung them up to dry over the sink, using my extendible
portable clothes-line. But when I went to unpack my bag, I found I had
not brought any extra shirt. I would have to wait until the one I had
washed had dried. So I lay down on the lumpy bed and slept for an
hour or so. When I woke up it was ten o'clock. The shirt was almost
dry: only the tails were wet. As it was now too late to go out and have
dinner, I thought I would put on the shirt and stoke up the Primus
stove: the shirt-tails would dry on my body and over the heat of the
stove as I cooked some nut cutlets and soya bean sausages which I had
bought from Shearn's in Tottenham Court Road.

Shirt-tails a-flutter, singing happily I bent to my little domestic
chore. The stove was soon fizzing away. I unfolded the handle of the
patent frying-pan, put in a knob or *noisette* of vegetarian margarine
from the plastic container, stabbed the sausages savagely but scien-
tifically with the folding fork, and laid them in the pan, where they
began to hiss gently and spit, expelling at times an almost cooing,
human sigh. I plugged in the coffee-percolator which was soon burping
away and making coffee smells – decaffeinated, of course.

I was very hungry. While the nut cutlets and the sausages were being
done to a turn, I flapped my clammy shirt-tails about over the pan,
receiving some delicious hot prickles of fat on my privates *von Zeit zu*

Zeit. But as I was removing the pan from the flame, somehow my shirt-tails caught fire. The pan was upset, sausages went rolling under the bed, boiling grease dripped from the rungs of a chair.

In a flash I had my shirt-tails under the tap. Only a few mild singes on my bottom, but oh what a nasty shock! And the shirt, my only shirt, ruined. The coffee was ready, anyhow. I devoured the half-raw sausages in silence, picking off the rolls of fluff from under the bed. The nut cutlets were ruined. My bottom was beginning to sting – were first-degree burns worse than third-degree ones? I could never remember from my wartime first-aid classes at the Royal Victoria Infirmary. Better ring for a doctor. As I went to lift the telephone, I saw that my 'Jazz' had stained almost black the glittering brass plug of the old-fashioned wash-basin. Now everything would be revealed. . . .

The scene with the manageress was painful in the extreme. I would have to leave next morning, to find 'more suitable accommodation'. Oh, these women's magazines! It is only women who should read them. When they fall into a man's hands, they conspire to destroy him.

The doctor was a crisply handsome, no-nonsense recent graduate. I was hoping he would rub my bottom with the cream he produced, but he said, quite firmly: 'Rub it in yourself.' He watched me, then: 'Fifty Schillings. . . .' All I had hoped to economize had gone up in smoke.

Totally alone in this strange, somewhat evil city, my life, divorced from that of other human beings, takes on an automatic air. I try all the automatic photograph booths, the sepia results of which make me look bilious, pouched, silly, mad. In one of them I have pictures taken of myself making gruesome or grotesque or plaintive faces, but these expressions of my multiple personality are hardly to be distinguished from those for which I display what I always imagine to be my normal countenance.

Then a glass of over-chilled milk from an automatic vendor is so deeply cold, so profoundly white and icy, it numbs my uvula, which aches with a dumb bleat.

The street photographers recognize me at once as one who has no one to send souvenir snaps to, and no matter how many times I walk to and fro in front of them, they ignore me. But I would so much like to have a 'natural walking picture' of myself: it would perhaps reveal something of his own undiscovered secret, tell him why he is as he is. But the photographers keep snapping happy passing couples, family groups, two pals out for a stroll, even a man accompanied by only a dog.

I walk up to a photographer who is busy lighting an expensive cigar with a Cartier lighter, and beg him to take me. The photographer agrees, with a faint smile of disbelief which has something insulting and contemptuous in its 'OK, I'm all right' twist of the lips round the fat, wet end of the cigar. 'Ready within one hour' is the legend on the shop door where I take my ticket. But it is late evening by the time my picture is ready. I don't dare look at it yet, but rush to a private cubicle in a record emporium where, with trembling hands, oblivious to Mahalia Jackson belting out the Lord's Prayer, I venture to take a peep at my hidden self, already embarrassed by the secret that might be revealed. In the gloomy curtained cubicle the photograph is whitely phosphorescent. I strain my eyes and see the picture of a comical monster that would be frightening, with its mad, wide eyes, furred ears and eyelids, finned shoulders and feathered head, if it were not so side-splittingly grotesque. I bend my fading sight over it, giving a grimace learned from the silver screen – the laugh that is the film star's symbol for weeping. The stretched lips grin, over teeth so perfect they look false, and salt tears dripping from the end of my red nose enter into chemical action with the wet acids and alkalis of the developer that will never dry. While Mahalia Jackson, in a hooty contralto, shouts and lingers balefully over 'For Thine is the kingdom, and the pow——ah, and the gloo——ry. . . .'

It's closing time. I go out into the windy, darkening street of a city whirring with versatile weathercocks. I feel a deep affinity with the top-hatted sweep, sooty face and carbonated shirt, his baggy turn-ups spilling out, at each step, the product of the day's chimneys.

Despite my dislike of the Viennese, on future visits I was to become fond of their city, which always seemed to be in a state of upheaval. People there called me 'Professor', just as the pimps in Montmartre hailed me as 'Docteur'. But of course even steeplejacks and picture-framers are given titles in Vienna. I grew to love the inner city, the old parts round the St Stephans Dom. The coffee-houses I haunted were also haunted by ghosts of Trotsky, Adler, Freud – Freud lived just a few steps from the Café Landtmann on the Karl-Lüger Ring. The Café Hawelka in the Dorotheergasse became my favourite, with its resolutely Bohemian ambience, reminding me of another favourite, the Caffé Pedrocchi in Padua, where I go for the Giottos and its convenient distance from Venice.

It was very curious how I kept running into the British in Vienna: Auden, Britten, Muriel Spark – always glimpsed at a distance, fortunately, and so easy to avoid. I remember meeting Spark one day in 1954, shortly after her conversion to Roman Catholicism, in a street in Camden Town. She invited me to have a cup of tea at an ABC, and I at once noticed a change in her that could not be explained by her no longer wearing one of her ultra-chic ladylike titfers of her *Poetry Review* editorship days, when she had seemed to me so fiercely dismissive and unkind, arrogance set like a mask on her enamelled face. Was it a white South African characteristic? Or a relic of 'I'm in my prime' Scots education? The very fact that she would allow herself to be seen with *me* was sufficient indication of the change in her. I noticed how all the unpleasant social manner had evaporated, leaving a shrewd but unaffected, attractive woman. After talking about Wordsworth (I had failed to contribute to her Wordsworth anniversary anthology), I ventured to comment on her transformation – 'How different you are! How much nicer you've become!' – and was quite alarmed when she informed me that her new-found, born-again radiance was the result of her conversion to Roman Catholicism. It seemed such a ninetyish thing to do, almost unbelievably old hat. But the change was genuine, not cosmetic, and it was without solemnity or pride. She seemed to be brimming over with bliss. But I have never liked her novels much: they seem soaked in her former acidulousness.

Auden was disenchanted by Vienna. He wrote:

> Standards at the *Staatsoper*
> steadily decline each year,
> and Wien's become provincial
> compared with the pride she was. . . .

But it was the provinciality I was beginning to like, caused partly by the lack of a certain civilizing atmosphere once created by the Jews, but also by the influx of refugees from Hungary, Albania and other Eastern bloc nations. I went on excursions to Bratislava and Budapest in the early seventies and was thankful to get back to Austria. After Auden's death, I wrote this poem:

Gay's the Word
(In memory of W.H. Auden)

So this is the room where Auden died,
in gay Vienna – and that the bed –

The management were nice about it,
didn't want the place
turned into a shrine or anything –
as he would have wanted, too.

I quite agreed, remembering Paris –
my ghastly night – and not alone –
on Wilde's deathbed, now all tarted up,
rue des Beaux Arts, Hôtel d'Alsace.

So this is the bedside table, and the lamp
he turned on never to turn off again
except in his own head – an act,
like a poem, purely of the imagination.

This was the very glass he drank
his last vodka martini from, on ice,
this the ashtray where the final cigarette
snapped that endless chain, the weakest link,

and was left to smoulder out
the memory of that dying inspiration, long
after his own extinction – that last sigh
of ashes to ashes, dust to dust.

And this is the pillow where he laid his head
as I lay mine, as if upon a wave of foam
or limestone shoulder – to dream, perchance to sleep –
the pills in an open box beside the lamp.

So let me lay my head, so let me, non-smoker,
exhale my ultimate breath, the smoking soul.
So let me drink my last Glenfiddich, with its
touch of Malvern Water, if obtainable. Please, no ice.

So let me write beneath the lamp
the line that never shall be ended –
so let me read the boring page
that never shall be turned –

in gay Vienna, O so very far from gay,
indeed, so ungay, I could die of grief,
as he did, longing, as we all must do,
for a world where gay

means truly gay – original delight – and not
lonely extinctions of impossible longings.

This poem was later reprinted in my collection of poems entitled *The Sense of the Visit* (1984) – 'New Poems by James Kirkup'. Not all that new, therefore, but at least fairly recent. Auden, whom I met several times, was the modern poet I admired most – among British poets, that is. The rest of the bunch of Macspaundays meant nothing to me. Today they seem a dusty lot, over-concerned with politics, that killer of literary feeling. Auden and Nabokov were two writers who distrusted the influence of politics on writers. Though I am by nature a kind of socialist-anarchist-pacifist, I have always refused to join a political party, and I have never voted for any politician, either local or national. I have only to look at the faces of politicians, both men and women (and their spouses), to hear their crude voices, study their cheap body language, to realize how ugly they are, and how shallow their principles of self-seeking disinterestedness. How could one possibly take an interest in a so-called discipline or 'science' practised by such unattractive human beings? When I look at Thatcher, I see Hitler; when I look at Kaifu, I see Mussolini; when I look at Major, I see Brezhnev. For politicians, life is one eternal Cold War, in which they alone are insulated against the freezing chills of terror, while the common people die of hypothermia and starvation – for those they have elected have deprived them of all power, and of their very voices, as Hitler did when he drove the Jews from Europe, as the Japanese did in Korea.

Back to the palm-house café in the Burggarten, the only place where I am always left completely alone. Even the waitress disappears for long periods. Some of the palm branches droop downwards with such subtle curves, soft as hair, long and sleek and almost wet-looking, with the central rib from which the fronds depend like a dead-centre parting, the lower leaves like a spiky fringe on the forehead of a Japanese gay boy.

If all space pilots lived as I do, in utter spiritual isolation – (and physical too, to a great extent), there would be no need to fear the psychological effects of protracted solitude. The lonely one is already preconditioned for space flight. Life alone with myself and my selves in outer space is my idea of an ideal existence. Unwillingness to return to this sad world would be my only re-entry problem.

I read a book about a man who bought a slave in Timbuktu – a book by James Morris. But then he released him. I plan a journey to the slave-market in Timbuktu, where I shall buy a slave and keep him.

But first, I have to return to Bath.

My return home was also a stroke of luck. Waiting for me was a telegram from Peter Brook, whose production of *Titus Andronicus* I had so much admired in Stratford-upon-Avon. I had been fascinated by Vivien Leigh in the mad role of Lavinia, in which she seemed to me even more beautiful than when she had first bewitched me as I stood in the gallery of the Newcastle upon Tyne Theatre Royal, watching with a packed house the first performance of Thornton Wilder's *The Skin of Our Teeth*. I felt an immediate affinity with Vivien Leigh – another example of the way I was drawn to emotionally unstable older women. Her beauty seemed to me to be on a par with another idol, Moira Shearer: I went to see *The Red Shoes* time and time again, and I still take every opportunity to watch it in revivals or on video. But what was this telegram from Peter Brook, which my mother handed to me with a trembling hand? For her, any of those little yellow envelopes could only mean some further disaster or ignominy had befallen her beloved son. But in fact it was good news: Peter wanted to know if I would be interested in translating Friedrich Dürrenmatt's new black comedy, *Die Physiker*, for a production he planned to do with the Royal Shakespeare Company. At once I telephoned him and said yes, and made an appointment to meet him in London at the Adelphi Theatre later in the week. I liked Brook at once – the face of a benevolent pixie, Puck in person yet cautious as Caliban.

Peter Brook took me out to lunch with his then assistant, the multitalented Robert Macdonald, himself a gifted translator, producer and actor, as well as a fine pianist. As we discussed Dürrenmatt's text, I learnt that Peter had chosen me because he had been impressed by my translations of various modern German writers, among them Christian Geissler's *The Sins of the Fathers*, a strange, violent novel that Barley Alison had commissioned me to translate for Weidenfeld & Nicolson. She had also been so good as to put other work my way: Ernst von Salomon's *The Captive: The Story of an Unknown Political Prisoner*; Herbert Wendt's *It Began in Babel*; and Simone de Beauvoir's *Memoirs of a Dutiful Daughter*. When I undertook these hackwork translations for Barley, I had no idea they would ever impress anyone, but they had certainly impressed Peter Brook.

I was given strict instructions to translate the play almost word for word. Apparently Dürrenmatt, with typical Swiss preciseness, had objected to the very 'free' translation of *Das Besuch der Alten Dame* (The Visit) which Peter had produced on Broadway with the Lunts in the main parts. For his new play, which was to become his best-known work, Friedrich insisted that he would allow Peter to produce it only if he, the dramatist, approved of the translation, which had to be an exact rendering of the original. I agreed to do the best I could, given these tiresome restrictions, and returned home to make a first draft. Boredom soon overtook me: I thought the play was rather cheaply melodramatic, and its ideas almost jejune, while its wit sounded ponderous and the situations repetitive. But I desperately needed the cash, so I persevered. Then unforeseen difficulties arose.

It was my father, a passionate admirer of George Bernard Shaw and the Fabian movement, who first pointed out to me something his hero had written about literary agents. This was at a time when I was seriously considering the possibility of finding an agent willing to take on such an unlikely lad as myself. My father was all against it. He regarded all agents, including insurance agents, as bloodsuckers, and, like critics, 'the lice on the locks of literature'. They were all linked in his mind with the Freemasons, for whom he had a lifelong contempt, claiming that they were responsible for the nepotism at the South Shields Town Hall. This is what Shaw said about literary agents:

> Agents are much more dangerous nowadays than publishers, because every author knows that a publisher's interests are opposed to his to the extent that the more the publisher gets of the price paid for any given copy of a book, the less there is left for the author; but many authors still believe, and almost all agents allege, that the more an author gets the more the agent gets. Yet if in his day's work an agent can place a dozen books on a 10% or 15% royalty he stands to get rich much quicker than if he spends the day fighting one or two books up to a 25% royalty. . . .
>
> To make the interests of author and agent really identical, the agent should give the author a percentage on his annual profits from all the books he places. Until this system is adopted, which does not seem very likely, it must be taken as a fact that it is in the agent's

interest to have a low rate of profit on many books, and the author's to stand out for the highest attainable rates of profit on his single book. That is, their interests are not identical, but beyond a certain point, flatly opposed.

These words of wisdom were written in 1911 for the Society of Authors, and they are still relevant to the deplorable present-day conditions existing between writers, publishers and agents.

Some years previously, I think around 1954, I had been introduced by Alan Pryce-Jones to a literary agent: Alan, then literary Editor of *The Times Literary Supplement*, had told me that if I wanted to get on in the literary world I must get myself an agent. So he sent me to Spencer Curtis Brown, and I was ushered into his office, where we had a chat and he at once extorted fifty pounds for me from Harvill Press, which had been witholding payment for my translations of the poems of Jules Supervielle. Spencer also negotiated slightly better terms for me on my next books. I did not take to Curtis Brown, and they did not take to me. At a later interview with Spencer, unaccountably adored by Elizabeth Bowen, I got the impression that he now regretted he had taken on such an unpromising writer who was never likely to produce best-sellers like Daphne du Maurier, on whose royalties the Curtis Brown empire was largely built. I detected a note of condescension in Spencer's offer to put me up at his flat any time I was in London – which I declined. What was he up to? I wondered. . . . I was 'farmed out' to a succession of people, starting with James MacGibbon, an amiable man who once took me to tea at the Savoy, where he begged me to 'write a novel with a story'. As it was my firm belief at that time that all I wanted was to write a novel that could never possibly be adapted for the screen, I shocked James by suggesting that I might write a novel about the life of a fly that changed into a human being – the very thought of which made poor James sudder with disbelief. A few years ago, I saw a highly successful movie about a scientist who changes into a fly, with horrifying results.* It seems I was before my time. . . . When *These Horned Islands* was published, James got it accepted by the Macmillan Company of America, simply because it happened to be lying on his desk when the American representative of that publisher called for a chat. James proudly told me that that was 'the gentlemanly way' to do business in the book world. I was not so sure that it was the

---

* David Cronenberg's SFX movie *The Fly*, a remake of the 1958 film.

best way, for he had given *The Only Child* to Collins, not to the Oxford University Press, as I had fully expected, and I trusted his judgement: but Collins inexplicably let it go almost immediately out of print, despite its resounding success.

When it came to making arrangements for a contract for my translation of *Die Physiker*, I ran into violent agency rivalries. I had told Peter Brook to get in touch with Spencer Curtis Brown about it. But when the news got out that I was doing the play, I had an urgent call from another agent, Jan van Loewen, who claimed he was Dürrenmatt's representative in Britain, and that I should allow him to draft the contract. When I told Spencer of this, he was furious, and at once a battle royal started between the rival agents. Neither would give way, and both invoked my aid in doing the other down. I was completely bewildered and bored by this controversy, and early on I withdrew from the fray, leaving the agents to fight it out between themselves. Spencer never forgave me for backing out, because in the end they had to agree to share the royalties, and a complicated system of payments ensued. In order to avoid any further unpleasantness, and in resentment at being made the whipping-boy for both parties, I asked Jan van Loewen to handle all my future dramatic rights, and this further alienated Spencer. From that time on, he did the very minimum for me. He never found work for me, never produced commissions or advised me on what publishers were looking for. He just went on taking his 10 per cent rake-off from contracts he had already made for me. So I began making my own arrangements, without consulting him: I did not see why he should take his 10 per cent from royalties for work I had found off my own bat.

After James MacGibbon, I was passed from pillar to post at Curtis Brown: it was Budd Maclennon who handled the Dürrenmatt affair, and as I had no one to go with to the first night I asked her if she would come with me, only to be rebuffed, with a look of horror on her face. She informed me she was going with Robert Conquest – very upmarket.

There was another curious incident connected with Budd. Through Barley Alison, I had undertaken the translation of a novel by the Polish author Jerzy Andrejziev, about the Children's Crusade. (It was later made into a beautiful but unsuccessful movie by Wajda.) I am not able to read Polish well enough to translate, so Barley had given me the French translation. However, when the book came out, she had omitted to state on the title-page that I had translated it from French, not

Polish, and this caused me a lot of embarrassment when reviewers, the eminent Peter Green among them, began praising me for my mastery of the Polish language – especially since the whole novel was written in one continuous sentence! Budd at once stepped in and had Barley send off a letter of apology to *The Times Literary Supplement*, giving the correct facts of the matter, as I had requested. However, many people – including the then literary editor of the *TLS* himself, Anthony Thwaite, seized the opportunity to accuse me of deceit, and I remember Thwaite gleefully recounted his erroneous version of the business in his gossip column in the *TLS*. I did not bother to reply: my motto had changed from 'I of All People' to 'Never explain, never apologize' – a truly oriental attitude.

To return to Dürrenmatt: I was so depressed by his play that I turned in a very scrappy first draft. At this point, Robert Macdonald came to our house in Bath to help me through this unenviable task, and I was forever grateful to him for all he taught me about what would 'go' on the stage, without departing from the original text. It was Robert who later suggested 'Humoresque' as the tune to be played by Einstein at the end of Act One. But the poem in the second act was interfered with by Cyril Cusack, who played another of the mad physicists. ('Nice face, hasn't he?' Peter Brook remarked of Cyril.) Cusack imagined himself to be a gifted poet who could improve on my own version, with disastrous results. But I was so fed up with the whole business, I let it go, though not without a shudder when I heard Cusack deliver my mutilated line. The play was a great success, and is still performed world-wide. I also turned it into a student reader for the Japanese, with an introduction describing my associations with the play, and this is still selling well in Japan, where the play has often been performed.

After the first night, there was a party on the stage where I met one of my new heroes, Linus Pauling, and his delightful wife, introducing myself as 'only the translator'. I remember I hinted that Pauling himself might one day appear as a character in such a play, and this at first seemed to alarm him, as if he thought I had already written it, but then, on his wife's prompting, he saw the joke.

On the morning after the first night, I met Dürrenmatt at his hotel, where we discussed the very favourable reviews, and, prompted by Jan van Loewen, I sounded him out about the possibility of translating his musical play, *Frank der Fünfte* (Frank the Fifth) for the English stage. He was quite willing for me to do it, but when I suggested that a new score might be written for the lyrics, he refused: the score had been

composed by a friend of his, a rather mediocre musician chiefly famous
for that ever-popular weepy, 'Oh, mein Papa'. There were various plans
to put on this musical, which had been a success in Paris under the
unintentionally comical title *Frank Cinq*. I once went to Oscar Loewen-
stein's flat to try to sing the score to him, but found it beyond my
abilities. When it was eventually produced during a disastrous Dürrenmatt festival at the Sherman Theatre in Cardiff, to which I was very
temporarily attached as a *dramaturge* (with equally disastrous results, as
will later be revealed), it was done so heavy-handedly and humourlessly
that it fell flat as a pancake under the fascinated gaze of Oscar Loewen-
stein and Frank Dunlop, whom I had mistakenly invited to be present
at this catastrophe. The only redeeming feature was new musical
arrangement by Charlie Barber. It was one of the most awful evenings I
have ever experienced in the theatre, worse even than the totally agonizing production of my version of Schiller's *Don Carlos* two years before,
at Cheltenham, with an audience of local old-age pensioners laughing
their heads off.

I was to adapt, rather than translate, several other Dürrenmatt plays
for Jan van Loewen. The next one, over which he seized complete
control from Curtis Brown, was *The Meteor*, produced for the Royal
Shakespeare Company at the Aldwych by Clifford Williams: it had only
a short run and no American production. After that, I translated several
of Dürrenmatt's works, including his very interesting version of *King
John*, followed by no production, as was the case with some of his plays
requiring very large casts, like *The Anabaptists* (which I consider to be
his best drama) and *Period of Grace* (Die Frist), another excellent play
still awaiting an adventurous producer and director.

But my other translations – *Portrait of a Planet, Play Strindberg* and
The Conformer – were all given good provincial productions before
London. *Play Strindberg* in particular was noteworthy for a superb
production by Gareth Morgan at the University Theatre, Newcastle
upon Tyne, starring an ebullient and brilliant Freddie Jones, who was
later to make an unforgettably moving impression as Peer in Gareth
Morgan's fine production of my new version of *Peer Gynt*.

I was obsessed by the theatre in all its forms, and longed to write a
real play of my own. Indeed, Peter Brook asked me to write one for
him, and I suggested the theme of a German family living in a house
divided in two by the Berlin Wall – an improbable setting, but one
which symbolized very strongly the Cold War divisions of those days. I
brought in a parallel scene from *A Midsummer Night's Dream*, and there

was the story of lovers parted by the Cold War – the man on the West, the girl on the East: she is gunned down when trying to escape to her lover. But somehow I had neither the time nor the energy to finish this project.

One of the reasons why I wanted to go to Vienna was to visit the theatres there in the hope of finding some new author, some new playwright I might translate. But there was disappointingly little of interest just then in the Viennese theatre, where mostly revivals of the classics – admirable in themselves – were holding the stage.

When Peter Brook brought his revolutionary production of *A Midsummer Night's Dream* to Japan in the sixties, I went to see it, and was dazzled by the great acting and the astonishing directorial vision behind that epoch-making staging. I thought again of my own play about a wall, and set about rewriting it as *The Language Barrier*, set on the demarcation line between North and South Korea, manned by international surveillance teams. But the cast was big, and the whole idea too ambitious for any British director. The only possibility was a radio production, but even that fell through: the subject-matter was too sensitive for the BBC. *The Fall of The Wall* might have been the title of a sequel to *The Language Barrier*, which could have been revived as a visionary commentary on the events in Berlin.

My Traveller's Heart

My traveller's heart is neither settled nor decided;
Many things fill it with vague unrest; am on point of doing what?

Li T'ai-po (trans. Florence Ayscough)

Spring Window

– On a rainy morning
Just after dawn
To rise and drink
The first cups of tea –
O faraway friend.

Tu Fu (trans.
Florence Ayscough)

Apart from the Lippizaner horses, I had found little to enchant me in gay Vienna. The pictures in the Kunstmuseum, the ballet and the opera and the plays at the Burgtheater all seemed by comparison unreal. Only those horses kept me from total despair, or I might have gone the same way as poor Bernard Spencer.

But when I got to Bath, at once I wished I were back in Vienna. Those formal streets, avenues and crescents seemed as lifeless as operatic artifices: at night, the deserted streets looked as if the Bomb had already dropped. The people of the West Country frightened me more than most British people: there was a darkness about them, something sinister that was alien to my Scandinavian Viking ancestral urgings. Even Vienna would have been better than this sullen, malevolent, gnomish countryside and these semi-rural towns and cities split between a cap-doffing working class and the Church of England gentry who, as Ackerley wrote in his fiercely concerned poem 'Micheldever' (it appeared in *Horizon*), – 'capitalized the land by force,/ And when the dispossessed cried out for mercy/ Choked them to death – judicially, of course'.

Bath was too full of agonizing memories of Dana, my father, my mother's descent into blindness, my own folly, the malice of my colleagues at the Bath Academy of Art, the West Country craftiness and muck-raking meanness of the Corsham clodhoppers.

But my mother appeared much restored after her holiday, and she was enjoying her new friendships at the Blind Club, an admirably organized institution whose manifold activities helped to keep her mind and body busy after the shock of my father's death and the realization that she was losing her sight completely. Our new flat in Hill House was spacious, airy and bright, and I had found a devoted servant to look after us – Agnes.

So I scanned *The Times Educational Supplement* week after week in the Bath Public Library Reference Room, a place that will surely be haunted by my ghost. I wanted to be free of Britain for good, and particularly of the Jane Austenish terrors of Bath and its environs. So I wrote away for details of posts in many parts of the world – Mali, Tunisia, Turkey, India, Hong Kong, Martinique, Brazil, New York, California, Amsterdam – anywhere that was not yet under the dread control of the British Council's heavy bureaucratic hand. Nothing came of any of these applications. But then one day I was invited to an interview in London for a post at the University of Malaysia in Kuala Lumpur – known to me then only through Cocteau's quip, 'Kuala l'Impure'. I think it was some university appointments board I had to steel myself to face. I had recommendations from Joe and Raymond Mortimer: a final appeal to Professor Girdlestone in Newcastle again went unanswered, so I was without any formal academic sponsorship. But the board, all men, were very amiable and seemed to think it would be a great joke to send me to Malaysia. I got the job, and at once set about getting all the medical certificates, inoculations and tropical outfits such a posting requires. My mother was surprisingly agreeable to my departure: 'At least, it's not as far away as that awful Japan,' she said. But I would be away for three years, and we had a heart-rending parting. As I sat in the taxi to the station, Bath suddenly looked so desirable, as I wrote at the start of the book I was to write about my Malay misadventures, *Tropic Temper* (1963):

September in the pale-golden, tranquil, ever-beautiful city of Bath, where the avenues of lime in Lansdown are heavy with leaf.

Over the trim-gravelled drives of Georgian houses lean the expiring rockets of purple or yellow buddleia, bougainvillaea, maroon and white valerian, the ballooning, soap-bubble clumps of hydrangeas, the massed glooms of laurel and blackish-green holly. . . .

That book recounts in detail the best and the worst aspects of the seven months that were all I could stand of Malaysia. As soon as I arrived, I knew I was not welcome, for there was no one to greet my arrival from Penang by the jungle train at KL's triumphantly Moorish railway station. But by a stroke of great good luck, I saw opposite the station the place that was to be my home for the next four months or so, the superbly British colonial Hotel Majestic – now, alas, swept away to make room for the capital's proliferating, high-rise cliffs of faceless glass and concrete. I proceeded towards this haven in the crippling heat, like some Victorian colonial administrator, followed by a row of native bearers burdened with my impedimenta.

Just crossing the road had me streaming with sweat: my inoculations and vaccinations never stopped playing me up in the most debilitating and depressing way. I was shown to a comfortable bed-sitting-room with a private bath, blissfully air-conditioned. After bathing and chang-ing into a cool sarong, I ordered a refreshing drink from the bar. It was brought by an elderly Chinese room-boy with a curiously camp walk: I used that word 'camp' in my descriptions of him in my book, and so was able to point it out to Susan Sontag after she published her *Notes on 'Camp'* as the first use of the word in a serious work of literature. I sat at my window sipping my gin sling like a seasoned Maughamesque ex-quisite, entertained by the antics of the monkeys on the jungly banks outside. I think I must have called the university to announce my arrival. No one there had ever heard of me, and I was beginning to think I was yet once more a non-person when I had a call from a junior lecturer, a pleasant enough Englishman who felt constrained to take me out to dinner with his wife.

I took my leave of them around ten and went up to my room to change, as I was soaked in sweat. Then, when I thought the coast was clear, I sashayed out into town, down past the mosque and the *padang* and the Moresque city hall. I soon found that the Malays are utterly charming and I thought them wonderfully attractive and good-natured. I was to make many friends among them, and find lovers, too. The Chinese fascinated me even more, and I created what I later realized must have been a minor scandal by advertising for a teacher of Chinese in the local press, when every other Britisher was swotting up Malay, of which I had already gained an offhand mastery by studying *Teach*

Yourself Malay on the long and tedious voyage out, in an ancient liner infested with tiresome American women and stodgy British Council types *en route* to Bombay. My only consolation was a cheerful British nurse bound for Hong Kong who really took me under her maternal wing and gave me a good time all the way to Penang.

The only people I could not understand in Malaysia were the Indians. But after a while, I started visiting their temples and festivals, practising yoga and eating Indian food in all its incredible variety, and I slowly grew to love and respect them – a process that much amused Mark Bonham Carter when he came to edit my book. This he did mainly by cutting the downbeat paragraph that unaccountably appeared at the end of every chapter, thus lightening the tone of the book considerably.

Those downbeat paragraphs were violent mood-swings from ecstasy to disillusion, from love to hate: but after all, a love-hate relationship is the only one worth having with a country. There was so much to love in Malaysia, and so much to hate: my hatred was directed entirely at the British, particularly the head of the English Department, a linguistics man. Of course no true writer ever bothers about fussy little grammatical points, and what style I have is devoid of formal grammar of the kind so laboriously taught in language labs and university departments of linguistics, where the discipline becomes a kind of mathematics – human speech reduced to algebra and trigonometry of the most baffling abstraction. This professor at once turned down my suggestion that I should do a course on Firbank, and held up his hands in horror when I proposed *Lolita*, then considered a pornographic literary jape. So I had to settle down with the usual boring Conrad and James and Eliot and, as a special treat, all those ghastly 'Angry Young Men'. I offered to barter these for Orwell but was told it was Maugham or nothing, except possibly Graham Greene – my two pet Mod. Eng. Lit. hates. I never bothered to prepare a lecture: as in Japan, I just took a book and went into the lecture theatre and talked. The students were darlings, and they seemed to like my unconventional methods and were open to my weirdest interpretations.

In Japan, foreign teachers are mercifully spared from attending academic meetings and staff consultations. But in Malaysia, I had to be present at these interminable and paralysingly boring confabulations, conducted with extreme formality, with rigid attention to the 'minutes of the last meeting' and so on. I slept through most of them, and in any case it seemed that nobody wanted my opinion. In the end, I started walking out after half an hour of unendurable balderdash, and this brought disapproving notes from the professor, who was something of a martinet. It soon became clear to me that the University of Malaysia was not the sort of place in which to waste the next three years of my rapidly disappearing youth.

I had one or two friends in the department and among the British business community who sympathized with me and were unfailingly kind and helpful. One of these was Ray Bramah of the Oxford University Press, whose beautiful native house I took over when he moved to more palatial surroundings. He arranged for me to buy a second-hand car, which I was unable to use until he found me a native driver. The car was very necessary, because the campus was miles away outside the city in those days, and there was only one bus a day, so I was spending a fortune on taxis driven by turbaned Sikhs who seemed to have the monopoly on that form of transport.

I travelled everywhere, all over Malaysia by bus and train, with excursions to the heaven of Thailand and several trips to Singapore, where D.J. Enright was now Professor of English Literature and apparently in constant conflict with the regime, which I thought was a great point in his favour. He came on a tour of inspection to see me when I was still living in the Hotel Majestic, and I was charmed by his Shelleyan appearance and Cambridge drawl. For the first time since we parted, I talked to someone about Dana, whose teacher Enright had been in Berlin. Enright's eyes lit up when I mentioned Dana's name, but I did not attempt to find out what kind of relationship, if any, they had had. Enright invited me to give a lecture at the University of Singapore, an invitation I gratefully declined.

The British Council in Kuala Lumpur was a place where I never set foot, and its officials avoided me like the plague:

> I can feel the flowers in the Lake Gardens
> Revolving with faint clicks.
> Clumps of telescopes
> Erect vermilion extensions,
> Bamboo fountains in a spray of fans.
>
> Dragging my grief, flesh and diamonds
> I trudge past the Central Electricity Board.
> I can hear bagpipes from the Campbell Road.
> Then to a model suburb, where
> Nothing happens, and I comb my hair.

Perfectly the Language Institute
Rivets earth and sky
With the clinking bolt of a regardless tower.
An old dog, my sweating shadow, stops and staggers,
Slogged by a thunder's rubber hammers.

The Railway Administration Building
And the Station, Edwardian-Moorish,
Suddenly exhibit cracks that steam.
Eyes averted, groping after a broken pencil,
I tiptoe past the British Council. . . .

(from 'Kuala Lumpur', *Refusal to Conform*)

Encouraged by Ray Bramah, I contributed to local magazines, and
wrote one of my best poems about Malaysia, 'Kampong', also in *Refusal
to Conform*:

Clusters of sultry palms
Limber as layabout brothers,
Lean with the sky's arms
Of cloud around each other's
Tawny necks and naked shoulders.

Loose-locked, random lovers,
On lazy hips they shag
Their ramshackle flywheels' windmill feathers
On warm trunks curved with the lag
Of kite-strings hauling on milky treasures.

Over the neat, brown-stilted houses'
Leaf-patched roofs and languorous verandas
The long legs in skin-tight trousers
Moodily flex their supple timbers,
Sighing for tempest-tossed surrenders.

It was quite daring to publish such an obviously homoerotic poem in
those days – and might be even more so in today's fundamentalist
Muslim Malaysia – but by distancing the sexiness of Malay boys into
the forms of palm trees I was able to get away with it. And how lovely
those boys were, so naturally loving and affectionate, their perfect,
slender bodies so enchantingly innocent and undepraved! The Chinese

and the Indians, too, offered heavenly gifts of erotic play, and I was never so happy as when I was lying some boy's arms, just stroking his silky skin and lightly pressing his voluptuous lips with mine. Of that side of my life, I have nothing but happy memories. But from an academic point of view, I was utterly miserable, as can be seen in this letter from Joe in Putney, dated 28 October 1961 and addressed to me at the Hotel Majestic:

But, darling Jim, what *are* you telling me? Surely you have entered the realms of fantasy? Accepted by the University, discredited before you appear, slighted upon arrival, ostracized and black-balled thereafter – surely this cannot be true, surely you exaggerate, – surely a single malicious voice, Mr Enright's, could hardly have had so sweeping a success? I mean it sounds not merely uncivilized but irrational, in fact perfectly dotty, to appoint a man and treat him thus on the merest gossip. Something else must be involved, besides the slanders of Mr Enright. It doesn't make sense that his words should have such power – and after all the money that has been spent on your transportation thither. I am so grieved and dismayed that everything (except the disconsolate Malay boy) should look so wrong so soon, but do give me a clearer idea of what you are up against and why. To start with, is the University European controlled or Malay controlled; are you employed by Europeans or by Malayans? Then, what sort of classes do you have, and what are the students like – idle or keen, intelligent or stupid – and how many do you have, and what are you teaching them? Is all that side of the matter satisfactory to you and them? Did you give your lectures on Henry James and were they a success? I happen to be reading him myself at present, *The Golden Bowl*, which I understand Stephen Spender is busy dramatizing – though I can't imagine how anyone could make drama out of so subtle and tentative a book. I do find it fascinating all the same – exasperating too, the wordiness and infinitesimal movement forwards and the endless turning over of every ventured thought.

Darling Jim, I have no great news and am a bit tired, so will not write much today. But I do hope things are not so odious and your colleagues so ill-mannered and offensive as your letter suggests – and that you will not do anything rash. It is sweet of you to offer your Bath flat, if available, and put yourself to the trouble of writing to your mother; we may try to avail ourselves of it; but this sad business drags on, and has dragged on now from a pleasant sunny autumn, into the beginnings of a cold and wet winter, and I wonder now whether, when the time comes, we shall not feel more melancholy and broody in Bath than here. Gorer says that if we go anywhere we shd. go to Brighton which is full of distractions and near to him. But Queenie lives still and we have made no decision.

> Bless you, dear
> Your devoted
> Joe.

It was a true measure of Joe's love for me, and of his loyal friendship, that he should have written such a letter to comfort and encourage me at a time when I may well have been hallucinating in the tropic heat during my first bout of malaria and under the continuing distress of all my inoculations and vaccinations. But it was certainly not all fantasy. I was in a state of almost total disintegration, and I could feel looming up that all-too-familiar sensation of impending doom:

> . . . Before dawn, in the deserted garden restaurant
> The table-cloths are sodden with the tears
> Of a million weepers, long departed.
> I sit alone in darkness deep and wet as a well.
> You can be sure of hell.

Again and again, I was to experience that sense of vastation, a feeling of being a void existing in a void. The only cure for it was a sexual encounter in the Batu Road or in the Oasis Coffee Shop. But often I refrained from touching the boys I most desired. There was one such who was a waiter in the Oasis, and I yearned to possess him (which would have been a simple matter of temporal, spacial and financial as well as sexual conjugation), but I deliberately abjured the consummation of my raging lust. I did not even speak to the boy, or smile at him, when he served my cup of coffee, but contented myself with glancing at him when he was not looking in my direction, thus preserving intact a memory of perfect and unsullied bliss, untainted by sordid lucre, sexual disappointment or – much worse – by everlasting regret.

I knew that poor old Joe had been worrying about Nancy, finances, health and, above all, Queenie, who was literally on her last legs, paralysed and unable to drag herself to the balcony to defecate with dignity. So I knew the value of that letter, written when he was harried and exhausted. But he was not satisfied with that: immediately after writing it, he must have written the next, also dated 28 October, but posted the following day:

Dearest Jim

I have decided about Queenie. She is to have her quietus tomorrow, if the vet can manage. I wanted it done today, but the vet is away at a dog show in Beckenham and won't be home till late. She is to ring me in the morning. Now that I have taken the decision I feel quite calm; it will be a great relief not to see her in her present state any more. She has dwindled and dwindled away and is as gaunt as Don Quixote; when I carried her out onto the terrace this morning and watched her trying to defecate and collapsing into her own drips of excreta, her hind legs being too weak to support her, I realized with absolute conviction (the thing I have hitherto lacked) that the end of the journey had come. The sense of pity has come, the pity of seeing her so helpless and abject; it is at last utterly clear that life is a humiliation and a burden to her; it is now easy to take it away. I shall miss her, as you may suppose, and until I do not have her I shall not know how much, but I think I shall be all right; the relief of no longer having to fight this so sad, so disappointing losing battle will be greater than the grief, I hope.

I posted a letter to you yesterday, and your sweet cards came this morning. I am so pleased that you have read my novelette [*We Think the World of You*] and liked it. I spent many years writing it, many years ago, and was satisfied with it in the end, it did everything I wanted it to do. Based as it is on experience, it is inevitable that my friends should read it as autobiography; but as pattern and plot took charge it became for me an objective work and the narrator an objective character. One of my friends said to me 'I would have enjoyed it if it had been written by someone else, but you made yourself out so *nasty*. I couldn't bear it.' The remark amused me; I saw that I had made of Frank a success. Personally I regard him as one of the best comic characters in fiction, and whenever I read the book myself almost everything he says and does, all his futile and absurd efforts to communicate his thwarted schemes, his impotent rages, his wild surmises, make me giggle. I wrote it as a funny book, above all, a kind of Charlie Chaplin, an irritable, frustrated figure perfectly determined to have his way and coming nothing but a cropper all along the line – in the end 'left with the dorg' as Isherwood laughingly remarked. Though I injected into it the utmost seriousness, heat, and drama, I intended it to be read above all as comedy, wry if you like, and I was particularly pleased with the passage where Frank keeps treading on the carrot in his flat, the canine equivalent of those human romances where it is the lingering perfume of the beloved lady which reminds the forlorn hero of what he has lost.

Nancy's card tells me you are wandering for a few days. How I envy you, dear Jim, how I wish you envied yourself. But I do hope and believe that if your new world is not to your liking at the moment, it will improve, with a little patience. *Think* how fortunate you are, darling, not to be sitting in Putney with a dying dog, or in Bath with a blind mother, or in England at all! Think, oh think, and tell yourself that, though you are not in Japan, you are still a fortunate boy.

I am addressing my letters now to the Majestic, partly because I have lost your University address, partly to save you the dismal prospect of calling at that horrid place.

Fond love
Joe

I remember weeping for poor, sweet Joe as I read that marvellous letter, and counting myself lucky to have such a friend. The trauma of Queenie's long decline and lingering death seemed to be a kind of watershed in his own existence. He must have seen in her end something of his own. Of course I wrote back constantly to him and to Nancy, trying to raise their spirits with a lot of trivial nonsense that I knew would amuse them, though my own heart was in my boots. I had never felt so ill, or so miserable, so alone, such an outcast from all-too-British Malaysia, one of those places like Hong Kong and Japan where the British character always seems more British than ever, and thus to me trebly dismaying and terrifying. But with the aid of artificial stimulants and regular doses of sex, I was just about keeping going. Indeed, sex had become to me like a drug, a craving for the human touch, however abstracted and impersonal its intimacies. Walking in the streets, I would let my hand brush lightly against the back of another, or I would bump as if by accident into someone, or in a bus I would sit with my knee gently pressing against the one next to mine, feeling a powerful current passing from my neighbour, the innocent provider of his stored-up vitality, through the taut transmitter of our tropic trousers into my ever-ravenous libido. Sometimes, in the crowded streets of KL my hesitant body would suddenly be confronted with another and we would perform a kind of side-stepping dance. On one memorable occasion, the young Malay I was trying both to dodge and to collide with resolved the impasse by laying both hands on my shoulders and giving me a dazzling smile, thus becoming my friend for life. In his *Psychopathology of Everyday Life* which I was reading at the time with great amusement, Sigmund Freud writes: 'Occasionally I have had to admit to myself that the annoying, awkward stepping aside on the street, whereby for some seconds one steps here and there, yet always in the same direction as the other person, until finally both stop facing each other . . . conceals erotic purposes under the mask of awkwardness.'

But with the encouraging letters of Joe and an occasional card from Raymond Mortimer, I thought I could hold out a little longer. Like my parents, Joe kept none of my letters, but I preserved as if sacred treasures all those he sent to me, and often reread them in moments of despondency and sickness, for I seemed to be running a permanent fever. Joe's next letter is dated 10 November 1961:

Dearest Jim

I have two extremely interesting and welcome letters from you, and a charming invitation from your Mother to Nancy and me to stay with her in Bath. She wrote it in her own wavering hand, sweet lady; I am deeply touched. I must take a day or two off and go down to see her, but not to stay, unless perhaps for a night. Queenie died on Oct. 30 and Nancy decided after all not to go anywhere. It is true that the clocks have gone back an hour, England is dark and cold and raining, not the most enticing time to move about; but that is not her reason, she says that she is so unused to going anywhere at all that it would now make her nervous to stay in anyone else's house. She is a strange woman. Fancy being nervous of staying with your Mother! But she is immovable over it. I suggested, too, that since Xmas will not be much fun for us in this haunted flat, we might fix to go and spend it with Gorer in Sussex, or Jack Sprott and his sister in Norfolk. But no, no, no, she could not do it, it would upset her and she would not be able to sleep. *I* could go if I liked, but not she. So we are not going anywhere, as I have told your Mother; Nancy will not budge and becomes visibly agitated if pressed.

I have begun to get over it all now, the misery of having to take the sweet girl's life, though it was done very efficiently and she never knew what happened to her; the shock is wearing off, but of course I think of her all the time and feel lost without her. But I managed to get away to Raymond in Dorset last weekend, and that has helped; I enjoyed it very much, the comfort and the talk. I did not take any more strongly to Desmond [Shawe-Taylor] than in the past, though I see he is a friendly, affectionate fellow; but I liked Raymond and Eardley Knollys, and we all talked of you with pride and love. Next weekend I am going up to Jack in Nottingham. Nancy doesn't seem to mind being left here entirely by herself, at any rate for short periods, which surprises and relieves me. What she will do in January I don't know, for – what do you think! – Morgan has sprung upon me the most exciting plan; he wants to send me to New York to represent him at the opening of his play there *The Passage to India*. Isn't that wonderful news, and the very thing I need. I do hope it comes off. I expect it will. He will pay my flight and everything and I shall stay there for a week or longer.

I am fascinated by your letters, dear; if you are still discontented at least you write very lively and have much of interest to impart. Lend no more money and get back what you have already lent. Do you always have to go to bed, à deux, in the 'Jungle'? It may be romantic, but hardly sounds comfortable. Are there no discreet hotels? I enjoyed one of your errors in typing: 'the Brutish Council'. But much of what you write makes me laugh out loud. The ipoh tree is clearly a problem; it is obviously better always to be the passive agent, underneath. I must go and see if there is one in Kew Gardens. But oh, dear Jim, how lucky you are; you do have fun beneath your trees, even if you ultimately turn to green jelly.

To take my mind off sorrow, I am looking through my old papers with the idea of trying to put together a small vol. of autobiographical essays. I remember a piece or two that might be worked up. We must work, as Tchekov remarked; it does help if one can.

Love as ever
Joe

A quarter of a century later, I cannot remember to whom I had lent money and from whom was having trouble in retrieving it, nor can I recall those escapades in the jungle under the ipoh tree, or why one might be turned to green jelly by standing underneath it. But I'm glad my nonsense made Joe laugh. I cannot now remember if Joe actually went to New York for the opening of Forster's play: if he did, I have no letter from him about it. The next letter is dated 22 December 1961:

My dearest Jim

Oh good. I'm so pleased the scene has changed for the better. I was feeling quite upset on your account, but everything sounds delightful now, almost nicer than Japan! I am reading your journal about that country [*These Horned Islands*]. The *Observer* asked me if I wd. review it for them and I said I wd. if I liked it. So I have a proof copy from them, I wasn't sure that I would like it at first, it seemed so profuse and long, but I have got on better as I have got in. So I will try to do a piece about it, though I ought not to be reviewing, I feel so dead and dull. But I can build it up by putting in lots of quotes from you. But where, oh where, is all the gaiety and rudery? Not a hint, not an innuendo, so far as I have got. These horned islands will disappoint some readers, I fear. I shall have to prepare them for the shock.

We drool along here very monotonously. The days seem almost unendurably long and there seem far more of them than there used to be. I can't write, don't even want to, and fill in time by slouching down the grey river side and going to films. Life has certainly lost its savour. Fortunately drink can be afforded and I can fuddle myself into insensibility twice a day. Perhaps America, if I ever reach it, will perk me up. I have a letter from Francis [King] suggesting that I should fly on to Japan from there for the Japanese spring. That would be towards the end of Feb. I suppose. It does sound a jolly notion, and since you too will be there about that time, I might return with you to Kuala L. on my way home. How long do you expect to stay in Japan? However, I am only turning it over in my mind as a pleasant fairy tale. I don't actually want to commit myself to anything more, at the moment, than getting to N.Y.; but if I leave the rest to impulse when I'm there, how shall I be able to pay my further fares? Perhaps I shall hear, in the next fortnight or so, whether my novel has sold there or not (it was published on Dec. 6); if it has – oh so unlikely – Obolensky might give me some money. Anyway, tell me what you plan to do in Japan and where one might get at you if one suddenly swooped down. I certainly don't want to linger long with Francis – had enough of that – Nara is a place I would like to stay in . . . but this is only a dream.

Xmas day

This time last year I was sitting in a cosy bar in Kurashiki with the Rev. Kinoshita, my little priest, and his papa, huge fat Japanese provincial geishas nudging us in at our too-small table. It was happier than today. I have finished your book, and my review. I hope you will like – and not mind – the latter. The further one advances into the book, the more interesting it becomes, but oh dear Jim you have not troubled much to accommodate it to what is called 'the reading public'. The profusion is too great in so long a book; the eye can take in effectively only a certain amount, in life and literature, and all those catalogues of objects you go in for, they may be Japan, but will they not bewilder the public? And there are no persons, no conversations, no sex – not even little sly jokes about it – nothing to break up the long descriptive text. However, there are also masses of interesting observations from which I have lavishly quoted, and although I had to put in these other opinions too, I think I have done a fairly 'selling' review of you.

Love as ever
Joe

The sadness and weariness of old age were descending rapidly upon Joe at this time. He was in really low water, and I was rather surprised that he was able to write the review of my book. I cannot remember what it said except for one thing that overjoyed me – he said I was 'innocent'. That in my opinion put paid to all my detractors. As for the sex he missed so badly, in those days it would have been impossible to write as frankly as I can now, and it would have implicated too many people whom I did not want to distress – including my mother, who, though she could not read, had Agnes and other helpers to read to her, and there were the Talking Books to which I had granted permission to record all my writings. As long as my mother was alive, therefore, I could not write as I should have liked. There are signs, too, in those last two letters, of a growing testiness in Joe, and I believe he had a terrific argument with *The Observer* for wanting to change his review in ways he would not allow. But I was grateful to him for the trouble he went to over the book, and wrote to tell him so. In fact, the fears he had that the general public would not like it proved groundless, for it was sold to an American publisher and went into several editions. It had excellent reviews. Many people who have come to work in Japan, or just to visit, have told me that it was my book which inspired them to do so. I wish I had kept a copy of Joe's review, his second for me: the first was an anonymous review of *The Descent into the Cave* (1957) in *The Listener*, after he could find no one willing to review it.

Did I go to Japan for Christmas? I certainly did, by ship from Singapore, calling at fairy-tale Manila on the way, then Taiwan and Hong Kong. I was longing to see Japan again. Seen from KL, it seemed like a lost paradise in those days, and after my stay there I decided to return as soon as possible. This feat I accomplished in the spring of 1962.

My departure was sudden, and unheralded, and is fully described in *Tropic Temper*. Only Ray Bramah and another non-university British friend were in on the secret. I got a visa 'for cultural purposes' through the kindness of Professor Muraoka in Sendai, who had to go to a notary public and sign an affidavit guaranteeing me. I got the visa from the Japanese consulate in KL. Then I had to have more inoculations. I went down with shingles. I was treated by a brutal British doctor who jabbed syringes into me with the utmost ferocity, a real sadist, but one whose aim was not to give pleasure through the infliction of pain. Then I found my Malay driver in bed with one of my male students in the basement of the house I had moved into. The old Chinese cook who had been engaged for me by my British friends was cheating me hand over fist at the market: this was common practice, but I did not like to feel helpless in the face of such wholesale robbery. Nevertheless I left a substantial sum of money for him when I finally left. I 'did a Kirkup' again. I got on a JAL plane at KL airport, seen off by only those two friends.

The university did not find out about my defection until several days later, when I was sent an angry letter by the Malay in charge of educational affairs – a man from whose bullying tactics I had suffered in the past. It was a long, furious diatribe, and he said among other hurtful things that he would see to it that I never got a job at any university again. This was typical of his very un-Malay aggressiveness. Ray Bramah, too, had warned me of this possibility, but I was past caring about any future in the teaching profession. I felt I would rather wash dishes or empty trash-cans.

I sent that letter to Joe. He fully agreed with the registrar's complaints and accusations, which I came to see were entirely justified – if only he had not expressed them in such a rabid manner. But at the time,

I was disappointed in Joe, as he must have been in me. I felt that I had lost an old friend, and for some months the flow of letters between us dried up.

As the plane took off from Kuala Lumpur, I felt that familiar lightening of spirit I always feel when finally escaping from some unendurably constricting situation. I still did not realize that all flight is useless – something I was to learn from certain characters in Simenon's more serious psychological studies of lonely outsiders and fugitives from the banality of a world in which they have no place.

My life was not so much fatality as deliberate choice. Whatever went wrong could be only my own fault, though my errors were provoked by what I saw as errors in conventional society. I could never come to terms with my inability to live in the world of others in the way they wanted me to live. I was filled with fear and trembling whenever I was near the British. I began to understand that the source of some literature is in fear, that writing is the act of confronting threats and anxieties and shame. And love was sheer malediction for me. I wrote to exorcize that shame, that fear, but succeeded only in augmenting their intensity. Whenever I published anything, even in the most obscure little magazine, I was seized with a mortal dread, so much so that I had to give up reading my own work in print, and took care never to read any review after the one by Joe appeared in *The Observer*.

But now I was on my way back to my beloved Japan, and for a while the torments were stilled. I had a little money saved up. I intended to try to make a living by writing and translating.

At Osaka, there was the usual long line in front of the immigration counter. Then something quite wonderful happened. The young clerk at the immigration counter beckoned to me, indicating that he wanted me to jump the queue. When I got to the counter, amid curious and furious glances from the waiting travellers, he said: 'Good-evening, Professor Kirkup'. It was one of my old students at Tohoku University. I had not recognized him in his uniform. He checked my passport and asked me how long I was going to stay in Japan. 'One year,' I replied. My visa was a 'cultural' one, valid for only one year, though it could be renewed. 'I hope you will stay longer than that,' he said, smiling as he handed back my passport.

And indeed, as things turned out, I did.

Living Dangerously

Believe me! The secret of reaping the greatest fruitfulness and the
greatest enjoyment from life is to *live dangerously*! . . .

He who fights with monsters might take care lest he thereby become a
monster. And if you gaze for long into the abyss, the abyss gazes also into
you.

Friedrich Nietzsche, *Beyond Good and Evil*

So on my second arrival in Japan I had again been met by someone
sympathetic. That immigration official was not dear Professor Kobayashi;
but he knew me, he had been my student at Sendai. The fact that I had
no recollection of him did not surprise me, for classes were very large,
and many students, after attending one or two lectures to see what sort
of freak I was ('Go on, take a good look,' I would tell new students at
the start of the academic year in April. 'Drink me in from head to foot,
then we can start the lecture!'), would drop out and turn up for only the
final weeks before their final examination. I never once failed a student.
Often I just gave them all 'A' grades, without bothering to look at their
papers. They knew they could depend upon me for an easy pass – and
why not? I was getting a sort of revenge on Girdlestone for having torn
up my examination paper in full view of all the other students and
invigilators during my finals.

I wanted to make my savings last as long as possible, for I really
believed that I would never find another academic post. So I went to
the Osaka YMCA. As soon as I signed in at the desk, the person in
charge gave me a strange look, and from under the counter produced a
copy of the *Orient/West* special number which contained my 'Gay Boys'
poem and the one about the strippers in Asakusa, 'Nippon's Non-Stop
Nudes'. The thought that he found these scandalous was a matter of
indifference to me; but being a marked man in Japan was very unpleasant. The news of the 'mad poet's' arrival spread like wildfire round
the Y, and I had hardly settled into my room when there was a knock at
the door and a youth wearing only his winter long johns entered and sat

beside me on the bed. I at once sensed that this was a kind of amateur entrapment, nothing serious or official, just somebody wanting to have a joke: he had probably been 'dared' to do it by his mates. So after a few minutes' chat, during which he lay back invitingly on the bed, I stood up and asked him to leave. He was quite attractive, and seemed insulted by my rejection, like all males who think they are irresistible to 'gays'.

The night was still young, and I had no intention of spoiling my first evening in Osaka by submitting to an ignorant cock-tease. I went out and had dinner at a Kirin Beer Hall, then wandered off towards the Gay Quarters, where I suddenly saw a small bar named 'Genet'. Could this be named after the Jean Genet whose poems I had translated? Or was it a tribute to Janet Flanner, whose *New Yorker* letters from Paris always entertained me so, under the pseudonym of 'Genêt'. That circumflex makes all the difference. It means 'flowering broom' (*Genista*), while Jean Genet's surname means a jennet. In either case, I felt that such a fine literary name was worth investigating: if the former, the bar would be full of toughs and sailors; if the latter, it would be the haunt of literary lesbians like Renée Vivien and Nathalie Barney. Perhaps even Djuna Barnes and Vita Sackville-West. . . .

Full of pleasurable expectation, I pushed open the door, and saw at once that it was not my kind of place: it was a 'sister bar', in which all the boys were decked out as pretty little geishas. I must have been the first foreigner ever to enter the place, because the sweet things made much of me, patting my hair, feeling my muscles, giving me playful slaps, while I tried to drink a small glass of beer – always the cheapest drink in such a place. But after a few minutes, when I wanted to pay and leave, I found that the bill was 5,000 yen – an enormous sum in those days. It was no use arguing in such a situation: those male geishas are pretty tough cuties. After paying the bill, I had only about 100 yen left. Osaka was obviously already too hot for me. I would have to get to Tokyo and find a job – any kind of job – though as I had been admitted on a 'cultural' visa I was not officially allowed to take up work.

On the way to Tokyo, I went to Kobe to enjoy the sleazy delights of the Gay Quarters there – Fukuhara, now depressingly cleaned up and sanitized, but in those days a real hotbed of all kinds of vice in the form of gay movie-theatres and scruffy strip shows in draughty tents set up on bits of waste ground or still-surviving bomb-sites. I loved the place.

Then on to Kyoto for a few days, where Francis King invited me to one of his literary evenings for his chosen students and professors. That was where I met a rather dim post-graduate university assistant who,

Francis informed me, was rather improbably thinking of doing a doctoral thesis on Joe Ackerley, and hoped I would give him some hints. But I knew the sort of 'hints' he was angling for, and refused to betray Joe in any way. 'You can't write about J.R. Ackerley,' I told him, 'because there are so far no critical works about him, and no Japanese can ever be the first to "discover" and write about a Western author. You are lost without critical references to fall back on, and to quote at length, or even slightly rewrite as your own original work – what we call plagiarism.' The man must have been extremely drunk or just stupid, because he just giggled and agreed with me, adding, laughing loudly in that curiously insensitive way some Japanese do when making a joke: 'Anyhow, he's not dead yet.' I made no response, and gave no reaction to his unpleasant sense of humour. Poor Joe, I thought, suffering agonies of loneliness, despair and ill-health in faraway Putney, how glad I am you aren't here at this gathering of academic imbeciles. I believe no Japanese has, as yet, written anything at all important about Joe: he is the sort of writer, like Nabokov or Compton-Burnett, whose style and humour and background are totally alien to the Japanese, and so forever beyond their comprehension.

Back in Tokyo, I stayed a couple of nights at the Dai-Ichi Hotel in Shimbashi, where I received my first obscene telephone call – from an American, not a Japanese. He must have noted my room number on the key I was carrying in the coffee-shop, for as soon as I returned to my room there was a telephone call, and a thick Mid-West accent saying: 'Oh boy, oh boy, have I got something big and hard now in my hand for you! D'you want my measurements?' I interrupted him to ask 'What colour panties are you wearing today?' and rang off. He did not ring back.

Maurice Schneps, the editor of *Orient/West*, invited me to lunch at the Palace Hotel, where he proposed that I should become his literary editor. I jumped at the chance, and when he asked me how much salary I would require, I rather foolishly belittled myself in his eyes, and in the eyes of his backer, a very shrewd and generous fellow-American Jew, by suggesting the ridiculous sum of 30,000 yen a month, half of the pittance I had received in Sendai. I think this was the real reason why we broke up about a year later.

But I got two cheap rooms at the centre of Tokyo's Bohemia, Shinjuku San-chome, for only 6,000 yen a month, without bath, sharing kitchen and a crouch-toilet in which the aged proprietor had affixed a Janglish notice saying: *Please put piece paper on the botton* [*sic*]. Torn-up squares of the *Tokyo Shimbun* hung on a hook alongside, and in this way I began to familiarize myself with some of the more common Chinese characters or *kanji* in the Japanese script.

Now that I was back in Tokyo, I was determined to have a good time. On the wall next to my bed I stuck these lines from Marcus Aurelius:

> Observe, in short, how transient and trivial is all mortal life; yesterday a drop of semen, tomorrow a handful of spice or ashes. Spend, therefore, these fleeting moments on earth as Nature would have you spend them, and then go to your rest with good grace, as an olive falls in its season, with a blessing for the earth that bore it and a thanksgiving to the tree that gave it life.

This, I felt, was a perfect expression of the Japanese concept of 'the floating world', and of *mono no aware*. I found the image of the drop of semen especially appropriate.

After a couple of months working happily at *Orient/West* I received, through the kind offices of Professor Rikutaro Fukuda, an invitation to start teaching some of Tokyo's most intelligent and independent young ladies at Japan Women's University in Mejiro, at a much higher salary than I had received in Sendai. And I was given a beautiful old semi-traditional house right on the campus to live in. It was the start of six very happy years. During these years I received many letters from Joe.

Francis King had warned me that there was a new British Council representative in Tokyo, someone he referred to as Tomb-lin. In a kind letter some years later, Francis compares him with Bottrall:

> Curiously, Bottrall was here (London) yesterday – on one of his visits from Rome. He was infinitely better than Tomb-lin while in Japan. Of course he is a bully and has *folie de grandeur* but he *respects* writers (as Tomb-lin never did) and also likes homosexuals (Tomb-lin hated them). Bottrall spoke well of you, yesterday – we were talking about autobiographies of childhood and when I said that yours seemed to me one of the best ever written, he at once agreed that it was 'remarkable'.

Before I moved into my two rooms in Shinjuku, I stayed a couple of nights at the Kanda YMCA, then a place celebrated for its homosexual activity, which went on all night long between foreign and Japanese men. I had told Francis I would be at the Y until I found a room, and he must have informed Tomlin, because on my very first morning I had a telephone call from the representative, checking out on 'what Kirkup is up to now' and obviously determined to exert pressure and control over whatever job I might find. I remember hearing him drawl: 'I suppose you want to find a job. . . .' I answered: 'Not particularly – and anyhow not with *your* help.' I rang off.

I never heard from him again, and on the one occasion when we were supposed to meet, a year or two later, I arranged not to turn up – it was at a party given by Japanese writers of the Japan PEN Club in order to present me with their first prize for a poem sequence. 'Japan Marine', which had won their award in an international literary competition to celebrate the 1964 Tokyo Olympics. The prize was presented to me, as the newspapers put it, 'in absentia'. Tomlin and the rest of the British Council were all there to steal as much of my limelight as possible. Tomlin was said to be a close friend of T.S. Eliot – enough to damn him in my eyes. I was involved in the mysterious disappearance of the typescript of one of his boring philosophical works, which he had written in Tokyo. I knew how the theft had occurred, but I had no intention of betraying those concerned in it. In the same letter, Francis went on:

I wrote a story in *The Brighton Belle* about the theft of Tomb-lin's great work. I made him into a Japanese and the thief into the Japanese's discarded English mistress. I've no idea what really happened but I feel that this could have been the answer. Bottrall told me yesterday that Tomb-lin is a voyeur. He once paid a woman to go to bed with his best friend and then tell him all about the friend's performance. . . .

Francis goes on to speak about Joe's letters, so it is appropriate to quote him here:

Neville Braybrooke selected which of my letters he used – I had over 200 and he used only 24 or 25. He also excised names where he thought that people might take offence. Joe would sometimes get exasperated with his friends and say very cruel things about them, as you know. One of his letters (unpublished) to me contains some

horrid remarks about Bunny and another some no less horrid remarks about Geoffrey Gorer. He also wrote very woundingly about
me to someone who made a point of showing me the letter! He often
spoke to me about your 'joy-injections' – in fact, when he got gloomy
in Kyoto, he said 'What I need is one of Jim's joy-injections.' How
we laughed when he read out to me a letter in which you said that
you were testing Helena Rubinstein's Anti-Wrinkle cream by rubbing it on your scrotum! (You *must* put that in your autobiography –
it is worthy of Firbank.)

So here it is, Francis! Thank you for reminding me of those 'joy-
injections'. What I meant by this were not injections of euphoric
stimulants, of course, but my own little jets of fun in the form of jokes,
Firbankian letters and the occasional young man, such as the ones I had
provided for Joe in Sendai and Tokyo, and who left him feeling
rejuvenated – except in the latter case, when he unaccountably fell
deeply in love with the boy I had asked to be nice to him at the Kanda
YMCA in Tokyo. Perhaps that was the cause of Joe's gloom when
staying with Francis in Kyoto – he knew he would probably never see
his young lover again. In that case, my joy-injection had had adverse
side-effects: but at least Joe had had one wonderful night of love. . . .
I have many letters written to me by Joe from 1963 up to his death in
1967. Here is one dated 11 June 1963 which was addressed to me at
Orient/West:

Dearest Jim
    So nice to hear from you from Koyasan. My last word from
Francis [King] was a card from there. The temple I stayed in was the
Daimyo-in. How far and long ago it all seems now. My health is all
right, I suppose, but my spirits do not soar. I feel so tired and know
not how to use my days, warm and summery though they now are. I
go to Kew Gardens a good deal, with a bird book and a tree book,
trying to learn about these things. Also a loaf of bread, to feed the
various birds. The water-birds eat from my hand; they are very busy
breeding; the beautiful black swans, with their flounces and red
beaks, have a large biscuit-coloured brood and are much photographed. We are having a good June and the flowers are wonderful,
the iris garden in particular, scenting the air all about, and the azaleas.
I just lie or sit there in the sun or in the shade throughout the
afternoon, not even reading; then I come home and get tight. Of

course other things happen, lunches, dinners, cinemas, plays. One has somehow to *make* each day as it dawns. What to do? Sometimes I take Nancy, out of kindness, though I prefer to be alone; she would like to go with me everywhere – Darby and Joan – but that I cannot bear. I often remember your remark about her in Bath, tapping along behind us on her stiletto heels 'like a woodpecker'. All that continues; if I reduced my pace more than I do to suit hers, I should be standing still. But she is much better. I took her to Weymouth for a fortnight in early May; she enjoyed it in a way but could not sleep, though she had a quiet room on the sea. And though we had some sun, a rather chilly north wind blew all the time. I devoted myself to her entirely for a fortnight; she is not the brightest woman in the world. But now her doctor has put her on to tranquillizers; she sleeps well, even dozes in the afternoon, and is much more tranquil: but still the bother goes on about wanting me to take her everywhere with me, because she 'doesn't like' doing things alone. I spend much time inventing engagements in order to get free from her. It is all death in life for me. I took Morgan to your Physicist play. It wasn't a huge success. The second act interested him, but the first act – which is indeed awfully long – bored him no end. I too saw through it on a second seeing. Now his own new adaptation is on, *Where Angels Fear to Tread*, and is rather good. It would have been better, I think, if my advice about the last scene had been wholly taken – I re-wrote it for Mrs Hart, the dramatist – but only a part of my suggestions was acceptable to her. A young Welshman, playing the part of Guido the Italian, carried the First Night evening, to which I took Nancy and a friend.

I'm so glad *Orient/West* has got on its feet again and that you are to be its Lit. Ed. If I could offer you anything for it, you may be sure I wd., but (I will look) I think I have nothing lying about except some sad reflections upon the wretched plight of that charming young tigress in the Children's Zoo in Matsushima, who upset me so much. But I've done nothing to article-ize them. Certainly use my Kobo Daishi article if you want it. I could send you a copy, and might improve upon it, perhaps. Morgan is too old to help.

In Sept., early, I go to Greece with Jack Sprott and his sister (if I am still alive). I shall stay on, I think, after they have gone. They go for 3 weeks, at most. I suppose I could fly on to Japan to you from there. What do you think? I am sure I shall not want to return to England. Much love, dear Jim,

JOE

I was trying now to reduce my multiplicity of selves to more manage-
able single figures, but without much success. Every time I looked in a
mirror, I seemed to see someone different. It was as if I were possessed
by a host of warring impulses and conflicting identities. At one moment
I was the poet, at the next the satyr; a saintly figure, then the image of
decadence; a man, then a woman; a child, then an old man or a witch.
Sometimes I did not know where I was or what I was doing. I was at
the mercy of all these swirling character currents and whirlpools of will.

What effect I was producing on others was something I never considered. But it must have been confusing, to say the least. Around this
time, when I first began working for *Orient/West*, an unusual number
of people were brought to see me, and I had the sense of being put on
display or even on exhibition like a waxwork: why were all these people
so interested in me? A certain journalist well known in the Far East even
bargained with the proprietor of the magazine to let him have a glimpse
of me, and this was done without my consent. I remember how he
turned up one evening at the office, without warning, with an almost
gloating face that seemed to be all *goguenard* eyes as he raked me from
head to toe with a knowing smile. I restrained myself from giving them
both a shot of the old evil eye, which I was trying to keep for more
important occasions: its effect was diminished if I used it too often on
people unworthy of it.

One of the gapers was Edmund Blunden, then Professor of English
in Hong Kong. He had often written me condescending little notes
when he was literary editor of *The Times Literary Supplement*. Now I
saw what a mean, trivial little person he was; and Maurice told me of
some grubby sexual scandal which did not interest me at all. But I was
grateful to Blunden because he brought with him R.H. Blyth, that
quirky scholar whose *haiku* anthologies became the bibles of the Beats
and made the fortunes of what is still little more than a vanity publisher,
Hokuseido Press. Blyth was very shy and silent but smiled as I praised
his *Zen and Zen Classics* and his remarkable *Zen in English Literature*.

It was around this time that Joe started signing his name in capital
letters, and I supposed this departure from his usual 'J' or 'Joe' was a
subconscious assertion of an identity he may have felt he had lost in part
after being retired from *The Listener*. Or he may have been trying to be
more affirmative in the continuing negative attrition of Nancy's possess-
iveness on his embattled but fading will. In the end, Joe never managed to return to Japan to stay with either Francis or myself, though
when I moved to my large house on the campus of Japan Women's

University I could have given him a very comfortable *tatami* room and the services of many charming young men who would have been only to glad to act as guides in return for Joe's mellifluous voice in patient English conversation. One of my old friends in Sendai, Takuro, to whom I dedicated *Refusal to Conform*, had moved to Tokyo: he had fought shy of meeting Joe in Sendai, where consorting with foreigners was looked upon with a suspicious eye, but in Tokyo he would have made an ideal companion for Joe's sightseeing whenever I was too busy to take him around myself. As for Nancy, many were the times on my returns to England when I offered to take her away for a week in Bath with my mother, to give Joe a little time to himself. Nancy always accepted these offers, but at the last moment would always find an excuse for staying with Joe.

I had been gathering English and American contributors to the literary pages of *Orient/West*, and succeeded in attracting William Plomer (who reviewed my *Refusal to Conform*), Ted Hughes, Charles Causley, Thomas Kinsella, F.T. Prince, Norman McCaig and a number of other poets. Naturally, I wanted something from Morgan Forster and Joe, but Morgan was past writing anything, and Joe was having difficulty in writing anything except letters and his diary. I suggested he send me some extracts from the latter, but these were not forthcoming. The essay on Koyasan, which had appeared already in *The Listener*, had been turned down by Maurice Schneps, and in a letter dated 19 July 1963 Joe reacted in a very typical way to this rejection, which was all my fault:

My darling Jim,

I am not *at all* surprised by Mr Schneps' opinion. I wondered what you could be up to, stocking your mag. with odds and ends from previous publications; *The Listener* too wd. never have permitted that – doubtless a reason why, in the long course of years, I got so worn out, having no assistant and only my own poor mind to rely upon in finding material which had always to be fresh and original. Killing work for one head, and in the end it killed me. You may be sure that if I can devise anything for you I will, for I love you and wd. like to help you adorn your mag., but the last two years have not invigorated my thought. However I am thinking of taking myself up into Bedfordshire soon for a few days to stay, perhaps in Dunstable, within easy reach of Whipsnade Zoo, which I visited this week for the first time and take an interest to explore more thoroughly. If some little piece on animals, including my memory of the Matsushi-ma tigress, came out of that I wd. submit it to you. No, dear, I cannot write about Goldie Dickinson, though oddly enough I am reading about him in Morgan's biography, which I have not looked at for many years: a beautiful book. *Appearances* I have read. He (Goldie) was in love with me when I was a young man and I had to disengage myself from an emotional relationship I did not want. He managed to sublimate it, as he sublimated all his unreciprocated passions. I have not thought of him or it for a great many years, preferring not to I suppose, until lately in my family memoir (*My Father and Myself*) I have been trying to examine and explain a psychology, my own, which was never able to be generous in such matters and which, although I could not and cannot help it, has been no pleasure to try to discern.

I have written to Francis who asks me to go out now and return with him on his P. & O. But, as you know, I am at present engaged to spend the last two or three weeks of September in Greece with the Sprotts. The plan wobbles a bit at the moment, for Jack's health is not good and is under medical survey. However, I hope all will be well. If we go, and Greece props up my failing mind to greater enterprise than it at present possesses, I might come and try you and your welcoming friends. A sweeter and warmer invitation than yours could not be imagined.

Love as ever
Joe

Joe's remark that *The Listener* would never have permitted reprints of already published work is not quite correct, for I remember he often urged me to send my poems to American magazines, and said this would not preclude their being published in *The Listener*.

I had been reading Forster's delightful biography of Goldsworthy Lowes Dickinson, as well as some of the latter's writings on Japan, so I had hoped either Morgan or Joe could have sent me an essay about him. But eventually, after many ditherings and autocriticisms of the most stringent kind, Joe finally managed to write, though still not entirely to his own satisfaction, his remarkable essay 'I Am a Beast'.

A letter dated 10 October 1963 gives an amusing account of his travels in Greece and offers some hilarious glimpses of our mutual friend M——, a charming scholar.

Darling Jim

So sweet to hear from you. This very morning. Indeed I had not forgotten you, in fact for the last six months – or so it seems – I·have been struggling with an article for your mag. But although it starts off rather bright and jolly, I simply got stuck and couldn't finish it, for the reason, I'm afraid, that I was never clear what I was trying to say. I took it to Greece with me (I returned only yesterday) and struggled with it there, in Nauplia, but without success, and I know now that I shall never finish it. Perhaps I will send you the bit that got done, *very* Japanese, just to show you that I have been trying to please you; but unless some inspiration comes to me – of which I now despair – it will remain forever unfinished.

Yes, I have been a month in Greece, first, for a fortnight, with Jack Sprott and his sister, touring the Peloponnesian sights in a bus and visiting Rhodes and Crete by air; then with M—— for another fortnight in Nauplia or Nafplion, whichever name you know the place by. I enjoyed it all very much, and am, in health, the better for it all, though M—— rather unnerved old Joe, too fast in his driving over all those precipitous mountain passes (he hired a car), and too fast and rash in his pursuit of sex, none of which did he seem greatly to enjoy, and some of which got him into unpleasantness. However, I am not so blinkered as to fail to see the rightness of those who, indefatigable in their pursuit of pleasure, are determined, at whatever risk, to wring from life's orange, or lemon, the last tiny drop. We got along all right, but while he prowled after chaps, never satisfied with their presents of money, I prowled after the famished stray dogs and cats, with a soap-box filled with inedible human food from our various hotels and restaurants – and they, at least, seem responsive to love. I am sorry to have left that lovely country, so warm and beautiful, sorry to be home – ah, home! – and of course I will come with you to South America in February, I would love it, I am always happy with you, as I was happy with the Sprotts; indeed poor old M—— is O.K., but for some reason I can't truly *like* him. Perhaps he reminds me too much of my younger self, of whom I am now critical.

Dear Jim, the news of your health distresses me. Pleurisy in Japan! And before the onset of winter! Well, I hope you are really recuperating and that the spot on the lung has been obliterated. It must be so delightful to have the small fingers of Japanese doctors smoothing away one's spots. Do write again, dear, and tell me more – and don't risk your health; it must be so boring to be in even a Japanese sanatorium. Unwanted illness is a great curse, and I'm sure you are the last person to be a wanter. Your letter was all too brief, yet why should I expect more, having been so poor a correspondent. However, the news of two books finished and soon to be published almost cancels out the rest. You are a darling to put me on your list and I can hardly wait for them, particularly *Tropic Temper* – an almost self-defensive title, unless the temper is elsewhere, but I hope it may be outspoken and tempestuous. Having lived for a month on nothing stronger than *oozo* [*sic*] and light wines, I am a little tipsy this evening on dear old gin, so forgive literary shortcomings.

Best love –
JOE

As far as 'literary shortcomings' were concerned, I could rarely find any in Joe's fluent, elegant, cool, humorous writings. Indeed, I was often amazed at the beauty of letters that must have been composed under the influence of 'mother's ruin' or Nuits-Saint-Georges. His writing had that pure and unadulterated *jet* of composition, as if he had just let his pen roam free, without almost taking thought. The result was that I could hear his mellifluous voice, so Cambridge still in timbre and languid mischief, casting its spell upon me, however far away I was from him in place and time. And there were almost no crossings-out: ' . . . he never blotted out a line'. I could not have continued with Jonson's praise of Shakespeare: 'Would he had blotted a thousand.' But of the 'sweet swan of Putney' I would have said with him: 'For I loved the man, and do honour his memory, on this side idolatry, as much as any.' Indeed, even more. . . . His next letter is dated 22 October 1963, and contains more entertaining gossip about 'poor old M':

Dearest Jim,
Such a lovely post this morning: letters from you, Jack and M——: yours miles the best, it made me laugh like anything, a sound not often heard in this flat. Jack and I lunch on Thursday (he is soon off to Ghana for 3 months); M—— is still in Athens enjoying the last of the year's sunshine and a satisfactory cross-eyed boy to whom a friend had introduced him. I am so glad he has found someone suitable at last, the long list of failures was becoming unnerving. I entirely agree about sex, of course, so long as it is gay and happy; it is the squalor from which I recoil – threats and violence, extortion,

physical insult (I forget the name M—— has for the boys who refuse to touch him in return: he meets a lot of those). The very thought of bargaining – 'a hundred drachma isn't enough' – which M—— seems not to mind upsets me so much that I prefer celibacy. But as M—— says 'Faint heart never won fair lady', and I'm so glad to know he now has one, even though she squints. Yes, though there is no law against homosexuality in Greece, there is a largely middle-class hostile feeling towards it (unmanly) and it remains difficult to introduce boys into hotels, excepting rather scruffy ones in the Plaka. M—— was twice obstructed by managements when I was with him, but sounds cheerful and pleased with his present hotel.

Darling Jim, your books have arrived   I kiss you for them – and I am well into *Tropic Temper* (as far as 'Some People'). It delights me, easily the best thing you've done, a perfect amalgam of your two gifted selves, autobiographer and poet. Every page is both exciting and beautiful with its wealth of imagery; you have really 'found yourself', as they say, and the book must surely have a great success. It is so amusing too – oh I am enjoying it. I have made a mark of especial gratitude on p. 59 – you will easily find the short passage. I wish someone had asked me to review it, but I must have been out of England when it was published and have seen, I think in Greece, only one review – Sunday paper? – I bought no papers myself, perhaps M—— got it. Anyway I can hardly wait for your 'Farewell to Japan' book and am sure that you have already established yourself as a wizard with words. Yet how sad to have sucked Japan dry – can there be anything left? Well, we will see. Fond love as ever

Joe

This was an air letter addressed to my new abode, Mariya Apartment 8, in Mejiro, where I lived for a few months before moving down the road to the house on the Japan Women's University campus. I was always thinking of saying 'farewell to Japan'. Life there increasingly exasperated me, but at the same time I felt as if bewitched and possessed by the country and the people, and every time I thought I could bear it no longer something or someone wonderful would turn up to make me stay. The review of *Tropic Temper* must have been the very appreciative one by James Pope-Hennessy in *The Sunday Times*. Perhaps, after all, on his visit with Lord Methuen to our house in Flemish Buildings, he had recognized me as the young man he had once picked up in

Piccadilly during the war, and rewarded with thirty bob?

The passage Joe refers to is this. I am describing an invasion of minuscule flying ants on the breakfast table at the Majestic Hotel:

I put a few crumbs of palest-amber cane-sugar on the tablecloth but they ignore them. The sugar here comes in large crystals, like square glass beads. Finally, one of the ants, instead of just bumping into a crystal and running past it, embraces it, crawls all over it and then rivets itself to its sweetness. A reflex makes it detach itself from the crystal and rush away to tell the others, but before it has gone an inch it is back again, sucking up the precious sweetness. A slightly larger ant comes busily running backwards and forwards through the sprinkling of crystals, but although it keeps bumping into them it does not acknowledge the sweetness and fusses away over the table-cloth's dull white desert to investigate a burnt-out match and a pipe-cleaner. But eventually it cottons on: anti-joy conquered by life's underlying, essential sweetness. It *is* so, or why do we go on living: it is not simply being glibly optimistic to suck life's quintessence whenever we can, to put oneself in shafts of sunlight whenever possible. But like those flying ants we sometimes have to be almost hit over the head with them before we realize the treasures at hand each day. And we are so conditioned to the bitterness and hardness and hopelessness of life that goodness and beauty, when they present themselves (for they are always there), go unrecognized, or are mocked because of their shining difference.

Joe's next letter is dated 31 October 1963, and is full of interesting news:

Dearest Jim

I have given your address to Sonia Orwell (can't remember if you know her, a nice, kind, unhappy creature, rather too much intellect, helped with *Horizon*, married George Orwell on his death-bed, then married Michael Pitt-Rivers after his emergence from Wormwood Scrubbs – Scrubwood Worms – now, alas, separated and divorced: she talks too much). She is now part Lt. Ed. to a new mag (don't know the name it will bear), financed by the wealthy wife of an English painter and birth-panging in Paris. Its object is to print good literature from any country, not by famous men but by those whose artistic worth has not been sufficiently acclaimed. Oodles of money, I am told. I could think of no one to suit their requirements, except you and me. On demand, I have given her a bit of my Family Memoir, my exploits in World War 1 (not much more than 5000 words – far too short for her but I can't do better) and directed her towards you. If you are interested – and Collins willing – *and* if she writes you – why not offer her something out of one of your two new books? *Something really special.* I can guarantee nothing, the set-up seems pretty dotty, what *she* likes (and she does have taste) her painter-supporters often don't, however they all appear to like me, and bloody well ought to like you whom I read with *envy*, and *oodles* of money are always worth trying for. I told her to read your *Tropic Temper* – but of course painters – abstract, I fear – may not like such rich, brilliant and kaleidoscopic wealth of colour and imagery. But do try, darling! I would love to be in bed with you in the same mag. You might also, perhaps, give a hand to some Japanese writer whom you admire – if you know any. Sideline: Were those cocoanuts [*sic*] smashed in the street human heads, as in my *Hindoo Holiday*, a Ganesh day, late January? I wondered as I read.

I loved your letter and Takuro-Dick's postcard. I wonder why he thinks so highly of me now when he came not near me in Sendai. I am reading a little book called *My Kingdom for a Donkey*, by Doris Rybot. Someone gave it to me because I fell so deeply in love with the ubiquitous little donkeys in Greece. It is surprisingly good, sensitive and not silly. She treats animals in the right way, allowing them to develop their personalities to the full, and gets the best out of even a hen. I think perhaps I was stupid not to move into the country after Queenie's death (two years ago yesterday). I might have had a little henny and whatever else came along. I am far more interested in animals now than I am in people. I feel closer to them. It is, in a way, what the article I tried to write for you was about. And for that very reason I find myself disturbed by the thought of further involvements in animal lives. I wish I had started all that when I was younger, instead of running about all the time after boys. Now I feel too old, also frightened. I don't think anyone should attempt to gain possession of an animal heart unless they feel as sure as mortality can feel that they will never fail it. To get the confidence of any animal and then let it down seems to me almost the worst crime anyone can commit; human relationships matter less, people understand people, suffer though they may; animals understand nothing, only loss.

Your Mr Pearson seems to have been rather a snake in the grass –

except that I am fond of snakes. You will have noticed how arrogant human beings are in having made use of the animals for almost all their terms of contempt, disgust, or abuse. I wonder if one could inject enough scorn into the word 'human' – 'You human!' – to make it sound insulting. I'm afraid one would only get a complacent smile. Has Mr. P. put you off poisonous S. America?

Joe's letter suffered an interruption of a couple of days or so, for his last page bears the date 2 November. He had been invaded by Ram Gopal, the great Indian dancer and choreographer whom I have once admired enough at the Lyric, Hammersmith, to write a poem on one of his numbers. 'Alarippu' – a poem Joe refused to print, though he liked it, because he was at odds with Ram over something in *Hindoo Holiday*:

I am now being asked by Ram Gopal to go to India with him in February. He has become immensely rich – a Maharajah, lately deceased, left him £150,000 in trust, 'for his great work as a dancer in spreading Indian culture throughout the western world'. He now has £10,000 a year, a house in Kensington, various servants, a chauffeur and a most uncomfortable motor-car. He wants to buy an option on the film rights of *Hindoo Holiday*; he also wants to take me to India to supervise the filming. He wants, he wants, heaven knows what he doesn't want, he talks endlessly and is stuffed with mad and mystical notions. However, he gave me champagne at lunch today. I do wish I liked Indians more. That your *Tropic Temper* softened towards them I was interested to note; perhaps my English temper may. I told Ram to read your book, but I don't suppose he will. 'You are a great genius,' he said to me, though I had scarcely spoken a word (there was little chance); he was quite vague about *Hindoo Holiday* when we discussed it, he had neither read nor heard of *Tulip* or my novel, and had entirely forgotten that I took him to see my play years ago. 'O have you written a play too?' What does one do with such shallow and trumpery people? Squeeze as much money as possible out of them, I suppose. Why do wealthy and philanthropic maharajahs not come *our* way, dear Jim? The *haiku* was charming.

Fond love as ever
Joe

Joe was quite right about Sonia Orwell's projected new magazine. It was indeed a 'dotty' set-up, and they lost all the material I sent them, which included my first attempts to translate the homoerotic poems of a young Japanese I admired and lusted after but forbade myself to touch, Takahashi Mutsuo. A few years before, I had run into Sonia Orwell in Paris, and was at once put off by her relentless, heavy intellectual chatter. She also disappointed me by repeating Connolly's snide remark to me: 'You never did get into *Horizon*, did you, Mr Kirkup?' – smirking as if such a failure was a disaster that must surely have cast a dark cloud over my entire life. As always when people insult me, I made no response, and this unnerved her: prattlers are always upset when they stop their prattling for a minute and find the other person does not prattle back. The 'Mr Pearson' was the biographer John Pearson, who had asked me to meet him on his arrival in Tokyo, where he was compiling some guide-book on the Far East. I'm afraid I was very naughty with him, and misled him with false information about a strip show in Shinjuku, which I assured him was performed only by very old men. As we passed the joint, two old men happened to totter out of it, probably the caretakers, for they locked the door behind them. 'Look!' I said to Pearson, 'there are the two top stars of the show!' He believed me, and put it in his book. As part of my 'farewell to Japan' I had been planning to go to Brazil, where the men seemed to be quite magnificently macho, but Pearson put me off. He actually asked me if I would write the Japan section of his book for him, but of course I politely refused.

This was the *haiku* I had sent to Joe:

> In movie darkness
> strange hands explore my privates –
> 'Nice place you have here. . . .'

'I might send you the 1st page of the never-to-be-finished article' is the teasing afterthought inserted beside the date (11 November 1963) of Joe's next letter:

Dearest Jimmykins

I forget if I sent you this new letter-card (airmail letter form) before; you deserve a nice picture for your enchanting Japanese p.c.'s which have given me a nostalgia unlikely to be engendered in you by this, our dear Mother of Parliaments. I don't think I *can* review your *Tropic Temper* now, my darling, it would take *ages*, I am such a fumbly old fool. I would have to recover it from Cambridge – Morgan, to whom I have sent it, then read it again, then construct a review which always costs me sheaves of paper, deep anxiety, and miles of time. I can *just* manage to do things if my mind is *at once* on the alert in such critical faculty as it possesses and I am receiving – and analysing my impressions. It is the same with letters, I like to answer at once (as now) while my mind and heart are stimulated; thereafter a sort of fatigue and hardship sets in. But I tell you what: if you cd. tell me when your Japanese book is to come, I wd. ask *The Observer* (with your permission) if I might have it. I am 'off' *The Sunday Times* (where, anyway, I expect Raymond will grab it) for I have just done, with infinite trouble, a review of a dog book for them, and although it was the exact number of words and they said it was 'admirable', they have massacred it in their columns without asking me to do the cuts or informing me at all. I do hate that, don't you, in a signed review, all one's carefully-constructed and balanced sentences ripped to pieces; 25 guineas is no consolation to my mind.

My friend Villiers David is going to Tokyo in December and I have asked him to look you up. Be sweet to him, he is a rich Jew, rather like Groucho Marx, but talented (a painter) and I am fond of him. Wealth has not spoiled him, he has a loyal and affectionate heart, but, though lively and enterprising, he is a *little* squeamish (I don't mind that): he cannot bear, for instance, *My Dog Tulip*. The 'coarseness' of life (if that is the right word), diseases and crudities of the body upset him a little, though he puts up as bravely as he can with me and my conversation, so spare him your shock tactics. The point of him here is that *his* news of S. America (to which he has never been) are positively glamorous and I am more inclined to believe in *his* experienced advisers than in yours. But if you don't go to S. America, why not come to India with Ram and me (assuming that we go)? I am sure I shall have plenty of time to go to all your 'M's' with you. But at the moment all is in the melting-pot. I lunch with my agent on Wednesday.

Joe's love.

On the back of this 'Alice blue' air letter form is a garish technicolour view of the Houses of Parliament from the Embankment, London – 'Photograph by courtesy of the British Travel & Holidays Association'. As Joe so rightly guessed, this did nothing to arouse nostalgia in my breast – an emotion in which I seem to be deficient, at least as far as

Thingland is concerned. But from time to time I get a wave of the old *saudade* for South Shields. . . . I cannot remember exactly what my 'M's' were – possibly Mexico, which I was to visit in the near future, Mauritius, Monte Carlo (always a favourite), Mandalay, Morocco and Maui – all later ports of call. It was Villiers David who objected so much to the portrait Joe had drawn of himself in *We Think the World of You*. He did not sound the sort of person I would ever want to meet, but for Joe's sake I agreed to do so. One of the perils of being stationed abroad, especially in remote places like Japan, is that people automatically assume one is always available to take their visiting friends on extended tours of one's adopted land. One learns a certain technique for deflecting these unwanted intrusions.

I felt worried about an apparent slackening in Joe's creative drive that seemed to manifest itself in his inability to write that article for me. But his very next letter, written the next day (12 November) contained a first and incomplete draft of 'I Am a Beast':

Darling Jim

All right, I send you this, unfinished and therefore unusable, as a little personal gift. After all, it was for you that I began it. The trouble, I think, is that it is an improvisation: I didn't know, when I started, what I was going to say or wanted to say. Then I saw that the muddle of my thoughts could be exploited, and it began to amuse me to tease the reader by exciting his interest at various points – then changing the subject. With all that I was rather pleased; I was even more pleased when the notion of Zen flashed into my mind. It was a happy inspiration – but no further inspirations have come to me I fear, though I have put myself into numberless trances, and I am left, as you can see, with lots of loose ends which I don't know how to tie together. Also, of course, there has to be a wind-up, but I seem to have no winch. I have scribbled a sort of finish – but oh so dull. Well read, and if you thought I *ought* to persevere I will have another go. I deeply doubt its success.

I never said, in reply to your cards, that I too know Mr Bond, not James but Ruskin. That is to say that I have corresponded with him in the past and was once on the verge of visiting him in India. But it came to nought. *Why* he started to correspond with me quite slips my slipping mind.

Bless you, Olympic James, my love is always yours.
JOE

It was I who had introduced Joe to Zen Buddhism by reading him Zen poems and taking him to some favourite temples for practice in meditation. But he must have got a mistaken idea about *zazen* and *satori*, for a 'trance' is not the correct state for getting in tune with the Buddhist nirvana: one has to be in complete possession of one's senses to balance on the fine line between temporal and eternal awarenesses.

Ruskin Bond was a man living in one of the Indian hill stations who started writing to me out of the blue and sending examples of his work, some of which I believe I put into *Orient/West*. Towards the end of 1963, Tokyo and the whole of Japan were agog and fizzing with the prospect of the coming Olympic Games – that dire happening which has succeeded in destroying any city it touches and was to be the spiritual ruination of Japan – and I had taken to signing my letters 'Olympic Games', which Joe charmingly mistook for 'Olympic James'. After he had sent me this fussed-over article, something went wrong. I believe Maurice Schneps did not like it, or disapproved of the title. Joe's letter of 25 November confuses me:

Dearest Jim
    but I sent you my little article – as far as it had got, about ten pages – nearly a fortnight ago. It must have gone astray – what a nuisance. 4/6 it cost me, and I remember taking care in writing your address. It was in a long airmail envelope. If you haven't got it and can't trace it, I *could* do it for you again, but it would be a second labour of love and do I love you twice? Yes, I do. Your little balls got through safely to me; I am sorry my balls did not get through to you.
    How sickening about your 'Kirkup-tells-all' book. Do resist cuts if you can. I wonder if the Bodley Head wd. take it. Or who is the publisher who is taking a risk over Fanny Hill? I doubt if even *you* could have gone much further than that. Have you read it, by the way? You should. It is extremely exciting – erotically – or so I found when I read it in Morgan's rooms in Cambridge, some months ago, although the copulations are all hetero. Morgan thinks that the pleasure we both derived from it is due to the fact that the organ upon which the most careful description is always lavished is the male organ. I wish I had an organ still, even a female one; yet what would I do with it if I had? Francis is here, already sorry for himself. He has rented a flat for a year, somewhere in Kensington. I took him to lunch at the Royal College last Friday and Morgan, whom he had not met before, joined us. Francis was very nice and they got on well

together. Not so Morgan and Cyril Connolly, who came in by appointment for quarter of an hour before lunch. He had asked Morgan to autograph his collection of Morgan's books; Morgan hates that kind of thing but had not liked to refuse so eminent a writer. So Connolly, fat and prosperous looking, appeared at the club by arrangement, carrying a satchel of some dozen books, and Morgan toddled off with him into a side room – and, after quite a long time, toddled back looking very vexed. It seemed that Connolly had not been satisfied with autographs, he had demanded inscriptions ('To Cyril Connolly from E.M. Forster'). Morgan complied, but thought him an awful cad, and stood him the smallest and cheapest drink available. All this was going on at about the time that the shot rang out in Dallas.

Ram Gopal is seeing my agent today about the option on *Hindoo Holiday* and is sending his car round to fetch me to lunch with him on Wednesday. He adores champagne, an excellent thing in a friend. I only wish he didn't talk so much; my head spins. He thinks that mankind must be cleansed in the fire: the next nuclear war he thinks inevitable. He also feels that anyone cruel to an animal should be put to torture or death. This, of course, is more agreeable to me, though I have never gone so far as he goes. With all this he is a 'joy-injector', like you. I try sometimes to imagine how you and he would get on together – that is to say when I am not wondering how he and I are going to get on together. I have never written a scenario. Is it easy? So glad Sonia took my tip about you. *She* talks too much too. How noisy the world is, and wd. be even noisier if our ears were able to detect the shrill ultrasonic cries of bats, mice and shrews. Love, darling Jim, as ever.

JOE

My 'Kirkup-tells-all' book was to have been *Japan behind the Fan*, a suitably provocative title, but Dent, to whom I had gone in a huff from Collins, who had questioned the printability of my first novel, *The Search for Love* (even though Mark Bonham Carter had been enthusiastic about my suggestion it should be issued with cover and illustrations by one of my favourite modern painters, zany Edward Burra), had demanded cuts of certain passages they deemed 'offensive'. The 'balls' I had sent Joe were those very decorative folk toys called *temari*, covered with brilliant silk threads in geometrical patterns. The publisher of *Fanny Hill* was Girodias's Olympia Press in Paris, to which Georges

Duthuit introduced me, and which had published Nabokov's *Lolita* and a few of my own erotic novels under an assumed name. That press was not suitable for my travel book, whose eroticisms were comparatively understated. As for Ram Gopal, I am sure we should never have 'got on' together: he was not 'my type', and I doubt if I were his. And I cannot endure people who talk too much. Joe's reference to his ears now seems prophetic, though I think he was already losing his hearing. We later debated which of the five senses we would part with most willingly: he chose touch; but I chose hearing, as I am not much interested in what people say, and I felt that the world was becoming much too noisy. I was willing to give up music for silence.

Joe's letter of 4 December 1963 clears things up a little; but ends alarmingly:

Dearest Jim,

So it did arrive after all! And what are you setting it up for? may I ask. Don't tell me that *Orient/West* means to publish it? In that case I must finish it. I have some notes, and will try to do so tomorrow instead of fiddling about with one of Ram Gopal's film scripts which he wants me to re-write for him – I sent him so critical a report of it. I must say I prefer revising other people's work to inventing my own, and am really rather bright at it, though I says it as shouldn't. Reverting to your piece, I suppose you don't happen to remember whether the animal in Balzac's story was a panther. It was one of the great felines, but I'm not sure which. 'Passion in the Desert' was the English name of the story, and Lord Wavell included it in his anthology of animal stories. My library hasn't got it, and I shall have to check up somewhere unless you happen to remember.

I have just had 3 stitches taken out of my scalp. So strange, I had a sort of black-out in my room late on Thursday night. Not drink, I think, my intake is always the same, but there had been a long wrangle with Nancy, a recurrent one which always upsets me, accusations against our char. for (Nancy alleges) using her cosmetics and wearing and stretching her shoes. As if it mattered! What worries me is that she may drive the char. – a nice woman, even if naughty – into giving notice again (she's done it once and I had to placate her), putting me to the trouble of finding another. *Anyway*, no sooner had I left Nancy than she heard a dull thud (almost midnight) and found me stretched pale, senseless and bleeding on my back in my room. Falling, I had struck the back of my head on my bookcase and was concussed. Poor girl, what a shock she must have had! A salutary one, I hope. As for me, I remember nothing about it, only how peaceful and comfortable the world seemed for a change (I've now been twice concussed and found both occasions quite delicious); some poor doctor was wrenched from her bed, a woman, and came and stitched me up as I lay on the floor. Nancy says I conversed with her quite rationally; I don't remember her in the least. Nor do I recall a thing about my stretcher-and-ambulance journey to hospital, to which she sent me. I have a vague recollection of an asiatic medical face bending over me there, and of saying 'are you Japanese?' He said 'Chinese'. I said 'I'm sorry' – but he quite understood me and rather unkindly remarked 'Yes, you've got me out of bed.' What they did to me there I've no idea. I simply felt wonderfully comfortable and happy. Nor do I remember the journey home at about 4 a.m. in a taxi they provided. I remember nothing, but woke up next morning at 11.0 a.m., feeling quite well and, covering my bandage and bloody scalp with a knitted skull cap, took Nancy and the Goronwy Rees's to lunch at my club, which I had arranged to do. Isn't that a nice story? Four or five times in my life I have been upon the outskirts of the Valley of the Shadow – once, indeed, almost in it, when I nearly died of Spanish Grippe at the end of the first World War – and the experience has *never* been unpleasant. Death deserves a welcome, just for the kindness which life is not so quick to bestow.

I am now off to celebrate Sir Herbert Read's 70th birthday at a dinner in London. He was a staunch friend of mine for many years, though I haven't seen him since my retirement. I like him and wonder what he adds up to in all his voluminous writings: not much, I fancy. But then I haven't read them all.

Another nice letter from you this morning (5/12/63) but no time to answer. Nor time to finish that article today. And I am going off for the weekend (Nottingham and Norwich). But I promise to send the end of it early next week.

Fondest love
JOE

Stop–press. Look, dear, I have done it for you, after all, this afternoon, well or badly I don't know. *Do* criticize! I only hope I have resumed where I left off. Can't quite remember.

How inattentive not to get the title of your book right: Times, 5/12/63.

This account of his 'black-out' is both comical and disturbing, because it gives a premonitory glimpse of Joe's end. But his attitude towards illness and death is so brave and comforting to us, the living. When I received news of his death in Tokyo, in 1967, I took out this letter and read it. I still have the last three pages he wrote of that article, in his increasingly unreadable yet neat and characterful scribble – another tiny script in my personal life, though not as neurotically compressed as Dana's. As these pages did not appear at the end of the article as it was printed in *Orient/West*, I give them here:

Yes, there are zoos and zoos and when I visited Kasch, of whom I had had good news, I found her reclining on the grass beneath a tree in her Whipsnade paddock, a sunken glade, roomy, arboreous, and provided with a pool and accessible caves. Shafts of sunlight fell upon her striped coat through the branches of the tree. She was watching her cubs, who were asleep in each other's arms in a sort of open Nativity shed some distance away. Tigers are rather weak in their sight and have a poor sense of smell; I was privileged to see her rise to her feet, pad over to the shed, mount to its raised platform and, to re-assure herself that her babies were alive and well, lick them awake and turn them over with her paw. As she returned satisfied to her grassy couch they tumbled playfully after her trying to catch her tail, then fell asleep again on the edge of the platform. A high metal fence guarded her from human interference; she seemed, in fact, quite unaware of the spectators above her, and was therefore able to live in her tiger character which, far from being aggressive, was of a retiring disposition, especially where man is concerned. The problem of zoos is not to protect people from the animals, which is the human fancy, but to protect the animals from people. Fences they must have, where there are no fences they are doomed; even behind bars they are not safe. A few years ago some small boys, out of the control of their supervisor, clambered onto the top of the cage in Whipsnade Park in which the lions had been temporarily segregated while their paddock was being cleaned. Taunting and provoking the lions they poked at them with sticks until one sprang up and seized the arm of his tormentor. He let go only when the supervisor arrived and struck him with an iron bar. Bulletins about the child's health, as he lay in hospital between life and death, were issued daily in the press. No bulletins were issued about the health of the lion, who had been struck on the head with an iron bar, and no one enquired after him. I myself wrote a letter of enquiry for publication, but I did not send it. I had not then reached enlightenment, and in the sacred hush that enveloped this child's sick-bed I was as scared as I would be to remain seated while the National Anthem is being played. Animals don't matter, only people matter.

I am a beast, but I would not have it thought that I hate people. Animals do not have hatred, only people have hatred. Are there any of my wild guises in which I have not readily responded to overtures of human friendship? It was man who disdained our relationship, invented for himself the terrible word 'human', and dubbed me with such cruel names as 'game' and 'pest'. And the higher he soars above me in his pride and power the lonelier he becomes. Yet vestigial remnants of the old world still exist, in Amazonia, for instance, where the Indians feel their kinship with the forest beasts, easily domesticate them and suckle the young mammals who have no mother as they suckle their own children. It is that that has been rejected and lost, the sense of belonging. Some eighty years ago a great American poet wrote 'I think I could turn and live with animals. . . . They bring me tokens of myself – they evince them plainly in their possession.' Now, in a world grown too small for man alone, what can he do with his tigers but shut them up in cages, a peep-show for children? If substantial profit can be made out of me, for profit is all that counts, I shall be allowed to linger a little longer, but I am in man's way, my days are numbered I know, and I would sooner end them, like Kasch, fed and protected in a comfortable prison than be left without a fence to a larger freedom and the greed of the only cruel animal in the world. The incessant wrangles of mankind interest me no more. They do not take me in. Do the Aldermaston marchers march for me? Why should I care about *apartheid* or who comes out on top in Africa? I shall never again belong with anyone, in the sense that I have lost. Today another seer, Mr James Baldwin, prophet of the American negro, has arisen, and leaves me altogether out of his philosophy. In his latest book he writes 'and if one despairs – and who has not? – of human love, God's love alone is left'. He spells my epitaph, and the epitaph also of the human race. God's love is left to them, for, without me, they will never get on together.

The title, 'I Am a Beast', becomes clear at the end. But my editor refused to print these final pages. I think he was motivated by a kind of American middle-class respectability, and a fundamental American lack of understanding of a certain type of British irony. I find those last pages unbearably moving: for all their extreme disillusion, they speak clearly of Joe's own consciousness of his approaching end. The recent black-out he suffered must have accentuated that perception. In reply, I wrote him a letter, the only one of which I made a copy:

Dearest Joe,

I write to you again for you were even more than usually in my thoughts tonight. A dreadful film, *Mondo Infame*, baleful with human tortures and even worse animal ones, in full hecticolour, was my lot tonight, and the Japanese looked on with bated breath and laughed at the most horrible bits. Alas, they are not as nice to animals as one would wish. At Matsue on the Japan Sea, there is a miserable cage like a large parrot's in the grounds of the gracious castle donjon, centuries old, that the newly-weds visit with ceremony and respect. As soon as they have done the castle and taken numerous snaps of themselves in newly-wed bliss – *momiji* time is marriage time in Japan – they betake themselves to the monkey cage where six poor, bored baboons with crimson faces endure their taunts and laughter with a resigned indifference that is something like genius – it has to be, as it is their only defence. There is nowhere for them to hide, they have only a couple of sawn-off boughs, slippery with scrambling. The newly-weds, relieved of the necessity of being awe-struck by the castle, rattle the cage bars, throw balls of paper they carry around in secret wads for all purposes, try to poke the poor creatures into entertaining life with bits of bamboo, or tease them with the lovely autumn horse-tail grass. The monkeys just sit and endure it all – they have developed a built-in boredom that defends them from callous intrusion and tittering malice. I gave one a banana and he didn't know at first what it was – he thought it was a joke. The discovery that it was a *banana*, a *real* one, produced such demented screams that I had to hold my ears, and I realized that the poor beasts were mad, stricken incurably with melancholia and the utmost despair. It was like a mad scene from Hogarth. The screams were greeted by the newly-weds as great entertainment, and they smiled and bowed to me for having provided them with such fun and subjects for interminable snapshotting. In return, I gave them my 'meaningless' smile and walked away.

Fortunately I walked out of *Mondo Infame* with a new-found friend, a Japanese who was more interested in his own anatomy than in that of the poor tortured beasts and humans in the film.

I was in luck that night, because the Kennedy assassination has cast the most tiresome blight on pleasure. The Japanese love to indulge in orgies of mass response, to join in totalitarian waves of feeling in which the individual can feel he is being swept off his feet like everyone else. This week, overwhelmed, as always, by a large public event, the Japanese have been regarding all Americans (which for them means all foreigners) as being in a kind of purdah of inextinguishable grief, and avert their faces and douse their smiles whenever they see me. It is simply maddening, and does so interfere with the more important nonsense of sexual caprice. Sorry as I am that JFK was shot, I can't stomach all the hypocritical fuss made about it – he was not all *that* wonderful, merely a well publicised figure, just another nice ordinary guy, power-mad, he seemed to me, and I must admit I felt relief to know he had gone, though I wish he had just quietly retired, as all politicians should. Then we would have no politics, a quite unnecessary expenditure of time and money. Or even better it would be if politicians were put in cages and fed uneatable rubbish instead of being put in luxurious white houses all with modern paintings and performing guests representative of all races and creeds.

Only the *very* sincere would then wish to run for election, and it would soon mean an end to politics and nuclear deterrents and 'working lunches' and 'briefing breakfasts' in which the starving world is being slowly and politely pushed, with every semblance of rationality, into ghastly horror. I think I shall seek asylum, on the grounds of cultural persecution, with the Flowery Kingdom of Peking, if only they would let me in.

Such are the thoughts provoked by *Mondo Infame*. Naturally, the Japanese have already made their own versions of these infamous 'corror firrums', not without some protests from the public, I am glad to report, but they play to packed houses. Like you, I cannot understand the world that takes such a savage delight in cruelty, I cannot think what it wants or where it is going. I can only understand people in bed, or in casual or intimate physical contact. That is the only meaning left to me. It is an abyss, but an unusually attractive one. It is real and honest and authentic, I can be sure of that. The rest of life seems to me witless and dull and mirthless and barbaric.

A recent remark in a letter from my mother ran: 'The weekend (of the JFK killing) was nothing but news, and so depressing I had to keep switching off the TV.' If only we could switch off things like that for good!

On that Saturday afternoon of the JFK assassination, where was I? I was standing at the back of a cinema in Shibuya which was fairly dark and had sometimes offered pleasurable contacts. It was on that afternoon that I met one of my most delightful and enduring friends – C___. We must have linked hands in the dark for the first time as the Dallas motorcade came under fire. A few moments later, after a meaningful squeeze, we left the movie-house and took our first good look at one another. Then I hailed a taxi and we were off to Yotsuya San-chome, where I had a house for a short while before being invited to occupy the house on the campus of Japan Women's University. As we were riding in the taxi, the news of the Kennedy assassination came over the radio. It was the beginning of a new era for me in the fields of love, and, as I said in that letter, the events at Dallas faded into total insignificance against the warmth and brilliance of my new love, which lasted for several years. C___ was only about seventeen, a high-school student wearing the Japanese scholar's black military-style uniform with stand-up collar. But he was already experienced, and he told me he had an American lover. That did not bother me at all: I was simply too happy to care, as long as C___ came to see me every few days after school. He was the only Japanese boy I have met who had phimosis, a condition he had to have corrected by an operation, towards the costs of which I contributed. After a while, he introduced me to his brother, a charming art student. I wrote about all these affairs in my letters to Joe, none of which have survived except the one I quoted above.

In a letter from Putney dated 9 December, Joe wrote to me about his article again, which Maurice Schneps now seemed unwilling to print. Schneps especially objected to the title, 'I Am a Beast', which I think shocked his rather middle-class Jewish American sensibilities. He also did not want to frighten his Japanese readers. But here is Joe's worrying and worrisome letter:

Dearest Jim

I sent off to you an ending, fairly short, to my beastly article on Friday. Please give my regards to Mr Schneps. This ending may show him more clearly what the article drives at and that my title is really the only one that describes it. I wonder why he shd. think it off-putting. It seems to me a striking title and an intriguing one. I fancy that if anyone else had written an article with so startling a title I shd. be curious to read it. But don't let that bother you, or him, dear Jim, and if it shd. emerge that the article is an embarrassment, let there be no tears upon your side, as there will be none on mine.

I wd. be interested to know, however, what *you* think of it and whether you have any ideas for elucidating or improving upon it. Is there anything you itch to change, even words here and there? I like collaboration. On reflection I think the end is not too bad; it was rather longer in the first draft, and brought in the death of Martha, the last of the Passenger Pigeons, a moving story of human greed and ruthlessness; but I thought that perhaps the ending I have sent said enough. Useless though it all is, I think it might effect a belated pause or two for thought.

If you are really setting it up, I wonder if you could do something for me, send a galley to Sonia Orwell, 38 rue des Saints-Pères, Paris 7. I don't know what she has done about you and your contributions to her mag., but she lamented the fact that my one contribution was too short and asked to see the beastly article which I had told her I was trying, then in vain, to do for you. Your last number, if it gets into it, comes in March; it could possibly be that, if she likes it, she could use it too without inconvenience to yourselves. I suppose that if you do use it you will be letting me see a proof? I wd. like to have a final look at it in print and, if you dislike messing about, wd. try to mess it about as little as possible. I am fairly good at proof-correcting, that is to say taking thought for the printers and their difficulties.

What will you do when *Orient/West* folds up? Are you still think-ing of leaving Japan? A lapse has occurred in my correspondence with Gopal and I am not sure at present where I stand. He gave me a film-script he had written called 'Thunder over the Himalayas' for my comments, which were far from enthusiastic; he then asked me to rewrite part of it, which I did; his views on that (and his cheque) have not yet reached me, and I begin to wonder if I have wounded him in his pride; however he did ask for what he got.

I am in Norfolk for the weekend (Velda Sprott) but hear from Nancy there are letters for me from Villiers David at home. I think he must be in New York, and hating it, but if he keeps to any near-schedule should be in Tokyo soon. I do hope you will make allowances for the peculiarities of a rich man. I adore your word 'genitalman' – it pairs with William Plomer's 'wombman' for woman.

Much love, dearest Jim
Joe

The infinitely cautious soundings-out, self-doubts and hesitations of the first part of that letter I now find both comic and pathetic. Joe is obviously trying to salvage his hurt pride at having his article even slightly criticized by Maurice Schneps, though quite rightly he had no scruples about hurting Ram's sensibilities, which being Indian would be even more on a knife-edge than his. Joe seems defensive and yet he tries to maintain a cool politeness to Maurice who had had the temerity to question the appropriateness of his title. But the letter shows what pains Joe always took with his writing, how he worried over almost every word and the balance of every sentence, paragraph, page and chapter. All this time he was, of course, working away rather dispiritedly at his memoir about his father and family, which was to have a success well beyond his expectations. He liked to appear pessimistic about everything, to cloak an undying optimism – an attitude towards fate that I have found in many of my Jewish friends: it was certainly part of Maurice's philosophy.

Villiers David did indeed arrive in Tokyo and I dutifully took him around my less squalid haunts. I think he enjoyed my company, though I did not really take to him as Joe would have wished. I remember taking Villiers to a specially recommended *sushi* restaurant in Tsukiji, which I had not visited before, and of whose location I was unsure. I had only the name of the place, and did not possess the little sketch-map one nearly always has to have when trying to find one of Tokyo's muddled addresses. We were in a taxi, and the driver thought he knew where I wanted to go, but at the last moment failed to locate the restaurant, though we were near.

I could see that Villiers was getting agitated, so I just leaned back in my seat and waited for the driver to get on with the job of finding the place. By putting him at the risk of 'losing face' before two foreigners, I knew I should get the best out of him. Villiers was fussing and looking all about him with frightened gaze, while I lay back and let events take their course. This is the fatalistic pose I always adopt in crisis situations, though the outward calm is deceptive. The baffled driver stopped the taxi at an intersection and asked a policeman if he knew where the restaurant was. By good fortune, the policeman did. He invited us to get out of the taxi and accompany him along a narrow passage where the taxi could not go, and delivered us, with a smart salute, at the door of the restaurant, where we were greeted by one of the most handsome young *sushi* cooks I have ever seen. The place was very expensive, and we were the only customers that lunch-time, but Villiers settled down to the exquisite meal and attentive service of the *sushi* boy with the relief that comes after extreme tension. It was worth the price, because on the way out I was able to make a date with the cook for a rendezvous that very night. For the rest of his stay, Villiers was agog with the way I handled difficult situations by allowing them, in truly Zen fashion, simply to resolve themselves without any interference from me.

That policeman had been very kind and polite to us. But this was not always my experience. In Japan, foreigners have to carry with them at all times their Alien Registration Card, a little booklet that is all too easily lost or mislaid. I was often stopped in the streets of Shinjuku and Shibuya by over-zealous cops hoping to make a catch – for if one does not carry one's card, it means a visit to the police station, and then one has to write a letter of abject apology, in Japanese, to the immigration police. There was a certain police-box in Roppongi that I began to make a point of passing and giving them impression of Bohemian, even drunken, insolence. This always provoked a cop to dart out of the *koban* and demand my card. Some of the cops were very attractive young men, and once or twice I wished I had the nerve to leave my card at home and get arrested and intimately frisked by one of those macho beauties, who seemed totally unaware of the power of their charms upon me.

One night, at Shinjuku San-chome, I had just emerged from the palpitating darkness of a gay movie-house when I was stopped by a young man in plain clothes who demanded to see my Alien Registration Card. With great coolness, I produced it from my back pocket and presented it to him with just the shadow of a bow. He seized it eagerly and scanned the information inside, which revealed that I had lived many years in Japan and that I was a professor at Japan Women's University. He spoke to me therefore in Japanese, saying: 'So you must be able to speak Japanese?' The first rule to remember in that kind of situation is to answer in English, or in any foreign language: one must never reveal that one can speak even a little Japanese, because that only prolongs the interview. So I disclaimed any knowledge of Japanese – speaking in English, of course. Without a word, he handed the card back to me and walked away. I now wonder if he really was a plain-clothes' dick: he did not show me any identification – but that is standard practice among the police in Japan.

Such incidents occurred with quite unnerving frequency. I began to feel I was a marked man, just as George Barker in Sendai had believed himself to be the target of the *kempeitai* – and with good reason, I expect.

It was in this period of general anxiety and insecurity that I was dismissed from *Orient/West*. I had suggested to Maurice that I should write a series of poetic essays about Japanese industry, for most of the magazine's revenue came from the big advertisements placed in its pages by giant firms like Hitachi, Sony, Toshiba and so on. My suggestion was turned down, so, with the help of a Japanese friend, Tomohiro, who was an excellent businessman, I started the first of my Japanese publishing ventures, Perfect English Publicity, which we hoped would soon be known by the attributive acronym PEP. During the next two years, we travelled the length and breadth of Japan, visiting all the great companies, and some lesser ones, while I wrote my poetic impressions of them and Tomohiro collected orders for the books in which they were to be collected, with profuse illustrations mainly supplied by the companies themselves. But *Orient/West* thought we were stealing a march on them, though I reminded the editor and the proprietor that we had offered them the idea in the first place, and had been rejected. They were furious with us, and I was then given my marching orders. But I had no regrets: I had sensed that the magazine was on its last legs and, soon after I left, *Orient/West* folded. Maurice went back to New York, where he got a job as editor with the Macmillan Company of America. When I took up my post at Amherst College, some years later, Maurice wrote to me and we met in New York, where all was forgotten and forgiven. I was very glad, for he was a fine scholar and philosopher and poet whose mind I respected.

I was already well into my first year at Japan Women's University, where I taught poetry, drama, criticism and the novel. As noted earlier, I never prepared a class: I would just walk in and start talking about *The Importance of Being Earnest* or *Arms and the Man* or Hopkins or Yeats. The lectures were all religiously recorded, I am ashamed to say, for sometimes my impromptus got me in the most awful muddles. But I was somehow able to hold the students' interest – and most Japanese have a very short attention span – for ninety minutes on end. I tried to stress the formalism of English comedy, for that was something the very formal Japanese understood. For example, I would carefully show them how characters entered and left the stage, how they sat down and stood up, why someone would remain seated when another stood, the niceties of the English tea ceremony and so on. There is a lot of sitting down and standing up in English comedy, especially in Wilde and

Shaw. Today, I simply cannot believe that I taught such advanced texts to fourth-year students: they would be utterly beyond the grasp of students now, such has been the decline in the teaching of English during the last fifteen years, with emphasis on linguistics and set phrases rather than on literature and spontaneousness, inventiveness, which are the life-blood of speech and writing. Today, an English exam consists of multiple-choice questions, and the filling in of empty spaces in standard sentences. No wonder the Japanese are less and less able to hold an intelligent conversation in English; few of them have anything interesting to talk about, even in Japanese, so their set phrases and robot-like language-lab Americanized pronunciation now make them among the most boring conversationalists ever known.

I had my university salary to tide me over in my many emergencies, so Tomohiro and I enjoyed ourselves visiting companies and preparing our two volumes of *Japan Industrial: Some Literary Impressions of Japanese Industry*, which was a genre never before attempted. I took as the epigraph for the first volume a quotation from Herman Melville's *The Tartarus of Maids*: 'Yours is a most wonderful factory. Your great machine is a miracle of inscrutable intricacy.' The second volume has epigraphs by Byron ('This the patent age of new inventions . . .', a whole stanza from *Don Juan*); a passage from Firbank – *Lady Appledore's Mesalliance*, which contains the delicious phrase '. . . a short essay on the manufacture of Strawberry-punnets thrilled her to enthusiasm'; and a quotation from John Davidson's description of Greenock from *Ballad in Blank Verse of the Making of a Poet* – '. . . where hammers clang/ On iron hulls, and cranes in harbours creak/ Rattle and swing. . . .'

The places we visited were Kurobe Dam (Kansai Electric Power Co. Ltd), Fuji Iron & Steel, Hitachi Shipbuilding, Toyo Kogyo, Nippon Pulp Industry, Noritake China, Kanegafuchi Spinning Co. Ltd, Nikkatsu Film Company Studios, NGK Insulator Co. Ltd, Yamaha Pianos, Kubota Iron Works, Sumitomo Chemicals, Toei Movie Studios, Takeda Chemical Industries, Tasaki Pearl Co. Ltd, Kyoto Nishijin Textile Museum and the Yamamoto Family, Kokusai Denshin Denwa and many others. . . . I found them all absolutely fascinating, and wrote excellent poetic essays about even the most improbable subjects – something that has always been one of my specialities, though in little demand. We had great fun making the books, and also made quite a lot of money out of them, for most of the companies ordered up to a *Mésalliance* hundred copies to present to foreign visitors. But by the time we had finished the second volume, I had become rather weary of the exercise, and though Tomohiro suggested we devote the next volume to folk crafts, which interested me very much, I had to call a halt to our lengthy expeditions.

Sayonara Joe

Every parting gives a foretaste of death; every coming together again a foretaste of the resurrection.

Schopenhauer, *Gedanken über vielerlei Gegenstände*

During these years I was also writing travel books, books of poetry, translations, textbooks and novels. I travelled all over Japan and South-East Asia for *Tokyo, Bangkok, Hong Kong & Macao, Filipinescas* and *Streets of Asia* (Korea, Cambodia, Vietnam, Laos), all published by Dent, who also published my book about Russia that raised many hackles, *One Man's Russia* (1968). It was no wonder that a Japanese doctor I went to told me I was 'mentally and physically exhausted'. He gave me an injection, the nature of which he refused to reveal, and at once I felt as fit as a fiddle again.

Yet with my dismissal from *Orient/West* I had a kind of nervous collapse, and when a Japanese professor friend, at my invitation, visited my mother in Bath, he made the usual Japanese joke about my single state, telling her that soon I would be marrying some nice Japanese young lady. My poor mother took this attempt at humour seriously, and wrote such a whining letter about my 'keeping' her 'in the dark' about my marriage plans that I decided it was time for her to leave Hill House, where her increasing blindness had begun to alarm Agnes, who had written to me advising that my mother would be looked after better at Green Park House, the model home for handicapped elderly residents that had recently opened in Bath. With the help of our good friends in Hill House, Mr and Mrs Evans, and of the Blind Club, our household goods were sold, including my library, which went for a song, though it included some valuable first editions of Dylan Thomas. Then my mother was gently removed to Green Park House, where she had a beautiful bed-sitting-room and some devoted helpers and friends. Until she died, I travelled back to Bath every summer to be with her, even though it meant a fresh smallpox vaccination and the usual cocktail

175

of inoculations every time I left Japan for Britain. It was a sad time for us both.

It was a sad time for Joe, too. He wrote to me from Putney, 'Xmas Eve. 1963':

Darling Jim

Your card and letter today, beautifully timed. This will have to wish you that far more serious wish: A Happy 1964. What a word 'Happy' is: I write it always with care, as one lifts an invalid. Anent plans for that year: Cyril Eland has sent me a card, very down in the mouth for some reason ('embittered' is the word he has about himself), in which he tells me that there is to be a very large British Book Exhibition in Tokyo in April, to which publishers are sending out authors to speak. Do you know anything about it? Would it be worth while your suspending admiration of your ravishing membrum virile for a moment and finding out about it? Whom could Collins employ more suitable than yourself, and might not the Bodley Head send me? Cyril says that 'Toynbee (the old one) and Aldous Huxley may come'; he is partly wrong there. It would suit me very well to go, expenses paid, and might suit you too. And how delightful that we should be together, united in literature. Anent literature: if you are really going to publish my article, an event I have scarcely believed in hitherto, wd. it be straining the resources of the American dollar too much to let me have, for myself, *two* proofs? I am a fumbling corrector, and like a second proof to clean up on. I wish you had been a shade more critical: is 'without me' in the last line what I ought to mean, or should it simply run 'for they will never get on together'? And in the Zen passage about the dog: 'less important than people like to suppose': is the word 'important' right? I have pondered it for months. I feel I need another word but know not what. It is an important word! Well, I am pleased you are putting the article in; I could not be cross-examined upon it, but I am sure it has something to say, even if I haven't quite said it.

How pleased I am that you and Villiers got together and got on together. With your wonderful exactness of image you have, of course, the appropriate word, his *spaniel's* eyes. The moment it is said it is seen to be the truth. Letters from him poured in for a time and have now ceased (it is the difference between Japan and the U.S.A.)

We have sent Xmas cards to your dear Mother and she to us. A turkey is in the oven, sent by the Duchess of Westminster. Her sister is coming shortly to help us eat it. The flat is crammed with booze, we shall drink champagne and hope to feel 'merry'; what a word is 'merry', I write it with care, for it is liable to hit back. Nancy has a heavy cold, so I have done all the work, peeling chestnuts etc. Tomorrow (the Day) we were invited to spend with Mr Gopal, but silence has fallen upon him. Perhaps he did not enjoy my last letter in which I required 20gns a week for turning his flabby writing into jewelled dialogue. Since beginning this letter I suddenly remembered the name of the Director of the Bodley Head, Max Reinhardt, and have written him a breezy letter asking him to send me to Tokyo in April. Now it is your turn with Collins, who cannot but think highly of you despite differences of opinion. What a bore for you they must be. A letter from Gerald Heard in California says: 'the evidence that consciousness goes on after the body is shelled off is too strong to be rejected'. With that encouraging Xmas thought I leave you, my sweetheart.

Your loving
JOE

I was beginning to feel somewhat exasperated by Joe's eternal fiddling with his article. I had written some mild comments on it for him. But I was certainly not going to expose myself to his wrath by telling him exactly what I thought of his dithering. In all my love for Joe there was an element of fear. I knew how he could wound and snub and vilify. It was for this reason I preferred gentle, sweet, dreamy Nancy. Underneath Joe's beaming exterior and mellifluous tones there was a suppressed violence and anger that would burst out unexpectedly from time to time. I often felt uneasy in his presence, fearing that some word might provoke the thunderer's fire and brimstone and unleash the ashes of Sodom upon my defenceless head. His name-dropping in his letters was also becoming a little tiresome – again the consequence, I feel sure, of his loss of self-esteem and self-confidence. His capitalized name at the end of letters became more frequent, suggesting a final desperate fight against the disintegration of his personality. As for attending the Book Fair in Tokyo, I am sure his tone was ironic: he knew I would never be invited to attend anything so officially OK, and that he himself stood very little chance of being given an all-expenses-paid trip. The idea that Collins would bother to send someone like me was so ludicrous, I could not help laughing, which is probably what he wanted me to do. The Collinses did arrive in Tokyo and sent a message saying they would like to invite me to dinner at their hotel, the Imperial, but I pretended to be away from home on a skiing trip. Then Geoffrey Cumberlege arrived with Ray Bramah, and we had lunch together, but nothing further came of that. I complained to Cumberlege about his letting all my books go out of print so quickly, and I think I upset him by showing him a reprint Tomohiro and I had made of my *True Mistery of the Nativity* (though with additional material), without his authorization. The Japanese printer had very skilfully reproduced the exact format and typography of the original, though the cover was different. This 'pirated' edition we published under the imprint of my next publishing venture, Orient Editions. It was a total flop.

Joe, of course, never got invited to the British Book Fair in Tokyo. I did not bother to go and see what it contained: I feel pretty sure none of Kirkup's Workups would be displayed there, as the whole thing was in the iron hands of the British Council. I consoled myself with a favourite quotation from Nietzsche's *Ecce Homo*: 'My time is not yet come; some are born posthumously.' I used the title *Ecce Homo* many years later for my collection of poems and translation about Pier Paolo Pasolini, *Ecce Homo: My Pasolini* (Kyoto Editions).

The year 1964 began with a letter from Joe dated 3 January:

Dearest Jim

I'm sorry that Villiers' conduct had displeased you, it seems to have surprised himself. He says in one letter 'My life here is very merry and exhausting. I behave really outrageously, as if Tokyo were not within talking distance of St James's Place! I cannot understand myself.' This, incidentally, explains his remark to you that I had 'made him afraid of meeting you'. The fear was the fear of indiscretion, your 'Kirkup tells all' side, for in London he is a secretive and nervous man: although I am his newest close friend I think I am perhaps the only friend wholly in his confidence. Yet he remains a bit scared of me too, that I might repeat things to others. Ordinarily he does not like outrageous behaviour; I think I told you that in the beginning; and he behaved with extreme discretion in Japan the last time he was there; indeed he baffled Francis and me, and so far as I know (unless perhaps with some old buddy) he had no fun at all. So this is something quite new. He is letting himself go. Personally I am rather pleased about it, and am sorry you take so severe a view. He is far from attractive and cannot have much of a life, in spite of his wealth. Now he is enjoying himself – at the expense of others! say you. Well, that is a question. It may, on the other hand, be the making of them; it is just as easy to take one view as the other, and personally I have never believed in moral corruption, and only doubtfully in the broken heart. I wonder if I morally corrupted or broke the heart of that little taxi-driver I took to bed in Sendai and never saw again. My Buddhist priest friend, Kinoshita-san, had bedded down with all the queers of Kyoto before I met him, and has doubtless bedded down with many others since; he was a serious-minded boy and stuck to me while I was there. I don't think Villiers is a man to let people down if he likes them and believes they like him. He seems to me to value friendship, though I agree that his taste as a collector of *objets d'art* is somewhat bizarre. But he is a *feeling* man, of that I am sure, responsive to feeling. No reservations enter his pleasure in meeting *you*, in his letters. I wonder why he fails with you, while dear old M——succeeds: perhaps you did not see the latter often enough. As you know, he became 'involved' in some Japanese boy, on small acquaintance, and got him to fly to S. America to meet him on some other tour he was making, paying his fare and all expenses. One day, or night, together there was enough to prove that the thing didn't work. I spent a fortnight with M—— in Greece and still have the story of that to tell you. I get along quite well with him, but I should have thought that if 'harm' is wrought by queers in their sensual and promiscuous saunterings – and I doubt the harm – he, as compared with Villiers, wins hands down and cock-up as an entirely self-indulgent sybarite.

Well, enough of that. The Bodley Head has enthusiastically put forward my name to the British Council as a candidate for the Tokyo British Book Exhibition April 14–17. They think I stand a good chance. Now I must write to Villiers, whom I have neglected. His letters, for some reason, have not stimulated me, possibly because he is enjoying himself more than I am.

Fond love, as ever,
Joe

That letter puzzles me. I cannot remember at all what Villiers did in Japan, and I feel sure that whatever it was it could not have been his sexual conduct to which I objected. Perhaps I felt his treatment of Japanese boys was just too commercial, lacking the finesse that after all comes only after long experience of their wiles and ways. Even the lowest prostitutes deserve respect and good manners, and I seem to remember this was something Villiers failed to show. As for M——, this was another example of Joe's jealousy. He knew we got on well together, but it was not a sexual thing at all: we never touched one another. It was simply that we were both crazy about opera and music in general, and this I think brought out the best in M——, in a way that sex never would. Our passion was musical, and I liked him because of all the anecdotes he told me about composers and performers he had known and written about so brilliantly. But Joe was jealous of the most unexpected people who came within my influence. A notable example was dear old Nancy. In his diaries, and to my face, he accused her of 'stealing' me away from him. I witnessed one or two horrifying scenes that acutely embarrassed me, in which he rounded upon Nancy and even poor old Bunny for 'seducing' me – 'You women, you're all alike! You want to catch every man by the cock. Take him, you can have him! The one friend I have left in life, and you drag him after you to the shops and heaven knows where else! Bitches, all of you!' That sort of thing usually broke out when Joe had been over-indulging in Gordon's gin, and it terrified me. I love Nancy, and liked going out with her to cinemas and vegetarian restaurants: but in the end Joe sometimes got so infuriated with her that, in order to spare her, I stopped going out with her, to Joe's evident satisfaction. In the flat at the Star and Garter Mansions, he would take me away into his own room after dinner or lunch, leaving Nancy to clear away and wash the dishes. She would often sit there alone for hours, doing nothing whatsoever, just waiting for a glimpse of Joe.

The next letter, dated 18 January, continues the previous themes, but ends on a new note when Joe reads for the first time *Gulliver's Travels*:

Dear Jim

You are now the best of boys once again, the boat rocks no longer, one may rest on one's oars and have a quiet chat, for the storm has passed. Indeed, it had passed before your letter came and I was experiencing some *faint* regret at having cast a spanner into your works. But then I reflected that, after all, as Lt. Ed. of *The Listener* I would never have dreamed of publishing a signed contribution without sending its author a proof, and would have considered myself as

richly deserving such spiky protests as I sent you had I ever done such
a thing. I have a pleasant unruffled note from Mr Schneps this
morning and am glad that I gave no offence in my letter to him (if he
ever got it, the box number may have been out of date), or, at any
rate, that he has taken none. You see, dear, I rather incline to share
his doubts about my article – doubts all the more unresolvable since I
do not have a complete copy of it and can't remember what I wrote;
and praise never registers with me; I think that my intellect (if I can
any longer call it that) is a sort of permanent invalid, perhaps a
malade imaginaire, one of those patients who actually prefer to be
always discussing their symptoms with the doctor or anyone else they
can button-hole, and are affronted to be told how well they are
looking or that there is nothing wrong with them at all. Well, enough
about that; I am glad to hear from Mr Schneps that the magazine is
not to end in March after all, and from William Plomer, with whom I
lunched last week, that he had reviewed your poems in it. He asked
me why you had renounced poetry and I told him that it had all got
into *Tropic Temper* and that he should read it. Poor Villiers drifts
homeward, somewhere between Hong Kok and Bangkong, more
and more deflated and now dejected by bad news of his London
domestic scene. It was naughty of him to stand you up on his last
evening (is that not part and parcel of the gay, capricious life of dear
Japan which you extol? 'I much prefer M——'s way of treating
everyone quite selfishly for one's own pleasure'); he will become
more serious and dependable when English standards impose themselves again; but he seems to deserve to get into your novel for that
alone, we shall both enjoy to identify him in it. Can't you squeeze me
in too? No one ever bothers to caricature me and it is the very lesson I
have always wanted to learn, the kind of figure one cuts. Indeed, I
have been lamenting it in my family memoir, the difficulty of knowing what impression one makes upon others. I am getting along now
to the end of that – and about time too, for it has been lying about
half-baked for a good thirty years, and I don't think I have a lot of
time left. It is quite a good joke; whether it is the truth is a different
matter. I have just had a wonderful experience. What do you think? I
have read one of our great classics for the first time. *Gulliver's Travels*.
It is *my* book, and I am glad that I have neglected it hitherto, it is a
book to which a mature mind and personal experience have to be
brought, and I think it must be more applicable to the present day
than to the day on which Swift wrote it. Do you ever lecture upon it?

Japan enters, as you doubtless know.

I didn't say that my publishers were sending me to Japan in April, I said only that I had applied. Not a sound yet from anyone. I will let you know if there ever is.

Fond love
Joe

This letter gives us the unusual spectacle of Joe trying to apologize gracefully without admitting he was at fault. It was all because of that wretched article for *Orient/West* which I had long ago begun to wish I had never asked him to write. It did eventually appear, with Joe's title, but in a truncated or revised form, and Joe had not been consulted or sent two sets of proofs simply because there was no time to do so. He sent me the most vitriolic letter I have ever received, which distressed me very much, not because of its vituperation, but because it had come from Joe's pen. I handed it to Maurice Schneps and the magazine's proprietor, then wrote a letter of apology to Joe which apparently mollified him and made him feel rather ashamed of himself. When Neville Braybrooke asked me for letters from Joe for his selection, I sent him some, and directed him towards the proprietor of the magazine for Joe's most startling letter. He sent it to Braybrooke, who printed it uncut. (Many of the letters had to be cut and names omitted because of the frightful things Joe wrote about even his best friends.) After Joe sent me the letter, our friendship was never the same, and he knew it. On my returns to Bath to visit my mother every summer, I often did not go to see Joe and Nancy in London. So our letters became rarer. The next letter I have after that virulent attack is dated 4 February 1964 and is in reply to one in which I pointed out that I had mentioned Swift, *Gulliver's Travels* and 'Zipangu' in *These Horned Islands*, and that it was perhaps a memory of this reference that prompted him to read for the first time one of my favourite books:

Dearest Jim

Thanks for your pretty p.c. It was stupid of me to forget *These Horned Islands* and *Gulliver's Travels*. As soon as you prompted my memory I recalled it, and have since looked it up. It was also a pleasure to look into your book again. Nothing much happens here, but we have been fortunate, these last four weeks, to have a mild winter. Not much rain, sunshine, cool air but not too cold. Really rather a pretty January. You will not enjoy your return of course, except to see your mother, but a 2-month torture is not long and I will slip down to Bath to see you both. No word yet from the Tokyo Book Exhibition, except a hand-out to say that the organisers were about to deliberate. I am glad Schneps got my proof. There was a ghastly error in it which, perhaps, would not have been noticed, the word 'understand' instead of 'instruct' on galley 2, col. 2, line 13. If that had slipped through it would have rendered all the Zen para-graphs entirely incomprehensible. Since then a friend of mine here has pointed out a few obscurities but they are slight and I shan't attempt to bother you with them at this date. So glad your mag. has found another backer and that William's review pleases (Plomer's review of *Refusal to Conform*). I have been seeing a lot of plays, chiefly because an old Cambridge friend of mine, Claude Colleer Abbott (did you ever meet him?), having planned for himself a riotous visit to London from Durham where he lives, and bought seats for all the best plays, difficult to get into, suddenly had a stroke and sent all the tickets to me. A mild stroke, he recovers, and tonight I start on the 3-part cycle of *The Wars of the Roses* at the Aldwych (Shakespeare's *Henry VI* et seq. done up afresh) which takes me back there tomorrow for matinée and evening performance. I have lately seen dear old Morgan (now 85) and on Thursday dine with M——, and perhaps spend the weekend with Jack in Nottingham. All that pleases me and stocks my empty life. And I have written an article about Queenie 'snarling', which I referred to in your piece, for a man named Neville Braybrooke who is editing a book of autobiographical essays called 'Authors and their Animals'. I am happier about it than I was for the thing I did for you. I wonder how negotiations over your own book develop. No further news dear.

Fond love as ever
Joe

Colleer Abbott was Professor of English at Durham University but I had never met him, though I had often been entertained by imitations of his Housman-like ballads recited by William Plomer at Joe's. Joe once or twice took pity on the elderly academic and printed his peculiar poems, in which he often appeared in the role of a milkmaid wooed by a Housmanesque rustic swain. In the best poems, there was a touch of Hardy – in the style of 'A Tramp Woman's Tragedy', with which Rosalinde Fuller used to enchant me.

I do not possess another letter from Joe until one dated 2 October 1964:

Dearest Chimbo-Jimbo

Your last packet (as you will note) has just arrived; I found it on my return from Italy the night before last, and I am hoping it is a response to my long-delayed letter to you before I set out, though you don't mention that. I say this only because your Kintama have rested (if they ever do rest) in so many places that I begin to wonder whether what I believed to be their latest address is still extant; there is no address on any of these cards. However, I am enchanted by everything you send, especially your excellent photo, which, sweet Miss Rieko alas cut away, would make, I should have thought, a good dust-jacket picture for your work-ups – but *not* especially your *semi* [Japanese cicada], which disintegrated between my fingers with a nasty little crackle when I lifted it out to see what it was. Nancy is pleased with your *Frisson dans le Dos*, which has given her a third perfume, for I brought back from my travels at her request a bottle of Robe de Nuit and one of Chanel No. 5 – said to be cheaper in France, where we finished up, but which nevertheless cost me (two tiny bottles) £2-10-0. I didn't greatly enjoy my elderly motor-tour with the Sprotts thro' N. Italy (a schedule affair, too much of a rush, and such a nice Italian boy in Vercelli who had to be left behind as soon as met), but it has done me some good. No gin or whisky, but only wine and a little Stock Brandy-and-soda at night. My morning nausea and hacking cough (nothing, it turns out, to do with smoking) have disappeared. A fortunate experiment, for now I can no longer afford to soak in spirits, my B.B.C. Security Pay has dried up and I am the poorer by £400 a year. At present I am drinking nothing but beer.

I am so glad you are happy, dear Jim, and often wish I were in Tokyo with you, but no more holidays for me henceforth, I fear; but certain things in your generally gay letter naturally worry me. Doctor's orders: are you under the doctors and for what? I must say that to be under a Japanese doctor sounds to me a consummation devoutly to be wished, but I suppose you are not there smiling with pleasure. Then I am sorry about your book. Quite right to withdraw it from Collins, but what will you do with it now? Secker & Warburg are enterprising: the nice man there is David Farrer (an excellent publisher too), you could mention my name. Have you an agent? I forget. If I myself can be of any use to you here you have only to say so. I would push the book about for you, if you so decided. I am sorry about your Mother, too, though the Blind Institute is wealthy and wonderfully good; they have always taken a personal and loving interest in her and, I am sure, will see her comfortably housed. I will go down and see her if you will let me know how things develop over the move and where she may be found. As you know. Nancy and I have the most affectionate memories of her.

I have heard from Sonia [Orwell], and you should have heard from her too by now – unless she has not been furnished with your latest address (do letters get forwarded in Japan, from one address to another?). She says that of what you sent her she preferred 'some very nice translations of Japanese poets which I hope we are going to be able to use'.

Write me again soon: your letters, with their fragments of Japan, are my greatest joy.

Love as ever
JOE

This letter made me feel sorry for Joe. His loneliness seemed to be increasing, and his appeals for more letters sounded plaintive. I cannot now remember who my girl friend Miss Rieko was – or perhaps it was Joe's misspelling of Reiko Sasamori, a Nikkatsu film star with whom I had been photographed when Tomohiro and I visited the Nikkatsu Film Studios for my essay in the first volume of *Japan Industrial*. The word *kintama* is a rather improper word for testicles, meaning 'eggs of gold'. I wished they could have been real golden eggs for Joe, struggling to support himself and Nancy on his diminishing pension.

I had started an office in Osaka with Tomohiro for Perfect English Publicity, which was doing rather well, and commuting to my classes in Tokyo by the Shinkansen, which meant leaving Shin Osaka in the morning by the first train, at 6 a.m. It was just a temporary stay, to get our name established in the Kansai region. Joe's next letter, dated 16 March 1965, was sent to my office address:

Dearest Jim
You see I am now becoming quite a good correspondent – better than you, in fact, for pretty though your post-cards are, they are rather short of news. However I am pleased with the present one,

pleased with your poem, pleased about your prize (why didn't you collect it yourself?) and pleased with the dish-wipe, if that is what it is intended for. So now that you have another letter and a large sum of money, buy an airmail stamp and send poor old Joe (who is not feeling very well today) a larger account of your life and your comings (and goings). Are you now a permanent decoration to the fortunate city of Osaka? Has Tokyo's tiara lost one of its brightest jewels? Were you expelled from that city? (I am still wondering why you didn't collect your prize in glamorous person.) Are you now what's called 'in business'? Have you an office and are you the Boss? And why Osaka? You see how little I know.

I am having a Japanese day here today, for the British Council (forgive me for mentioning it) has bidden me to a cocktail party to honour Yukio Mishima. I don't know how they thought of me; perhaps Francis King (now living in Brighton) put my name forward. I liked the only book of Mishima's I've read – a queer one – and from his photo he looks an attractive man. Tomorrow I transfer myself to Villiers' St James's Park flat for three nights to keep Anna, his pussy-cat, company. He is in Hong Kong. It is rather fun for me having a London house as well as a country one (Putney), and of course it is cheaper to drink someone else's gin and whisky than to drink one's own. Jack Sprott and his sister – perhaps Nancy too – are to dine with me there on Thursday and go on to a play. Feeling that the dear dark angel is close at hand, I am pushing on with my Family Memoir so as not to leave it in rags and tatters. It is terribly sad and rather funny. And what are *you* hatching, sweet Jim? Oh yes, of course, I remember, the same sort of egg upon which I sit.

Spring seems to have arrived and my little sycamore – a dried-up looking old brown stick only last week – now has tiny green swellings on it. I am moved, and rather envious; *I* have no swellings to greet the spring.

> Much love, darling Jim
> Joe

I had not accepted in person the prize for my Japan PEN Club Olympics poems because it was to be presented by Tomlin of the British Council in Tokyo, and I had secretly arranged with Kawabata Yasunari, the great Japanese novelist who at that time was President of the Japan PEN Club, to be given it *in absentia*. Joe never got to the

British Book Exhibition in Tokyo, I suspect, because the suggestion
had been vetoed by Tomlin, who hated homosexuals.

I had met Yukio Mishima at various official gatherings as well as in
gay bars (once at 'Ibsen' in Shinjuku), gay saunas and the Kanda
YMCA, where we had a brief romp in bed together. I did not like him
at all, and his novels even less, apart from *The Temple of the Golden
Pavilion*, and that chiefly because of the beauty of the translation by
Ivan Morris. The book Joe refers to as 'queer' is Mishima's *Confessions of
a Mask*, a pretentious piece of youthful garbage.

It was good to know that Joe was pressing ahead with *My Father and
Myself*, but I could tell from the tone of his letter that he felt he was not
much longer for this world. It was at Villiers's flat that Joe had a
comical encounter with a randy Indian gentleman who called upon
him there one day while he was acting as caretaker for Anna, and on
entering the drawing-room at once unzipped his fly and produced an
enormous penis, saying, proudly: 'What do you think of that?' I think
Joe was for once inarticulate.

My next letter from Joe is dated 17 July 1965 – our letters were
obviously becoming rather less frequent; but it is a long and very
interesting one:

Dearest Jim
a nice letter from and an idle morning: the best combination in the
world. I have finished typing out my Family Memoir and have also
read and reported on a large ms. (the racy autobiography of an
Indian resident in England) for the Bodley Head. So now I have
nothing to do but write to dear Jim and finish reading Mr George
Schaller's book on the dear gorillas, which I recommend to your
attention, so much more interesting, and infinitely more pleasant,
than reading about people: *The Year of the Gorilla* (Collins – your
least favoured publisher). 'Young apes need the same kind and
amount of attention given human infants. Zoos which cannot or will
not provide their charges with such care should not be permitted to
keep them, especially now that some species like the orang utan are in
danger of extinction. If nothing else, man should show some ethical
and moral responsibility towards creatures which resemble him so
closely in body and mind. But then man has never learned to treat
even his own kind with compassion.' You will see that young Mr
Schaller lives in my street. If dear Rena were as idle as a gorilla I
would write to her more often, but her good-natured habit of

answering letters the moment they arrive is too exacting. The distance between Gainsborough and Osaka allows for breathing space; London is too close to her busy typewriter.

Poor old Morgan's health is very dicky: do send him some little Japanese memento (King's College, Cambridge), he would be so pleased. I expect I should reply for him, for I go along every week for a couple of days to help him with his correspondence. He goes from slight stroke to slight stroke, though he gets about in between. I sat with him in Clare College Garden (such a pretty garden) last Wednesday in the only burst of sunshine we have had this wretched summer, and a Peacock butterfly came and rested on my knee between us. He said 'How appropriate that it should go to your knee instead of mine'; but the butterfly's selectiveness had a simpler reason – my trousers were light in colour and his were dark. He paid his first visit to London the other day since his bad stroke in Coventry some months ago and I stayed with him in his Chiswick flat. He wanted to see the John Osborne homosexual play *A Patriot for Me*, for which I managed to get seats, and we had a good day, lunch at the Royal Coll. of Art, a rest at the Reform Club, then smoked salmon sandwiches and drinks with Villiers in his flat – he too was going to the play with a friend, and took us all along to it in a taxi. But Morgan paid for his pleasure with a slight stroke next morning; I had to summon a doctor, who managed to keep him in bed for 24 hours. Then I got him back to Cambridge. We enjoyed the play very much, with reservations. The famous drag-party scene (men and boys dressed as women) doesn't really fit, also it goes on far too long and becomes silly and boring. Apart from that and one or two other errors of judgment it is a riveting play and has feeling, while it is sticking to its narrative. I fancy you will look down your handsome nose at these remarks and will be further horrified when I tell you that I am in correspondence with John Betjeman, whom I knew of old, and am to lunch with him soon near the Old Bailey where he lives. He has a remarkable poem, mis-called 'Narcissus', in the current number of the *London Magazine* which took my attention. What is happening to your new travel book since its long sojourn at Weidenfeld & Nicolson? I want so much to read it. Why not send it to James Michie at The Bodley Head and name me as literary adviser, should such an animal be needed? It wd. add excitement to my dull declining years. Of course it might also add one to your list of untouchables, but I am half-way there already through managing to like Francis and

Villiers besides your sweet self. It is possible that I may be returning to *The Listener* in September as Lit. Ed. for two or three months. They may be in a jam: the new char (Anthony Thwaite) departing, the old char (myself) has been sounded as to whether he wd. consider returning with his mop and pail until another new char can be found. The old char has said yes, since he is priced at 10gns. a day at four days a week. If this occurs I hope you will send me some poems and a whole page of rubbings of Japanese pricks. But I am not in the best of health, so perhaps I shan't reach September. I am always surprised and far from pleased when I wake up each morning.

Now don't say your old Joe doesn't love and think of you; it isn't often he writes such a long letter as this, and only to the Chosen.

I don't like your new notepaper at all, nor does Freud, he has just told me so.

Blessings
JOE

One of the reasons I had decided to live half the week in Osaka was that the men of that vigorous region are much more forthcoming than those of Tokyo or Kyoto. Osaka is still my favourite big city in Japan, though it is not nearly as sexy as it used to be, when there were dozens of gay bars and saunas, gay working men's dormitories like the Take-noya in Imaike where I used to go slumming, some very dark, packed movie houses at Umeda and a lively park culture to prowl at night. There was also a sort of lonely-hearts club for men where one could contact the sort of partners one had specified in what the Japanese call an *enquête* (they used the French word – for once, correctly), to mean a survey or an inquiry. The membership fee was moderate, so it attracted quite a lot of working-class men and youths. Thus I was able to meet some charmers. The Japanese have a tradition of preserving the form of any remarkable fish they catch by painting it with Chinese ink and impressing it on white hand-made paper. I think I was the first to apply this age-old craft to perpetuating the memory of erections by brushing with black ink while still rigid the engorged member – some were very ticklish – and then pressing it on some virginal white *washi* (I wrote a long poem on the subject for *My Blue Period* – still unpublished.) I soon had quite a collection, and I sent some of them to Joe and Morgan. Morgan also delighted in the little frilly hankies I used to send him, imprinted with photographs of dewy young Japanese male singers and film stars.

Osaka was noted too for the feverish gay life on its trains, particularly the first and last carriages on the subway at peak hours, which seem to last there all day long, and in the last carriage of the surburban trains in their perpetual rush-hour. This promiscuousness still goes on in trains, particularly on the Chuo Line in Tokyo, again in the first and last carriages, where both hetero and homo *attouchements* have become so common and accepted as part of urban sprawl that no one takes any notice of them. But there is the tale of a foreign woman, the favourite target of *chikan* or bottom-rubbers, who, on feeling a hand creeping up her skirt seized it, held it up and shouted: 'Whose hand is this?' To which the unfortunate Japanese gent replied, in English: 'Not mine!'

Joe's letters all through 1965 have a slightly hectic tinge, as if he were perpetually tight or on drugs. Here is one from Putney dated 10 August 1965:

Darling Jim

Your divine gifts arrived this morning. Oh Fanny dear, how pretty they are! Nancy is delighted with her (as it should be) superior one and is going to write to you. This should be a great treat for you, since she never writes to anybody, having nobody to write to. But she intends to put pen (not mine, I hope) to paper, she is so pleased. Could you perhaps send her a warm day too, Fanny, so that she might fan herself? You, who settled upon my knee as a butterfly in Clare College Gardens, could easily manage this, and really our summer has been, and continues, disastrous. Instead of a fan, one resorts to the gas fire.

Your wonderful, beautiful, terrible Gainsborough pen-pal, whose type-writer cries out for mercy, has also written me by the same post. It seems you have tumbled upon something of such international importance that it will be Headline News, all over the world. What can it be? I am agog. I am also frightened. What can you have discovered? Have you found Hitler masquerading in Osaka as a geisha? Or an unpublished poem by Edmund Blunden or Ronald Bottrall. Or a Japanese cock a yard long? Or a Buddha carved by Rossetti and Michaelangelo [*sic*]? Or a Japanese plot to overthrow the United States? I should not be surprised in the least. We saw yesterday on T.V. the most appalling film about Japan I've ever seen. Mr Dimbleby, *Panorama*. It was based on Nagasaki. The Japanese Navy expanding and marching about and no longer exciting hostility in the inhabitants. And then a terrible popular movement is everywhere, and of great power – called something like 'Sokagakkai'. Parades and demonstrations and what-not. Its aims were said to be peaceable and intelligent, but in appearance – mob-drill – it was terrifying, Mosley and Hitler. Someone called something like Komeito appeared to be at the back of it. Calm my fears about this, my darling, Japan is my favourite country, as you are my favourite Japanese boy, I don't want militancy there. Of course, if Japan and China could *somehow* manage to wipe out the western world without injury to themselves – or to the animals, that is of prime importance – nothing could please me more, but I doubt if that is the card up your sleeve, for you would not let it out. At any rate Rollicking Rena repairs hither some day next week with your bomb-shell letter which, preferring foot-notes to head-lines, I am *not* agog to see, nor competent to deal with, having no connection with the Press, excepting *The Listener*, and no acquaintance in the newspaper world, excepting Terence Kilmartin, Lit. Ed. of *The Observer*. Rhapsodical Rena says: 'I am writing ahead in case there is anything you can do in the meantime.' Superb sentence, when I haven't a clue to what she's going on about.

We are just off to see the new Beatles film, of which I have ill report. Morgan is in London but largely in someone else's care. He sends you his love. His health is not very good. I had a pleasant lunch with John Betjeman on Monday in the shadow of the Old Bailey. On Sunday I go to Brighton with your old buddy Villiers David to call on several of your other old buddies including F. King and J. Haylock. We shall be speaking of you, no doubt, in suitable terms. *My Dog Tulip* is an alternative Book of the Month (September) choice in New York. Shall I come to see you in Japan on the proceeds? Love,

JOE

Joe's reactions to the Dimbleby *Panorama* programme about Japan were over-excited, and I remember I wrote to tell him that things always appear worse on television. However, what he calls the 'mob-drill' in Nagasaki is something that has spread and increased over the years. Now all schoolchildren are regimented to perform mass displays on sports days, in emulation of the Moscow Olympics exhibitions of mass athletics. They are also herded into standardized educational routines. Japanese people are doing more and more things *en masse*:

housewives even go on shopping sprees in large groups, and families band together to go hiking by the hundreds through the helpless countryside, led by a flag-waving guide with a megaphone through which he bellows warnings and advice. It is a chilling sight.

I had taken to sending paper fans to people during the summer, which explains Joe's use of the word 'Fanny'.

As for Rena's uncontrollable excitement, I think this is also a case of over-reaction. I cannot remember its cause, but feel sure that it was all a joke on my part: I was pulling Rena's leg and she took this *farceur* seriously. Rena and her husband Roger Clayphan were the most wonderful friends to me, and Rena's death from cancer, against which she had long waged a courageous but losing battle, was a great sorrow for me.

While I now found Joe's letters over-febrile and unnaturally agitated, he at times confessed to lethargy. I suspect he was taking some kind of pep pill which often left him feeling depressed when its euphoria had worn off. Here is an example of the mood-swing in a letter dated 21 February 1965:

Dearest Jim

I have instantly written to Mrs Clayphan to welcome her to come for the Feild portrait whenever she likes, and told her we will give her a meal here if it should suit her. I am sorry about you. You have, fortunately for yourself, forgotten what England is like and the numbing effect it has on the spirit, especially in winter. I have often started to write to you, but it is one thing to begin a letter, another matter to finish it. The darkness soon descends, and the fumes of alcohol rise to meet it. Nothing else rises ever. But your card is another spur and I must manage to complete this letter while the mood remains. What are you up to, then, in Osaka? And what is 'Perfect English Publicity'? Correcting 'sand witches' on Japanese menus? A real need. Is it an enterprise invented by you, financed perhaps by Mrs Clayphan – or by those Japanese industrialists with whom you flirted in that amusing and amazing book [*Japan Industrial*] you sent me? Have you left Tokyo? Lethargic though I have become, I long to know all – and am indeed, through my lethargy, a greater sufferer than you, for I have deprived myself (as I said to Francis some time ago) of the most amusing letters that have ever been written. He has now left London for Brighton, with his Japanese servant, Siamese cat, and Pekingese dog, so I have temporarily lost sight of him; but he told me that, as literary adviser to Weidenfeld & Nicolson, he had read your travel book, removed from Collins, and also recommended some shortening and cutting. What has happened since? Francis is not a person to cut for prudery, you may be sure, so I hope that whatever his advice was, met with your approval. It now occurs to me that I shouldn't be telling you this, so pray regard it as confidential if it comes to you as a surprise. Francis may be anonymous in that publishing firm, which I believe to be somewhat slow in movement – so you may not even have heard from them yet. But I hope you have and that the book is under way, for I want to read it. A friend of his, and mine, lives in Osaka. Perhaps you have enough friends of your own, but in case you should care to call, his name is ——. He is an extremely plain, one could almost say ugly, queer Japanese, exceedingly good-natured, obliging and kind, and speaks excellent English. I believe he now teaches it. Francis thought more highly of him than of any other Japanese he met, and I liked him too, so give him my love if you happen to see him. We called him 'Fucky'. It was a misfortune for the good boy, and for us, that he was so very unattractive. I think his health – kidneys, perhaps – was not good either. I paint a rather gloomy picture, but he is a really nice and helpful chap.

I don't think I have much news of self – not much anyway to raise that smile or laugh which it is the social thing to do. Villiers is away in Bangkok, so I am especially lonely, since I have been living more in his strange, dramatic life than in my featureless own. I seldom set pen to paper, even, as you say, for letters, though I do like getting them, Kirkup-san, so though you may question my health (mental), do not question my heart. No, never. My *Tulip* book is, at last, to come out in the States this year, so though the cards are stacked against it selling, I hope for money, which, like you, I begin to need. (Money tends to become so terribly *fluid*.) The trouble with the book is that it falls between two stools: the dog-lover, who does not want to take his dog seriously, and the intellectual, who doesn't want to take dogs at all. It is addressed to both of them, and irritates or disgusts the former, and fails to attract the latter (dogs), though he would enjoy it if he looked, for I have a high opinion of it. Morgan keeps fairly well – I stayed two nights with him in Cambridge this week and read over again all his unpublished erotic stories, which gave me – that now rare thing – a lustful feeling. He occasionally deplores that no one else writes such things, because he would like to read them. Why don't you oblige? Too busy trying to make money, as we all are, no doubt. Though not wealthy, he has always had private means; one may doodle on those. Still, other writers also have private means and do not doodle or rudle for our pleasure.

No more, dearest Jim – at least, I can't remember any more. As my life passes it vanishes, as in a kind of following fog, and is never seen again. This is the story of your loving

JOE

I never really expected Joe to return to *The Listener*. But his letter of 19 August 1965 brought me the welcome news:

Dearest Jim

decisions have now been made: I am to be Lit. Ed. of *The Listener* again during the month of September. Have you any poems you wd. like me to see? If so, do send them. Send them to Putney or to Broadcasting House, c/o *The Listener*; if to the latter address, don't forget that all letters to the B.B.C. are opened unless marked 'Personal'. It is bad enough to return to my *Listener* vomit (which I wouldn't have done without the lure of £10 per day), I don't also want to be cast into gaol. Furthermore, what about your Japan Marine sequence? Has it been published anywhere? I couldn't publish it all, but am specially fond of V. Bitter Peace, also of VIII, The Sea Within – though it is the *sound* of the latter, rather than its meaning (which I find enigmatic), that attracts me. Would you be agreeable to my publishing one or both of these sections, out of sequence? Probably separately? If so how would you like them titled? 'Bitter Peace' and, underneath, 'from Japan Marine, a poem sequence'? – or just 'Bitter Peace'? The editor might step in here with objections to large headings. Perhaps 'Bitter Peace' 'from a Japanese poem sequence'? Say what you think. I don't think I shd. be allowed to make remarks about your prize – but I wd. try if you desired it.

Roger and Rena have just been to call. A most pleasant visit. We liked them both very much. I can do nothing about your scoop. It doesn't interest me. Assuming that your bones are the bones of murdered men, publicity would only re-open old wounds and lead to more recrimination – of which our world contains too much already. I should have thought that the less said about it the better – unless you pop it into one of your next travel books, an item among much

else. It will only stir up trouble, for your Buddhist monk and everyone else.

I am in rather a hurry, darling Jim, so excuse

Your loving
Joe

Yes, now I remember my 'scoop'. It was something about the bones
of Allied prisoners of war that a Buddhist monk friend had discovered
somewhere in Ikoma, and did not know what to do with. So I was not
pulling Rena's leg. But on Joe's advice, I did not follow up the matter.

My poem sequence 'Japan Marine', which had won the PEN Club
Olympic prize, had been published in a Japanese anthology of the
prize-winners, so I was quite willing for Joe to print those two sections,
and eventually he sent me the proofs for both of them. Only one, 'The
Sea Within', appeared during his brief stopgap editorship, and when
the new editor took office the proof of 'Bitter Peace' was scrapped and
the poem never saw the light in *The Listener*, where no more of my
work was allowed to appear. I did not care. In my opinion, after Joe left
that magazine, it went downhill and became banal and boring. The new
editor was Derwent May.

The next letter I have from Joe is addressed King's College, Cambridge, on Morgan's writing paper, and dated 9 November 1965.
Though the letter was written by Joe, it was dictated to him by Forster,
whose signature, a shaky 'Morgan', stands in the middle of the page:

Dear James

I write to you by Joe's hand to thank you for your letter and for
what used to be called a 'doyley'. You say that the latter represents
your favourite pop-singer. I should have thought that it represented a
'popess', but anyhow I am delighted with it. I have been ill, so write
by Joe's hand as I said, which is certainly much better, and, being
Joe's, well expresses my emotion.

With love and I am so pleased to hear from you and will write in
my own illegible hand later on. Do please write again.

Morgan

Then Joe continues in a footnote:

Dearest Jim

I *have* neglected you rather – yet I haven't. I was thinking of you all through Sept., when I did my month with *The Listener*, and published one of the Marine poems, leaving the other in galley behind for Derwent May. Did you get a copy of the one I published, 'The Sea Within'? It must have been sent to you, the issue in which it appeared, but although I thought of an address for your cheque, I never thought of an address for anything else. It was only at the end of my stint that I wondered what addresses they had for you, and looking in the book found masses of them, but not your Osaka one. That I have now supplied. I asked Rena where she thought the cheque shd. go, and she named your Bank in Bath (Barclay's? I forget) and I took her advice, I don't think I edited your poem very cleverly. I was in rather a tizzy for some time. I gave it the title you gave it in the sequence, and a number of people found it obscure. I should have called it 'Nagasaki', then all would have been clear as crystal. I think it a very beautiful poem and carry it always in my pocket book, together with Edwin Muir's 'The Horses'. Your *Japan Industrial* came this week; I have looked at the pictures but not yet at the text, but I will in time. I hope you're making lots of yen out of it. My *Tulip* book is having good reviews in the States and has gained the alternative choice of the N.Y. Book of the Month Club. I hope to get some dollars out of that. We are worried about Rena. She has not been at all well – vomiting and so on – and has stopped answering our letters. That does seem to me an anxiety. She was to have gone to Paris with Roger a couple of weeks ago but couldn't make it. He phoned us on his way through, making light of it, but that is what worried people sometimes do. Morgan was pleased with your doyley or handkerchief but thought the boy was a girl – hence his joke – not as good as the one I suggested but which he rejected 'Can it be a boyley?' I am not very well today myself, so shall proceed no further. Morgan has improved since his last September stroke, in part at least, but he has trouble with his speech and is very forgetful. We live too long, no doubt of it, the doctors oblige us to, though to be very old must be perfect hell.

Much love, dear Jim
JOE

My dear old friend was nearing the end of his days. His last three
letters to me are almost unbearably sad, in their determination to be
sprightly and gay. Here is the first of them, written on New Year's Day,
1966:

Darling Jim
    I owe you a letter and this seems an appropriate day for turning
over a new leaf as a correspondent and writing it. I wonder where
you are, having a heavenly time anyway I am sure, and I hope that
this time you will manage to publish your travel notes, for we are
badly in want of something to read. Xmas has been ever so dull. My
Duchess half sister sent us the customary turkey and Nancy said it
needn't go in the fridge, so for five days it occupied the bathroom
and went secretly bad there – the liver, which Nancy had searched the
bird's interior for in vain, must have been there all the time. On Xmas
morning the secret was out and the bathroom unenterable. Nancy
tried washing out the creature's inside with boiling water and that
made the stench even worse, so we had to roast the thing at once,
although we had intended to cook it on Boxing Day when we had
guests for lunch, Villiers and his new boy-friend Gérard, and a young
Irish novelist friend of mine, John McGahern. The bird still smelt
even after cooking, but fortunately it was only the inside that was
affected, and when we had dismembered it and thrown away the
undercarriage, the rest, the larger part, was quite all right. Nancy
then got into an ill-humour, so we scarcely spoke to each other at all
on that rejoiceful day, the birthday of Our Lord; but Boxing Day was
jolly and happy. Since then the days have been indistinguishable in
their monotony and the weather, of course, foul. However, the
shortest day is over, so we have that small pleasure, the lengthening
of light, to look forward to. I have read a good deal, in a rather dull
desultory way – nothing new, for there seems nothing new to read,
but taking old books from my shelves at random, Hester Chapman's
life of Charles II, Maurois' *History of England* (to educate myself, for I
suddenly realized that I have never read a history of England in my
life, not even at school), Lermontov *A Hero of Our Time*, Aksakoff *A
Russian Gentleman* and *Years of Childhood*, and a book on *British
Amphibians and Reptiles*. This last gave me most pleasure, and I
started to make notes on toads and frogs, newts, lizards and snakes,
hoping that by such means I might, for a change, keep a little
knowledge in my head. Did you know that the tadpole of the

common frog has 640 teeth? Not as large, I expect, as yours and mine, dear Jim. They enable the creature to rasp its slipping food and they are constantly and gradually shed. Two of my own teeth were extracted on Xmas Eve – I had developed a palatal abscess, and my kind dentist left his golf-course to attend to me. Painless but unpleasant; a pity we do not have teeth like the adders and snakes, who do not go in for roots and sockets, but drop their teeth when they are bored with them, replacing them with new ones which push the old ones out. I have, in short, been dreadfully bored with only Nancy for company and I cannot take to drink as heavily as I would like, it is so bloody expensive, nearly 50/- for a bottle of gin or whisky. Even so I spend £10 a week at least on those two drinks alone. Rena seems to be improving in her health, she rang up at Xmas, and Morgan (up in Coventry with his friends the Buckinghams) is much stronger and better, walking now without the aid of a stick. I go on Friday to stay with Jack in Norfolk for four nights. No more now. A dull letter, but you can't make a silk purse out of a sow's ear.

Much love, sweet Jim
JOE

I thought it was a wonderful letter, so very atmospheric, it made me shudder to think of the sort of Xmas I had missed. I was interested to read of John McGahern, whose short stories I had begun to enjoy, and who was to become a magnificent novelist. The comedy of Nancy and the turkey from the Duchess of Westminster was somehow so typical, and I could almost smell the wretched bird – which vegetarian Nancy must have hated to explore – and feel the dear woman's ill-humour, those pouting sulks she always did so prettily. Many years before, I had introduced Joe to Russian literature, and he was especially taken by Aksakov's *Years of Childhood*, which we both found deeply moving. He liked Turgenev's *First Love* so much, I suggested he should try dramatizing it for the stage or TV, and the idea seemed to set up a faint glimmer in the back of his brain, but nothing came of it. It was saddening to me to think that Joe was hard up, and the next time I returned to England I took him some duty-free booze. But I suspect he had been voluntarily cutting down on spirits, as they clouded his intelligence too much and gave him filthy dreams. It was good to read, at the end of the letter, that he would soon have some relief from Nancy and Putney by going to visit his friend Jack Sprott at Blakeney, where he had retired to a country cottage.

I wrote back to Joe as soon as I could from Japan Women's University: my Christmas and New Year had been spent in a rapturous first visit to the Philippines, which was to provide the basis for my new book, *Filipinescas* (1968). Joe replied almost at once, on 31 January 1966:

Darling Jim
Lovely letter from you, books, postcards, photos and invitations. The p.c. of the Philippinos [*sic*] dancing I sent on to Morgan during an icy winter spell ten days ago, so that its charm and warmth and gaiety should brighten his room in which he was hibernating. After the horrid blows (thrice believed at point of death) dealt him by 1965, the present year has opened well for him, he is wonderfully spry and vigorous, even walking without a stick; his eye-sight is the chief disappointment, he has much difficulty in reading, books or letters. He was pleased to get a copy of your *Tokyo*, [1965], as also were Joe, William, and Francis; I asked *The Listener* if I might review it for them but was refused, it is to be kept with all other such books for the next Travel Book Number, which means, I suppose, that it will have to wait about a year. Actually I haven't read it yet, only read *into* it, noting your joke about 'I like penis', for I left it on poor Villiers to comfort him. (He is mad about your letters which I sometimes show him, urging me never to destroy them – which I never do.) 1966 has not opened well for *him*, for he has been in bed since New Year's Eve with a mysterious temperature which, though not high – round about 101 – has weakened and depressed him by its persistence. At first it was thought to be pneumonia, but treatment for that was ineffective. Then dark glances were cast at Anna, his 'treasure-heart', his beloved cat, and it was said to be 'cat fever'. This enraged him – and me. Now she has been exonerated, and his illness has been diagnosed, without absolute conviction, as Malta or undulant fever, which, passed into the system as a bacillus in milk, butter, or cheese, comes not only from the goat but also from the cow. Since he does all his shopping at Fortnum and Mason round the corner this casts grave aspersions on that illustrious establishment. He is now thought to be on the mend, but it has all been a great inconvenience to me, for he and his flat are my nearest refuge from the monotony of Putney, and his illness and irritable humour have largely excluded me from them for a month. Whatever you may think of him, I am deeply embedded now in his strange eccentric life, and it

has been a bore to be separated from him by this tiresome illness. However, I have got about a little, to Cambridge and to Jack in Nottingham – nothing so glamorous as *your* get-abouts, but the happiest that my life here offers. What fun it would be to come and stay with you in Tokyo, heavenly Japan, but can I afford it? I doubt it. At the moment I am overdrawn in my current account, though I have some money on 4% deposit, but I try not to shift that, I want it to make its interest. In February or March I expect a cheque from America, and I think it might be a large one, though I don't know; I believe my *Tulip* book has sold fairly well there, in spite of transport strikes in New York, and is to be published here again in England by another publisher, The Bodley Head, this spring, in both board and paperback. So I ought to get a decent amount of cash, some £700 to £800 – though whether I would then dare to spend it on a flight to Tokyo and risk the aftermath of ginlessness in this lamentable country I don't know. To have constant booze, which now costs the earth, more than half my income, is my main anxiety. I really couldn't live without it. You will understand that.

Fondest love as ever
JOE

. I could understand how Joe felt about his dwindling finances and his gin, though at that period I was a vodka man myself, when I wasn't in low dives drinking cheap Nikka whiskey, *sake* or *shochu*, a drink from Kagoshima made from sweet potatoes, and terribly potent. It was just about this time that I discovered the Ohsawa macrobiotic diet, and soon I was to abandon vodka and all spirits for good, and stick to *sake*. It seemed to me Joe was slowly turning into a chronic alcoholic, and I remember sending him advice about diet and drinking – though not about smoking, for Ohsawa claimed that all long, cylindrical things were good (he meant vegetables) and even extended this idiotic notion so far as to claim that 'cigarettes cure cancer'. But I do not think Joe could be bothered with a change in diet: he felt that all that was now too late.

As for his never destroying my letters, this was not true, for after his death when I asked Francis King if Joe had kept any of my letters he said they had all been destroyed, except for half a dozen or so that Joe had sold to Villiers. The illness from which Villiers was suffering interested me, for I was also rather under the weather after my return from the Philippines, where deep-throat kisses had given me glandular fever. But I was soon on the mend, whereas poor Villiers's sickness went on and on. As I write this, the Japanese press is giving out the alarming news that cats are Aids carriers, though whether they can infect human beings is not yet certain. Fortunately, my wandering life has never allowed me to keep either pets or plants: I like to be free to take off for any destination at the drop of a hat. I had suggested Joe do the same and come and live with me in my lovely old house on the campus of Japan Women's University. I even offered to find teaching jobs for him, for his mellifluous Cambridge accent would be sure to charm Japanese listeners. But he doubted his ability to teach, which was absurd, for anyone can teach in Japan, as can be seen from the thousands of totally unqualified foreigners now making fortunes in fly-by-night 'conversation schools' and 'English conversation coffee-shops'. Joe seemed so much at a loose end that I had also suggested he take up some kind of voluntary work, for example looking after animals at an animal dispensary, or taking care of paroled prisoners or delin-quent boys. But he was too switched off and weary to think of doing anything. In the end, though I offered to send him money for the trip, he never succeeded in reaching Japan again. The pull of Putney, gin and Nancy all seemed to be exerting a dead weight upon his life, and I think he was just allowing himself to sink fatalistically into permanent de-spondency and death.

The last letter I can find at the moment from Joe is dated 11 October 1966, and it is terribly *triste*:

Dearest Jim

Your card today. I'm sorry not to have written earlier to give you on your return to Japan a welcome which (if your previous card speaks true) may otherwise be lacking. Naturally that news disturbed me, though it did not seem to disturb you, and since I feel both worried and puzzled I hope you will let me hear more of it very soon.

I can't write a long letter, for I have nothing to say. Your coming was, of course, like a visitation from heaven, the alighting of a bird of paradise, and now that you have returned to those horned islands from which you came we have sunk into that spiritless lethargy from which, for a moment, you aroused us. Shall I see you more? I doubt it. If my bronchitis, soused in nicotine and alcohol and already protesting, don't cough me this winter into a shattered heart I shall suffer the even worse fate of becoming a chronic invalid. Anyway, in

November I shall have had 70 years of life, more than enough. Morgan is back in Cambridge, well I believe; he was much pleased with your gifts, especially the Scandinavian booklet of boy nudies. What he will do with his pineapple fibre shirt, I know not, nor what I shall do with mine.

Tell me about your Japanese future.

Love as ever
Joe.

When Joe signed his letters, he never put a full-stop after his name, at least when writing to me. Now in this letter there was a full stop after 'Joe' and I sensed it was a sign of another kind of ending. I wish I had not bothered him with my own worries, which in the end proved to be baseless: I had forgotten to obtain, on leaving Tokyo, the necessary re-entry permit from the immigration authorities, and feared that on arrival at Yokohama in my cargo-boat I should at once be deported. However, my good friend on the staff of Japan Women's University, Mrs 'Kitty' O-hara, was there waiting to welcome me at the port offices, and with her influence managed to steer me through Customs and Immigration without a hitch, though the immigration officers asked me to write them a formal letter of apology for my foolish oversight, something Kitty and her staff concocted for me in beautiful calligraphy and high-sounding Japanese. So I had got through another scrape. 'You'll always fall on your feet,' my Irish grandfather had told me, looking at my palm. I wished I could say the same thing to Joe now, when he needed more than ever a bit of luck in his life. He had no fear of dying. But I was possessed of unspeakable terrors all the days of my life.

Joe's were such wonderful letters, and they helped me so much in my exile from Britain – even though it was a very willing exile, it was not always a happy one. Yet when Joe died, Roger sent me photocopies of the letters he had written to Rena, in which he speaks unkindly and harshly about me. Perhaps again he was jealous, and wanted to put dear Rena off me. If so, he failed, for she remained loyal. And she remained loyal to Joe, too, for she never revealed what he had said in his letters about me.

I shall end this section of my book with one of my rare letters from Nancy, written from Putney on 4 July 1967, just after Joe's death:

Darling Jim

Thank you so much for your dear, sweet letter. I know how dearly you loved Joe, and I feel as sad for you as I do for myself – it is so hard to realize that we shall never see him again – One always felt – at least I did – that he would always be there, and that one could not possibly go on living in a world with no Joe in it – I still feel that of course – but everyone has been so marvellous and kind to me and anxious to help in every possible way, that I feel I can't let them down and take an overdose of sleeping pills which I so often feel the urge to do, and I am trying to put on a brave face to the world, altho' I am weeping inwardly all the time.

I long to get out of this flat. It haunts me – but as the rent is so terribly cheap I may have to stay – I don't even know yet how much money I shall have to live on. As I expect you know Joe had an annuity and an old age pension both of which died with him – apart from that I have a pension of £4.8.0 a week (thanks to Mr Wilson) which I only managed to get about a month before Joe died. He was so pleased about it, but he also said 'Well I'm damned, you're getting more than I do!' That was the extra 8/-. Then he had some money on deposit in the bank and some investments which might bring in between 5 or 6000 if sold.

Francis King is Joe's literary executor – I know you don't like him but he has been very kind and helpful to me and I do think he is very honest and a nice man. Geoffrey Gorer has also been very kind and good to me and has offered me the services of his broker. Sonia Orwell has been an absolute darling to me – propping me up all the time and constantly rushing down in her minicar laden with bottles of booze and flowers – and taking me out for lunch or dinner at a restaurant called 'The Hungry Horse' where all the waiters are queer and very charming and wear mini aprons and very tight pants! You would love it! Darling, do write and tell me how you got on in the U.S.A. I'm sure you will hate it! And do remember that I love you, and so does Rena, although we are both very poor substitutes for Joe.

Bless you
Devotedly
Nancy.

It was my first trip to the United States. I was going for the summer, to be inspected by the staff of Amherst College, where there was a possibility that I might be invited to become Poet in Residence for a year.

What interested me most in Nancy's letter was the name of that restaurant, The Hungry Horse – for that was where Joe had once taken me and Dana for lunch. I had forgotten the name – and the occasion – until Nancy clairvoyantly recalled it to me.

Now, twenty years later, never a day passes without my thinking of Joe. He often comes to me in dreams, as Dana does. I shall end this chapter with the final paragraph of Morgan Forster's *The Hill of Devi*, a passage which, as Friends say, 'speaks to my condition':

> One of the puzzling things about the dead is that it is impossible to think of them evenly. They all go out of sight and are forgotten, they all go into silence, yet we cannot help assigning some of them a tune. Most of those I have known leave no sound behind them, I cannot evoke them though I would like to. He (the Maharajah of Dewas Senior) has the rare quality of evoking himself, and I do not believe that he is here doing it for the last time.

Joe, too, still 'evokes himself', in his letters and books, and in my memory.

A last memory of Joe at the end of his life. It was just after I had returned to Britain from Nagoya, on my annual visit to my mother; on the way to Bath after a year abroad, dashing through London, which even then I could hardly bear to look at. Rushing across Putney Bridge and up the High Street to take a quick look at Werter Road, my home for a while (remember Morgan Forster's aunt and Arnold Bennett's novel set here – was it *Mr Prohack?*) then up the hill where Watts Dunton defused dear sozzled Swinburne at 'The Pines' – a poet reduced by one pale ale a day.

Then back down to the Thames to spend a day with Joe; turning the corner at top speed making for the Star and Garter, blind with sun and traffic as I fly over anywhere but the sobering zebra crossings – there he is, smiling, slender, by the public convenience, Joe, amused, faintly sad, retired from work but not from life, Joe perched on the car-park wall, cigarette in bony, angled hand (pure Don Bachardy), unexpectedly waiting there for me.

A long kiss at last, full on the lips but quite platonic as his cleaning lady (the new char) used to comment: and then, as we stroll towards the lift to his top-floor flat, 'Jime dear, how are you darling?' Said with that crooked smile, the question is rhetorical.

'And how, dear Joe, are things with you?'

Things ain't what they used to be, until, of course, you came in sight around that corner. . . . A vision, dear, a perfect vision of delight.'

'The lift is slow in coming,' is my answer. 'The story of my life' – he laughs – 'I always came too quick.'

'But Joe dear, why were you sitting on the wall beside that boring pisshouse where nothing ever happens?'

The lift arrives. On its slow way up he puts an arm round my waist and sighs: 'To get away from Nancy for a while. When I'm expecting friends, it's an excuse. I don't wait for them in the flat. It's so interesting, watching them coming round that corner, across the road, and thus, for a few minutes before they see me there I have them all to myself, before dear Nance gets her claws into them . . . the males like you, dear.'

Well, I couldn't help asking as we stepped out of the lift and paused while Queenie barked her head off and Nancy nattered at her behind the door, 'Tell me, how did I look, Joe' – seeing in him at that moment one of those surprising shop windows, a passing mirror at the butcher's or on the door of a wardrobe crossing the pavement to a removal van.

'Marvellous, darling, too divine, just so miraculously funny as you blazed through the traffic with your big blond head turned back to look lustfully at a young policemen's passing bottom in tight-buttoned trousers of serviceable serge.'

'What are you two laughing at?' was Nancy's first remark, as I gathered her in my arms and kissed her on both cheeks while Queenie jumped and barked, and Joe hid his jealousy by playing with her cunt.

It is that memory of Joe sitting all alone on the low parking lot wall outside the Star and Garter pub that stays with me always. That more than anything else showed how he had changed since his retirement. I felt for him the sort of pang of love, sorrow and regret that I used to feel for my blind mother as I conducted her round the streets of Bath. As Dana had so percipiently remarked that lunch-time at The Hungry Horse, Joe, who had once been so surrounded by friends, was deeply lonely now – perhaps had always been so beneath the social surface. Perhaps it was my own loneliness that drew him to me, and me to him – 'Because it was he, because it was me.' I wish I could have taught him, at the end of his days, what I had had to learn from childhood on, that other aphorism of Montaigne's: 'The greatest thing in the world is to know how to be self-sufficient.'

Part Two
Gay Go Up and Gay Go Down

Une dentelle s'abolit
Dans le doute du Jeu suprême
A n'entr'ouvrir comme un blasphème
Qu'absence eternelle de lit!

Stéphane Mallarmé

. . . Sans plus il faut dormir en l'oubli du blasphème . . .

Stéphane Mallarmé, 'L'Après-midi d'un faune'

Et la bière et l'alcôve en blasphèmes fécondes
Nous offrent tour à tour, comme deux bonnes soeurs,
De terribles plaisirs et d'affreuses douceurs.

Quand veux-tu m'enterrer, Débauche aux bras immondes?
O Mort, quand viendras-tu, sa rivale en attraits,
Sur les myrtes infects entre tes noirs cyprès?

Charles Baudelaire, 'Les deux bonnes soeurs'

Another Side of Joe

The fathers have eaten sour grapes, and the children's teeth are set on edge.

Ezekiel 18:2

The poet is egoistic to the point of narcissism. He sees himself as a fixed point around which the notion of life circulates. He is compacted of imagination, to quote Shakespeare. He is obsessed by language. In fact he is a man of frequent and diverse obsessions. Often he shows a paranoid character, with some reason. He suspects that he has numerous enemies who are really trying to put him in jail or the lunatic asylum. Frequently he really lands in such places. He has a supremely guilty conscience, born from his ego and his passionate desire to know more than his senses tell. He experiences frequent pure states of mind, pure love, pure rage, pure knowledge. He is a man of infinite discipline (something which only other artists know about him). He is capable of great cruelty and something akin to saintliness. He is in love with heresies and regards the forbidden as his rightful province. He is nevertheless the most pious of men. He is both the most infantile and the most sage of creatures. He exploits his defects. . . .

. . . He is dogmatic and deliberately immerses himself in the occult. He is effeminate and, as the public often thinks, often worse. Sometimes he is physically and, as I think, deliberately, dirty. He tends to speak with authority, as if he were a kind of god. He is a hypochondriac who is not yet averse to ruining his health for some whim. He is, history shows, frequently suicidal, frequently alcoholic, frequently a victim of one of the known types of sexual aberration. Yet these are characteristics of other men as well. We can only say: the chief characteristic of the poet is that above all he is obsessed by the desire to write poems.

Karl Shapiro, In Defense of Ignorance
New York, Random House, 1960

Joe's last two years are amply covered in Neville Braybrooke's selection
of his letters. From 1966, these became ever rarer. I had been hurt and
disappointed by the way he had fussed and complained about that
wretched essay I asked him to write for *Orient/West*. I remember I
wrote to him saying I did not want to meet Francis King's cast-offs in
Osaka and Kyoto, and that his description of the rather depressingly
ugly young man (22/2/65 letter) showed a lack of understanding of my
needs, for I wished only to surround myself with life-giving, attractive
people. He was hurt in his turn by my refusal to follow his advice, and
there was a general cooling in our long relationship. There was no point
in keeping in touch, and I even stopped writing to Nancy: I was afraid
Joe's jealousy might make life even more difficult for her. There were
times when I did write to Joe: when he wrote from hospital to tell me
he had been knocked down by a taxi while visiting Georges Duthuit in
Paris, and on the anniversary of Queenie's death. But our letters were
now few and far between.

   Whenever I returned to Bath to see my mother, I used to spend a day
or two with Joe and Nancy in London or in Bath, but in the summer of
1966 I felt I could not face Putney again, and went straight home to
Bath after my Trans-Siberian trip from Nahodkha to Moscow and
Leningrad which was to form the basis of my book *One Man's Russia*.
Rena showed me all of Joe's letters to her, and the one he wrote on 10
July shows he wanted to know where I was:

Dear Rena,
   it's long since we heard from you, and you from us. I do hope all
goes well with you. My particular reason for writing is to ask if you
have news of Jim. I have been out of correspondence with him for
some months – through my own clumsiness perhaps. I long to see
him of course and wonder if you have definite news of his date of
arrival. If you happen to be in communication with him, will you
give him my love? I have an extra worry – the possibility of muddle
and missing him – because next weekend, July 16, Nancy and I go to
Brighton for two to three weeks. A friend of mine in the Royal
College of Art [John Drummond] has given us his house there while
he visits Russia. The address is 92 Montpelier Road, Brighton. The
phone number Brighton 28601. I should be deeply sorry to miss Jim,
so if you see him or are in contact with him will you give him this
information? I could actually put him up in my Brighton house if he
cared to come. What I am afraid of is that he may ring Putney and get

no reply and know not where to go after that.

I have only lately returned from a 12-day stay with the poet Richard Murphy on the west coast of Ireland (Connemara). Very beautiful, very desolate. I wonder if you have ever been there. Such local life as there was was centred on fishing – the unfortunate lobster, too expensive for our own table there where the almost unvaried diet was bacon-and-eggs. The lobsters all go to France. It would have been dull for me, had there not been a gay and friendly dog, named Nero, who took me for walks. But it was a nice change from Putney.

Nancy is well and sends love. I do hope you have now recovered all your health and strength and that Roger also is in good form.

Love to you both

Joe

I find this letter both sad and amusing. In his reference to his own 'clumsiness' Joe is adopting his usual tactics of self-excuse. He knew he had treated me badly and written to me in a way no true friend should do. There is sadness in that, and in his rather pathetic attempts to fill his empty days, for I was not the only friend who had started drifting away. Yet there is humour in the use of that very Morgan Forsterish word 'muddle', and in his references to the lobsters and the dog Nero. All the same, a deep sadness seems to seep through the surface of his words, and a regret for his destruction of our friendship.

This was Joe's last letter to Rena, or at least the last that has survived. Joe would be dead within a year, on 4 June 1967. Rena herself was dying of cancer, bravely and defiantly, almost with joy. She refused to admit defeat, and even dashed off quite a good romantic novel, *The Thorns of Love*, dedicated to me and Roger, that was published by Robert Hale through the good offices of Jan van Loewen, to whom I had recommended she send it. For one deliriously eventful weekend, I had been to stay with Rena and Roger and their lovely daughters at Gainsborough, during which Roger said I 'needed fathering', and took me with him to the local pub on Sunday morning to sip Guinness 'with the rest of the lads'. His complete confidence in me, and his uncondescending acceptance of my 'difference', made me his friend for life. There was nothing of what I call 'otherism' in Roger: he was sensible and down-to-earth, yet sensitive and warm-heated. He was good-looking, too, and showed his sheer goodness by never acting like other 'straight' men in my presence, as if they expected me to rape them on sight. No wonder Rena adored him. That weekend, they drove me all over the wonderful Lincolnshire countryside, and fed me enormous meals, perfectly cooked and presented with fine wines, which tasted even better in such generous company, so seldom my lot in life.

Rena had warned me that Joe seemed to be going into a decline, and that he had written some harsh and spiteful things to her about me. I knew, of course, that this was Joe's way of trying to overcome his jealousy of any woman who came close to me: he denigrated me and my work to Rena in a way that shocked her, but did not shock Nancy when she told her about it, for Nancy had suffered the same treatment from Joe with regard to my love for her.

After Rena's death, I asked Roger to let me have copies of Joe's letters to her, and he sent me nine, though I suspect there may have been more, so bitter in their attacks upon me that he did not want me to see them, for he was like a real father in that he always sought to protect me against hurt.

I shall give here Joe's letters to Rena in chronological order: the first is dated from Putney 1 April 1965.

Dear Mrs Clayphan
    on April 12 I have to be up in London at 6.0 pm for the evening, which means I shall be leaving Putney at 5.0: up to that hour I shd. be available here. On the 13th I am entirely free and you can come whenever it suits you. Also in the morning of the 14th. My phone number is above, so you may ring me when you arrive – and tell me what will suit you best. I am a bit doubtful how to guide you here from Maida Vale, which is a fairly large district. We are more conveniently served by buses than by trains. If you are near the Edgware Road, your best way, I think, would be Marble Arch and change there to the No. 30 bus which runs direct to Putney (about 35 minutes). I rather think there is a No. 16 bus down the Edgware Road which runs down Park Lane from the Marble Arch to Victoria. The No. 30 bus also goes down Park Lane; so if this arrangement suits you, you should ask the conductor of the 16 bus to put you off at the last stop in Park Lane where, without trouble, though perhaps at a different bus standard a few yards away, you would pick up the 30 bus to Putney. If you are able to take this 30 bus, you book to Putney Church. Putney Church is on the far side of Putney Bridge – don't muddle it up with Fulham Church, which you will pass on the

near side of the bridge as you start over it. Get off at the Putney Church stop (which is on the bridge, just before the church is reached) and cross the road to the other side (a dangerous road, so take care!). You will then see, if you look over the parapet of the bridge, a large building, quite close, down by the riverside. A cock crows on it for 'Courage' [the beer], and Star and Garter Hotel is also written on it. That is where James's portrait resides. Turn the corner of the bridge, walk along the Star and Garter on the road (not the river) side, *pass the Hotel entrance* and, further on, towards the end of the building, you will find a smaller door with 'Star & Garter Mansions' inscribed on it. You have then arrived and we are at the very top of the building.

If all this bus business doesn't suit, there is a Maida Vale underground station (can't remember exactly where) which wd. take you to Paddington. There you will be able to get another train to Putney Bridge Station direct. Putney Bridge Station is, unfortunately, on the Fulham side of the Bridge, so you wd. have to take another bus (No. 93 or 85) over the Bridge to Putney Church – or of course you could walk it. Over again, looking over the Bridge to the right, you wd. see the Star and Garter Hotel. I do hope all this is clearer than mud (see map, if you can call it that).

Jim has depressed me with his book on England – a Japanese publication – called, I think, *England Now*. A sillier book I have seldom read. There is much to be said against the western world as viewed from the East – but *not* in the way he says it. I like him to be silly, but not as silly as that. I'm afraid he may injure himself, even with the Japanese. Yours sincerely, JOE ACKERLEY

There is something very touching and indeed comical in those detailed and almost neurotically precise directions which take up nearly four small pages of Basildon Bond. Joe is a bit on the defensive, as he has not yet met Rena and Roger, but it was surely unnecessary to go into such minute details for a couple of intelligent adults. Yet there is a lot of Joe's fundamental niceness in the trouble he is taking with a couple of strangers who are coming to rob him of his last relic of darling Jim – the Maurice Feild portrait in oils that had been slowly kippering over his fireplace for the last fifteen years or so. I had asked Rena to send it to me in Japan: she took one look at it, and gave it to an art restorer friend who cleaned it within an inch of my life. After reaching Japan, it passed through several hands, and finished up with

Takeyoshi Yamaguchi, an old librarian friend from Japan Women's University. When he died, my assistant extracted it from among his belongings in Tokyo, and brought it to Kyoto, where it has lain in a cupboard for five years: I do not have the courage to unwrap it and look at it.

As for the little book, *England, Now* (1965), on which Joe pours his uncritical scorn, he forgets that this, like all my other textbooks, was specially commissioned for Japanese students and teachers, and was not intended for British intellectuals and sophisticates. I had to write it in a very simple style, with a reduced vocabulary – an excellent exercise for any writer, by the way – and I had to catch and keep the interest of readers with the world's shortest attention span right from the start. So the book presents a continually surprising and unconventional view of Britain, and the Japanese, accustomed to the usual dry-as-dust official handouts from the British Council, the British Tourist Board, the Conservative Party Headquarters and other stodgy institutions, were at first shocked (shocks always delight them) and then captivated by the kind of frankness and personal quirkiness they would never dare display in their own writings about either Japan or Britain or America. The book was a big success, and a long-time best-seller, going through innumerable editions, and it is still being used in schools and universities. It must have sold millions of copies, and made my name more familiar to the Japanese than any other modern English author, for it reached an audience totally bored by Graham Greene and Somerset Maugham and the monstrous regiment of British women novelists. It is only one of about a hundred of similar books I have written for the Japanese over the years, nearly all of them best-sellers or 'long-sellers' reprinted every few years. I remember Joe wrote me a letter about the book, deploring my essay on 'James Bond's Britain', in which I described my wartime encounter with Ian Fleming. He was not Joe's kind of author, of course; nor was he mine, for I find his work trivial, but because his hero was so familiar to the Japanese through movies and translations of the novels, it was an obvious theme for my presentation of my native land.

Joe's next letter to 'Mrs Clayphan', as he was still calling her, is dated 6 April 1965: apparently she and Roger had still not arrived. As always, enthusiastic Rena had replied to Joe by return of post, and had written in her usual exuberant style:

Dear Mrs Clayphan

I'm glad you mentioned the rush hour; it begins at 5.30 pm and is to be avoided if possible, the out-going traffic on Putney Bridge, over which you will have to pass, is practically at a standstill between 5.30 and 7.0. The drive back into London presents no difficulty. Start out to us at about 3.0 if you can, it will give me time to have the little afternoon nap that retired old gents get used to.

I'm glad you criticize dear Jim, but does he listen? He seems to me sometimes to have a deaf ear for criticism, and certainly to have no sense of self-criticism. His travel books, which contain excellent things, are always badly in need of the blue pencil, but he cannot apply it and doesn't like anyone else to apply it. I have *Japan Marine* and liked it. I'm not in favour of him doing more autobiography. Autobiography does need other people besides self, and he doesn't seem to me very interested in other people. More and more does he become self-absorbed and self-defensive, and I am worried by it. But I confess that I haven't read his other two autobiographical books; I tried the childhood one but got bored; I thought it indeed a fantasy, like so much else in his life. *These Horned Islands* and *Tropic Temper* are good books, which could have been better if he had a little more self-discipline; that sort of book, and poetry, are, I think, his métier; that he should look out, not in, is my notion. *England Now* was looking in (to his own prejudices) not out. I can't see what possible help a prolonged stay in England could be to him. Is it good for any of us to live in our own private hells?

Yours sincerely, JOE ACKERLEY

There are some fascinating things in this letter. It seems Rena and Roger were going to come to London by car to pick up the rather heavily framed painting, and were anxious to avoid the rush-hour, about which Joe again gives them detailed instructions, though he does not advise them where to park – always a problem in Putney.

What Joe says about my work is justified when considering my work at that date. But Joe was not a poet, despite some promising early attempts. Naturally, like any other writer, and like Joe himself, I am self-absorbed. It is true that I am not very interested in people, but I do try to take an interest in a few chosen ones, which I think is all one can really expect of one person. I do not like humanity *en masse*, especially in Japan; but I like to look for the individual face in the crowd, and often find one I like, even if only in passing. I like to preserve my privacy, but I am not what Americans like to call 'a very private person'. I am no hermit or recluse, as some people imagine – a view sedulously pushed by the British Council in Japan when approached by foreigners wanting to meet me. In this regard, one of my favourite poems is Walt Whitman's 'Out of the Rolling Ocean the Crowd', with these great lines:

> Out of the rolling ocean the crowd came a drop gently to me,
> Whispering, *I love you, before long I die,*
> *I have travel'd a long way, merely to look on you, to touch you,*
> *For I could not die till I once look'd on you,*
> *For I fear'd I might otherwise lose you.* . . .

That can hardly be called looking in rather than looking out – whatever Joe means by those rather vague words.

I find it necessary to look inwards as well as outwards, like every other writer and artist. Joe is quite right about the diffuseness of my writing: I am incapable of cutting my own work, though not of self-criticism. I think my love of discursive, erratic and sometimes almost random writing derives from my studies of oriental literature, from forms like *zuihitsu* (stray notes) or the wandering, journal-style alternations of poetry and prose (*haibun*) of the *haiku* poets; or simply from my own preference for disorganization, an illogical taking of chances. It depends on what one expects from literature. Joe, with his obsessive neatness, well exemplified in these first two letters to Rena, had what might be called the anal-retentive view of writing, whereas I was all for letting everything go as and where it pleased, in my life as well as in my work.

At the same time, I can detect a note of sour grapes in poor old Joe's comments: his own flow had dried up, though it could hardly be called a 'flow' – more like the rabbit-pellets of diverticulosis, a painful stool.

Obviously Rena had been encouraging him to speak out. Here is the next letter, dated 20 April 1965, after Rena's first visit:

Dear Rena,

I can't say 'Dear Rena' unless you say 'Dear Joe'; friendship must keep a balance. How clever we are at concealing our feelings. I had no idea you were feeling nervous. I'm glad it wore off and you enjoyed your visit too. I have had no word from Jim and don't deserve one, not yet having answered his last letter, but it is on my mind and will doubtless get done in time. His *Peace News* write-up (I suppose you got it) did not please me: Mr. Jebb [*sic*], if that was his name. It is all right to say Jim is a neglected poet, but not to take pot-shots at less neglected ones. It seems an article more likely to stiffen the front against him – if there is a front, which I doubt – than to win his enemies – if there are any enemies – over. However, disinclined for honesty, I doubt if I shall say any of that when I write. One doesn't want to shoot any more arrows into poor St. Sebastian, even though, in art, he never seems to mind them much. Sweet of you to ask me to Gainsborough; if a chance should occur I will let you know. I have no plans at present for Nottingham, and think I may spend Whitsun in Brighton. I am thankful I was not spending Easter here. We have huddled here in front of our gas fire. So glad the Egypt book isn't indigestible. Nancy joins me in sending all good wishes.

Joe

Joe is nearer the mark here, when he talks about the unfortunate essay on me written by a certain Barry Tebb (*not* 'Jebb'). Barry Tebb was someone claiming to be a poet who wrote me fan letters and to whom in my usual way I replied whenever he wrote, which seemed too often. I never met him. Later, he collected my letters and books and sold them without asking my permission, at a handsome profit. He must have been hard up, and the letters were of no significance anyhow. But he turned out to be a sneak, and when he invited himself to Rena's for the weekend she was horrified by his behaviour. So much for looking out instead of in.

Joe's next letter to Rena is dated 5 May 1965, and already shows signs of weariness at her relentless epistolary attack:

Dear Rena,

I'm sorry to be so late in answering you; as Jim may have told you I am a rather erratic correspondent, inclined to put off till tomorrow what ought to be done today; also a lot of not very welcome things have fallen into my plate, such as numerous visits to the offices of various newspapers and other publications to trace and copy out the reviews of a book I published nine years ago (perhaps stupidly I never keep cuttings) and which is now to be published in America this year. The American publisher wants English critical opinions (which were mostly favorable) to put on the jacket. It is a little smelly book about my dog, *My Dog Tulip*, easily the best dog book ever written, but it failed here and I expect will fail in America too. I haven't written to Jim yet either; I made a start, which is easy enough, like birth; it is getting to the end that is so difficult. So when you write to him again tell him that I *have* started a letter and will finish it one day if I live long enough. I don't know how you will get over your dilemma with Barry Tebb. Perhaps he should be advised to read Jim's books more attentively. I don't of course know how much reliance one should place upon what writers tell us about themselves, but is not Jim always saying now that he prefers his own company to that of anyone else? It is not a strong enticement to visit him, so I wonder if Mr Tebb is wise to want to go. My friend E.M. Forster is seriously ill and I am waiting on telephone calls, so will write no more. How tiresome the weather is. I hope your back has left off being that.

Nancy is well and joins me in affectionate good wishes.

Joe

That Barry Tebb was contemplating coming to visit me in Japan was certainly news to me. Perhaps he was trying to get money for the trip – or for the supposed trip – out of Roger and Rena. I would not have put it past him to extort the money and then not use it to the ends for which he claimed it was intended.

It was indeed true that I increasingly preferred my own company to that of tiresome intruders, just as Joe preferred the company of an Alsatian bitch to that of his friends. I had a few close friends in Japan, and did not have time to bother with any more. But Joe seems to forget his own preference for animals over human beings, and I was by no means rejecting the human race as he did, or claimed he wanted to do. Increasingly Joe's letters to Rena show weariness and disorientation, and betray a sense of hopelessness and approaching disintegration. The next is dated 22 June 1965:

Dear Rena

I suppose out of sight *must* be out of mind, for I lost your last letter and have not come across it yet. However here is a new one, and it seems to be getting an answer, which is far from common in this flat. Can I sustain it to the end? Time

Dear me, three days have passed and whatever Time was going to do in the above par., it is short now for I am just off to Cambridge for my weekly two days. Yes, I woke up to Jim's claims at last and have had a masterpiece of exuberance in reply. He really is worth tapping that rubbery tree for its generous fluids. I must do so again. I have been very busy at my typewriter, cleaning up an old ms. so that my literary executor, just appointed, won't have too ghastly a time in the present muddle of this flat, which I aim to tidy up generally in case the dark angel should be concocting my draught. Better not to be taken unawares, if one can help it, and whilst tidying up old Forster in Cambridge I may as well do the same to myself. Also there is a pleasantly savage satisfaction to be found from tearing up the rubbishy past. I'm glad you keep your end up with such wonderful energy and enterprise; the forward look, I have it not – the fewest possible hours of consciousness are my own ambition. Your post-operational treatment must be horrid, worse than the operation itself; I hope you will soon be back to normal. I didn't understand the last two verses of your Coffee Party poem – Tupperware and 'burping' kids. Perhaps I live too much out of the world. But I'm glad Michael Bullock liked it. I am in the train, which says 'You shall write no more.'

Love from
Joe

Trying perhaps to disengage himself from so relentless correspondence, Joe did not write again that year until 10 August. Rena had had a mastectomy, but we (Joe and I) were both amazed at her resilience. This letter is confined to one small page, and concerns the POW bones I had discovered in the temple at Ikoma:

Dear Rena

I don't like the sound of that at all and can't imagine how I could be of any use, for I know absolutely no one connected with the press. Even if Jim had discovered a new play by Shakespeare or that Hitler was living in Osaka disguised as a geisha, I should not know how to proceed, and don't see any paper giving headline news to anything without investigation. However, I shall be hereabouts all through August and shall welcome you if you come.

Love
Joe

But only nine days later, Joe was replying again to torrential Rena, in a rather longer (three-page) letter dated 19 August:

Dear Rena

How tiresome is old age with its decaying faculties: up to almost the last moment of your departure I was telling myself not to inform Nancy of the lovely present of eggs you had brought her. In the last moments memory failed. She is delighted, as am I. We have just unpacked them. Heavens, the hen who laid the largest, should it not have a medal – or a medical examination? May its exertions to please not have incurred a fissure or a fistula in ano? It seems incredible that any hen could lay so large an egg without some sort of rupture. Is it your hen? I assumed it was, and feel quite worried. Do thank the creature, and try to find out if it has over-exerted itself. If a nursing-home should be necessary I wd. gladly pay.

It was delightful of you to bring your Roger. I hope – and believe – he liked us as much as we liked him. Wd. that the sun had beamed upon us. So happy a party deserved it. Bring him and yourself again when you can. And get rid of that limp, it won't do.

I changed my mind and have written to Kirkup myself. *Two* letters from me within a week! Can you imagine? No you can't. But I so deeply dislike his 'scoop' that I must stiffen myself up to say so. I will have no hand in it at all, and can't imagine why he should want to stir up trouble, to the monk, the temple; and the Japanese generally wd. certainly suffer. Roger was perfectly right in thinking it was squalid to try to make cash out of such things. I will give him a little money for some poems if he will send them. I have said all that.

Bless you, take care of yourself, and love to you both.

Joe

I no longer remember what exactly this 'scoop' was that I was hoping to bring off. I must have been in low water and in need of money if I was wanting to make cash by selling an exclusive newspaper story that was bound to create a sensation. But now, from a distance in time, it all seems another of Forster's ugly little 'muddles'. Did Joe ever offer me money for some poems? I do not think so. In any case, I should have refused to accept it when I knew he, too, was having a struggle financially. However, Joe's next letter to Rena makes it clear that he was alluding to the poems for *The Listener* during his temporary caretakership. It is dated 3 September 1965:

Dear Rena

thanks for letter. I've taken two of Jim's poems, from his *Japan Marine*, will re-examine the rest and the ones you sent later. Do you happen to remember what the prize he won was called: was it Japanese PEN Club? And have you any idea what he would like done about the fees for his poems when they get published? Cheques to Japan? I forgot to ask him this. I am glad to have got some of his poems into an English publication; he will feel less persecuted, I hope.

I have had 3 days in *The Listener* office and am worn out. The secretary – such as she was – is on holiday, I am now quite on my own amid a mountain of books and a mountain of finicky detail – anyway it has undergone many changes during my seven years of retirement.

I hope you didn't have in Egham today the weather we had – are having – here. It has been a proper wash-out.

Love to you and Roger

Joe

It is noticeable how Joe now always referred to Roger, and one gets the impression that he had found Rena's husband very attractive – as who would not have? – and that he was putting up with Rena for the sake of another possible sight of Roger. Joe sometimes accepted the company of certain women because they had attractive husbands or boy-friends: but he was genuinely fond of Rena, too, as Nancy was.

This was Joe's penultimate letter to Rena. The last one, dated 10 July 1966, is the one with which I started this series of letters. It will be interesting to see Joe's entries for this period in his diary, if ever the sequel to *My Sister and Myself* is published, for that extraordinary book goes only as far as July 1957. The penultimate entry reads:

Upon the concrete verandah the bars of my cage are cast, cast by the sun as it sinks below the balustrades. How pretty the pattern they make, the bars of my cage. They lie beside me, bars of shadow, bars of brightness, on the concrete ground, they lie upon my body as I sit in my deck chair and upon the body of my dog beside me. We are within our cage together, the cage we have chosen, as happy as it is possible to be with death drawing closer.

We had been friends, off and on, for about twenty years before Joe Ackerley suddenly asked me, *à propos de bottes*, 'Can you describe me in a single word?' Apparently he had been asking this question of several close friends, as if in a desperate last search for an identity, and none had given what Joe considered to be a satisfactory answer or a worthy reply. Morgan Forster had answered: 'Kind to be cruel'. Jack Sprott: 'Alienated'. William Plomer with typical ready wit applied to Joe something he had said about me: 'A mixed-up Id'. And Georges Duthuit: '*Un joli laid* – which does *not* mean a jolly lay.'

I am no good at repartee and hate snap judgements. But on this occasion I brought forth, without effort, the word that had always entered my mind when thinking about Joe: 'Baffled'. At least it had the merit of being only one word, as Joe had stipulated.

He obviously did not like my view of him. There was no reaction from him. I was expecting his familiar convulsive giggle, with its jerking shoulders, but there was only stony silence. I considered trying to retrieve my *faux pas*, which had apparently hit uncomfortably home, with frivolity – 'A penis too frequent', one of my old jokes – but thought better of it. My poor old friend seemed in no mood for jokes. We both sank into silence so prolonged, as the sun sank over the Thames and cast the shadows of the balustrades over the veranda, that Queenie, lying beside us, became uneasy, and I had the brilliant idea of asking *her* Joe's tiresome question. Her answer was a sharp, high bark ending in a growl and the snarl Joe tried to interpret as a smile. On hearing this comment from our dumb friend, both Joe and I fell into helpless laughter, in which Queenie joined with ecstatic barkings and tail-waggings. 'You wicked old girl,' Joe cried, fondling her tits and her vulva, 'you're the only one who made an intelligible answer.'

Don Bachardy's portrait of Joe on the cover of *My Sister and Myself* only hints at what I saw as bafflement – with himself and with others. At times he appeared to be searching his mind in vain for an explanation of himself or of something I had said. Indeed, the Bachardy portrait is a rather gloomy, unflattering sketch, in which only the position of the right hand holding a cigarette, knuckles out, in arthritic fingers, is really characteristic. Joe looks properly down-in-the-mouth, as does poor Nancy relegated to the back of the jacket (she should have been on the front, with Joe on the back) in the companion picture, a gruesome Darby and Joan, a Philemon and Baucis without the visitation of Jupiter. I could have wished for a more lively aspect of them both: Nancy with her lovely, dazzled, sweetly-silly, uncomprehending smile, Joe with shaking shoulders and displaying all his tombstone teeth in an infectious titter at one of his own self-deflating quips. Joe had arranged for me to be 'done' by Bachardy, who was in England on a visit with his companion Christopher Isherwood, but when I saw what he had made of Joe and Nancy, I declined the honour and the invitation, much to Joe's annoyance. He wanted a portrait of me to replace the one by Maurice Feild that had been spirited away from him by Rena and Roger.

As I browsed through the compulsively readable selection (almost too tactfully edited by Francis King, who has the unenviable task of being Joe's literary executor), that word 'baffled' returned to my mind again and again as I followed Joe in his attempts to thrash out for himself the nature of his relationship with his 'harem' – sister Nancy, old Aunt Bunny and the monstrous bitch that dominated all their lives, the glamorous, demanding, everlastingly jealous, nasty, neurotic Alsatian to which I gave my pet name for Forster, Morgan le Fay.

But as I read these sad and comic diary entries, another word surfaces from my never very deep subconscious – 'bamboozled'. Poor dear Joe's agonizings were all so unnecessary. It was a supreme irony that he, the worshipper of the male, had to confine himself for most of his life with females. He had perhaps through some masochistic spirit of self-denial let himself be as thoroughly bamboozled by his witchlike womenfolk as any working-class het by the female members of his family. They form a suburban family group that is a mixture of Ivy Compton-Burnett and a Giles cartoon, with Joe as the elderly, incompetent husband, Aunt Bunny as Grandma, Nancy as a nagging wife, and Queenie as a demanding adolescent daughter. Forster appears as a tut-tutting provincial uncle, and myself as the 'butterfly of Bayswater' or 'the Firbank of Fowler Street' which I once tried so hard to be, unfortunately with some success.

At the heart of this book is Joe's anguished relationship with his sister Nancy, which verged on the platonic-incestuous. I remember once cruelly teasing Joe, when we had both had too much Gordon's gin, by saying: 'Why don't you just throw her on the floor and give her a good fuck? She'd never bother you again.' I shall never forget the appalled and 'baffled' look in Joe's steely blue gaze when I suggested that vulgar remedy, which I at once regretted having made. 'But Jim darling, I'd never be able to get it up!' he finally said. 'That would be the whole point of the exercise,' I saw the pair of them as other couples I had read about: Eugénie and Maurice de Guérin, Kleist and his lesbian sister,

Walser (Robert) and his sister Lisa, Nietzsche and his own horrid
female sibling. I replied.

I think a lot of Joe's agonizing over this delightful but, as he often
said, 'not very bright' woman – elegant, shrewd in an appealing child-
like way, but far from helpless – was the result of old-fashioned Cambridge or Bloomsburian worritings over 'the importance of human
relationships', which are worthwhile only if one refuses to see them so.
In Joe's pact with his sister we see something of the chronic alcoholic
and his co-alcoholic, intent on poisoning one another to death. We can
also plainly see the superficial imposition of conventional heterosexual
standards of bourgeois married life on what should have been a homosexual or bisexual freedom from all ties. After all, what is the point of
homosexuality if one tries to impose middle-class heterosexual conven-
tions of 'our home', 'our dog' and other symbols of married 'normality'
upon it? One is homosexual or bisexual in order to escape all the dreary
family commitment, and to enjoy the freedom of endless loneliness
under the everlasting spell of one's own company, one's own thoughts,
one's own conversation with oneself. *Vivre? les serviteurs feront cela pour
nous* (Living? The servants will do that for us), in the immortal words of
Philippe-Auguste Villiers de l'Isle-Adam. My own version of that is:
'Living? Let the working classes do that for us!' As I am myself working
class, I feel entitled to adopt it.

This essential freedom of the homosexual is something I tried again
and again to explain to Joe, but he always responded with that baffled
gape, his thin lips slightly open in shock, blue eyes cold and hard with
fright behind the cheap horn-rims. 'One cannot serve both God and
maman,' I told him – my poet's credo. Then I would sing 'Bewitched,
Bothered and Bewildered' to him, with a wealth of inappropriate
gesture that made Joe choke with laughter. When he came to stay with
me in Sendai, I had a recording of the song for him, sung by my
favourite canary, Anita O'Day. We once heard it being played in a
downtown bar, and with a sudden smile he turned to me and said:
'Listen, Jim, they're playing *our* tune.' 'You mean *your* tune,' I retorted.
Poor Joe, so worried about me and irritated with me at various times in
my extravagant career, sighed and said: 'Yes, I'm afraid you're right.
Nothing ever bewitches, bothers or bewilders flighty, fickle, frivolous,
feather-pated Jim.' 'Flatterer!' I cried, as he jotted down his phrase –
which he seemed to find rather good – on the back of a packet of 'Hope'
cigarettes.

In the Joe-Nancy relationship I recognized some of the familiar problems I had with my own darling but over-possessive mother, who tried to cling to her only child with subtle emotional blackmail, of a pathetic kind whose obviousness almost broke my heart. But break it did not. Certain curiously flat, vaguely discontented and disappointed and even disgruntled tones of voice in Nancy when trying in vain to extort some sexual or emotional tribute, or simply a few kind words, from Joe, sounded to me exactly the same as my mother's voice, deliberately devoid of interest, yet seething with unspoken jealousy and resentment, if I as much as mentioned a girl-friend's name. (She was slightly more indulgent towards my boy-friends, and even asked me to bring them home for tea and a night of bliss.) Joe's relationship with Nancy was like mine with my mother, only much worse, because I was able to treat my mother with compassionate dispassion, firmly but with love in spite of everything, and with sympathy for her ignorance and aberrations. I think I showed the same understanding and love to Nancy, who was only one of a number of highly emotional and mentally confused older women in whom I brought out the mothering instinct mixed with sheer predatory sexuality. (I was raped by an older woman – then by a man – at the tender age of three.)

One basic reason for Nancy's behaviour was jealousy of Joe's continued success, even into old age, with boys and men, while she, though still exquisitely beautiful, could no longer hope to capture the male admirers who once had swarmed around her charm, her fashionable elegance and the intoxicating sexuality that never quite left her. When we were alone together, she would recall those early triumphs in London, Paris and New York, and she would be transformed. It was a Nancy Joe never saw – a faded, sensitive beauty who could talk with graceful passion and gentle irony about her conquests, her fashion modelling and her lost youth. There was something elegiac about it, like *Twelfth Night*, from which I used to sing her the haunting songs about death and the loss of youth, love and beauty.

We were so often together, and so very close, that Joe sometimes became irritable and jealous and would accuse her of stealing all his friends – an absurd accusation, as most them were intellectuals interested only in boys, and were generally bored to death by what they considered Nancy's vapid chatter. In a 19 August entry, Joe wrote, with what one feels is only just-suppressed rage: 'I also said somewhere, "I do the best I can for you, old girl. I give you money, roof, and occupation. And all my friends. I can't do more than that. You must have patience and courage. That's all life is. You must wait for things to grow. You've already attached one of my friends, Jim, to yourself. . . ."'

Nancy had complained that she was not invited with Joe and me by Siegfried Sassoon to stay with him at Heytesbury House in Wiltshire, or by Jack Sprott to stay in Nottingham.

'And you can tell Jack from me,' she said, 'that he should have asked me too.'

I was quite shocked. 'I don't think I'll tell him that, old girl,' I said after a pause.

She then said: 'And Siegfried should have asked me too.'

I said: 'But he doesn't even know you.'

'He didn't know Jim but he asked him.'

'But he did know Jim in a sort of way. Jim had been in correspondence with him. Why on earth should he have asked you?'

'I'm your sister.'

'But he hates women,' I said. 'He's going through torments over his own woman already. He's a sort of hermit. He would never have had you in the house.'

She took no notice of this. 'Then you should have suggested taking me away for a holiday yourself. You never thought of this. You never think of me at all.'

These remarks quite shatter me. 'Never think of her at all'! – and I begin to shake inside and feel like saying, 'You bitch!'

That 'shaking inside' was one of the symptoms of Joe's rage, always terrible to behold. It once or twice terrified me. It was to lead to that near-fatal fall in his study after another of his squabbles with Nancy. Joe's use of the word 'bitch' is revealing. He sometimes used it in my presence when addressing Nancy, to my acute embarrassment. 'And yet,' he once told me, as Nancy fled weeping into the kitchen after he had used this word to her, 'it is an insult to the honourable name of bitch – isn't it, my old girl?' he cried, bending down to tickle Queenie's gaping vulva, and letting her lick his beaming face when she jumped up barking at this attention.

On 11 September 1949 Joe wrote:

Last night after dinner, Nancy said, 'Oh, I do miss Jim (Kirkup). Every time I think of him I have a pang. He was the only friend I had in this godforsaken place.'

The bitch! What does she mean by remarks like that? They are aggressive. Frustration and aggression. '*You're* no bloody good' is implied.

Sometimes, I half expected to hear that after the previous night's painful scenes, Joe had murdered Nancy.

It was an awkward triangular relationship for all three of us. I loved Joe, in a purely platonic way, but I was infatuated by Nancy. If Nancy showed me any special attention, like knitting me a muffler or baking me a cake, Joe had to pretend to be pleased, but I knew he was seething with jealousy and rage. On the other hand, if Joe took me somewhere for the weekend without Nancy, there were sulks and recriminations from her on our return — usually laden with presents for Nancy, but these were no substitute for our company. It got so bad that I gave up visiting them for long periods, and Joe would ring up asking me to go round from Werter Road, because 'Nancy misses you so, and so do I, darling Jim.' Even Queenie got into the act, giving my hands and ankles little nips and snarling at me if I got too close to Joe – 'Don't worry, Jim darling. She's only smiling – aren't you, you old goose?' He writes, again on 11 September 1949: 'Queenie not only menaces Nancy when she tries to enter my room, but, if she herself is outside when Nancy goes in, hurries in ahead of her, nipping her ankles on the way, to get in front of her and obstruct her progress. These jealous ladies!'

In his next entry, a few days later, Joe was to go so far as to compare Nancy with a tapeworm infesting his existence.

But I saw something else in Nancy, something Joe and his sophisti-cated friends could not possibly see, or refused to admit. It was one of the love affairs of my youth, and one that left no bitter after-taste of remorse and spite. Joe deeply resented Nancy's ability to attract a certain type of Firbankian young man, as I must regrettably confess to having been in my dissi-decadent way. (I am now the Cardinal Pirelli of boring old Kyoto-con-moto – *ma non troppo*. . . .)

I worshipped Joe, in a totally asexual way, for he did not attract me physically; but from the start I fell in love with Nancy. When I first met her at Joe's, I told her I was going to pronounce her name in the French fashion, as I felt 'Nancy' (or 'Nance' as Joe sometimes called her, to our disgust) was cutting a little too near the bone of my hyperaesthesia. For her part, Nancy was delighted and intrigued to hear herself named after that supremely elegant French town, and I believe that she took on a new personality when we were alone together and I pretended we were French. I looked forward to her sweet, soft, welcoming embraces and mothlike kisses much more than I did to those of the often rather bristly mouthed and gin-reeking Joe. Sometimes, I thought his long, narrow mouth gave him the look of an iguana or a monitor lizard.

Nancy and I soon discovered a common interest in vegetarian cookery, fashionable clothes, opera, hair-styles, scent and jewellery. She lent me her pearls, I gave her a set of 'antique' twenties marcasite clips, which put Joe in a huff, as all I had given him was a monocle with a black, watered-silk ribbon, very Nabokovian, which he never wore, though it suited him to perfection. Nancy knitted me pullovers and diaphanous, trailing, rainbow-tinted lambswool scarves *à la* Isadora Duncan – indeed a tough barrow-boy once nearly throttled me with one when I got too intimate. Nancy and I shared her make-up, because we both had the same colouring and fair complexion: I was always a dedicated *maquilleur*, like Pierre Loti and Ronald Firbank. When I found the complications of glove-knitting were too much for Nancy's dear little scatter-brain, I settled for a gorgeous Edwardian feathered muff she found for me in a Fulham antique shop. I have always advocated muffs for men. I think I must be the only British male to have gone through all the winters of the Second World War sporting a beaded fur muff, which William Plomer claimed must have once belonged to Queen Marie of Romania, and I was certainly the only one in the staid late forties to wear a twentyish brilliantly feathered muff in Fleet Street. Nancy also bought me a small pearl-handled revolver – a cigarette lighter in disguise – to put in the little silken pocket inside the muff, which was lined with turquoise 'ruched' brocade. (Those were the days when everybody smoked.) I shared my joints with Nancy, who did not notice the difference – nor did I, much, for poets are born 'high'.

When I later introduced Joe to marijuana, it merely increased his despondency and innate lethargy, though years later we grew hilarious on dexedrine tablets – such a pretty shocking pink – that I brought back from the pharmacies of Kuala Lumpur, where they were still on sale without prescription in the early sixties. In fact, Nancy seemed impervious to all artificial stimulants, though she could grow adorably, quietly tipsy on Joe's headily generous Gordon gin-and-tonics.

Right at the beginning of our friendship, when I had just gone to live in Werter Road, Putney (which I was amused to find in Margaret Drabble's fine biography of Arnold Bennett), I tried to persuade Joe, in despair over Nancy's attempted suicide, that electric-shock treatment was evil and totally wrong for her. There was even talk of the supreme horror of lobotomy, but I am glad to say I managed to talk him out of that disgusting practice. A diary entry describes one evening when Joe began to have doubts about the advisability of having Nancy, in hospital, undergo electric-shock and insulin-shock treatments which misguided doctors had advised. Joe went to see her in Worthing Hospital. He was in a state of intense self-hatred, and wrote, on 21 February 1949:

> I went to see her yesterday. I dreaded the visit. What should I find? Would she have hysterics at the sight of me? Would my visit bring about another collapse. Before going, on the Friday, I'd had a new crisis of nerves – something James Kirkup had told me, that the electrical treatment was a dreadful thing and a mistake. I ought never, I felt, have allowed it – these medical experiments. . . . I phoned Brodie (Nancy's doctor) and upset him I think. Could I take my sister away on Sunday when I came? He said it would be most unwise, that in any case she would not come. I did not perfectly comprehend her state, he said. I wanted to ask him to stop the treatment – convulsing this wretched, senseless body, this body that wanted no sense – but had not the courage for that.

Joe kept having attacks of panic and self-loathing, during which I would sit beside him, holding his hand, for he seemed on the verge of suicide himself at times. I told him one can best express one's contempt for existence by facing it, not by giving in to suicidal despairs and thus admitting the importance of life, and I think that saved him. Nevertheless I told him the truth as I knew it about such barbarous treatments of the human brain, for I had already known women, and men, who had received such treatments, and who for a while were in a wretched, quiet daze, but who gradually reverted to their old condition of near-lunacy, infinitely preferable to their zombied mind-blown silence.

But Nancy suffered those shocks again and again in what I indignantly told Joe was brute mental rape. For a while, she seemed calmer and almost carefree, but the effects soon wore off, and she became sad and querulous and interfering – and how Joe loathed interfering women! I have heard him lash out at poor old Aunt Bunny, a jolly ex-actress and opera singer of the Edwardian period, with a barmaid's music-hall voice and a saloon-bar laugh, for amiably fussing over the tea things or for pestering Joe with her theatrical reminiscences. We used to sing duets from *The Bohemian Girl*, one of my mother's favourites learned from my Irish grandfather – Balfe's enchanting melodies, of which the most famous is 'I Dreamt That I Dwelt in Marble Halls' – 'With vassals and serfs by my side. . . .' Bunny and I would act scenes from Shakespeare, which she had once known by heart. But her memory, at eighty, was failing, and when we did the balcony scene from *Romeo and Juliet* she could remember only Romeo's lines, so I had to be her Juliet, which I didn't mind at all, perched on Joe's kitchen table out on his veranda's extensive stage, and jeered at with delicious coarseness by the body-builders in the gym opposite.

It is wonderfully funny, in the diaries, to find Joe's many references to my past self, the self I am no longer, for I change every year almost with the seasons, especially in leap year. He mentions my comical 'persecution mania' – which, after all, in my cop-haunted days and nights had a basis in reality – and how I always seemed to encourage it, provoking attack by deliberately flouting the law, and arrest by smiling at any good-looking stranger. I liked to encourage abuse, criticism and ridicule by putting on the masks of other people's misguided, preconceived notions of the kind of person I was said to be. This thrill of self-inflicted punishment, a kind of intellectual masochism, from the hands and pens of total strangers is something I still relish, and something Joe could understand without bafflement, for he was also self-destructive, but without the wild, manic fund I derived from my self-abasement. I tried to explain it as being the result of an undying yearning for the unequivocal, brutal sexual assaults of the Tyneside rough trade, the tough Geordie corner-boys who were the heavenly torture of my delicate, sheltered and permanently lustful childhood.

I was convulsed with laughter at Joe's descriptions of my eccentric clothes: those white socks I affected and which so touched Morgan Forster when I crossed a tanned, slim ankle over a knee are now commonplace, but in those grim post-war days seemed outrageous. He writes about my long, pale-blond hair and what he calls my 'homosexual gait'. There was, however, nothing camp about this way of walking at a sort of smooth, rapid glide, like Lady Macbeth in a hurry to get home. It started off as an imitation of the unique level-headed *glissement*, almost catlike in its surreptitious stealth, of my youthful heroes the Geordie pit-laddies. They developed a curiously smooth way of walking when down the coal-mines in order to avoid bumping their heads against the low roofs of seams and galleries, and this gait became second nature to them, so that they brought it up into daylight with them. Even in his best suit, one could always recognize a Geordie pitman by his hynotically spellbinding glide, which of course made them such divine tango partners. I too cultivated this walk until it became a parody of slinking sexual provocation. Then I got tired of my pose and started my 'slimming stride' while I was in Malaysia (see *Tropic Temper*). But it had no effect, so I adopted a sort of Henry VIII venereal stumping. It was much too tiresome to keep up for long, so I now walk just like the hets, with as little effort as possible, which does perhaps produce an effect of mincing languor.

Towards the end of his life, Joe had the disconcerting habit of sitting on a low wall outside the Star and Garter Hotel and watching the approach of friends. One evening, he greeted me by saying 'You walk like a drunken sailor', which was understandable, as I had been on a long sea voyage from Yokohama by Dutch cargo boat. The crew was of mixed nationalities, but the officers and engineers were Dutch boys. I have always adored the Dutch, perhaps because of my own Friesian Viking ancestry, and they were perfect to me.

Joe had a novelist's keen eye for such physical details, and for the follies and foibles of his friends and enemies. I well remember our screams of laughter as we played one of Joe's favourite parlour games, imagining our most-hated persons 'at stool', in the act of defecation: our favourite victims were T.S. Eliot, C.P. Snow, Winston Churchill, Edith Sitwell and the Archbishop of Canterbury. What a pair of cads we felt ourselves to be, yet how we enjoyed it!

But we also used to describe our own defecations – 'Only a few Maltesers this morning, Jim dear, so light, like ping-pong balls, they refused to flush away.' 'Mine were like best butcher sausage.' In my hysteria, I would imitate Firbank: 'The Cardinal produced such a curious, whining, parsonical fart . . . like a fluty *pax vobiscum*.'

And we used to describe to each other our encounters and misadventures in those temples of trivia, public conveniences. Once on my return from Japan I was suffering from culture shock in London, and had a close run-in with the police in the vast subterranean gents in Waterloo Station. I was on this occasion performing my legitimate business, sitting in one of the cubicles, when someone next door started to push a mirror, about six inches square, under the considerable gap between the partition and the floor. What on earth can he want? I wondered, peering down into the glass and seeing a large red face reflected from next door. What was I supposed to do? I stared back. Then the mirror was hastily withdrawn, and I heard the person next door leave the cubicle without pulling the flush: he was informing someone outside that I had been 'trying to see into the next cubicle'. I thought I had better investigate this matter, so I hitched up my pants, unlocked my door and stepped outside, where a policeman had taken up his station, waiting for me to emerge. He gave me a suspicious look. I did not even bother to glance at the person who had been next door. At that moment I was on the verge of being arrested. But my quality was such, the copper just stood aside and let me pass without comment. I gave him *such* a look! – my special *mirada fuerte* had the effect of hypnotizing him into total immobility. This look is similar to that Andalusian heritage attributed to artists like Picasso and Dali, as well as to the poet Lorca, a gaze of such strong intensity that the eye could almost literally 'feel' the object or person looked at. John Richardson describes its power in his *A Life of Picasso*: 'For Picasso this demonic Andalusian birthright would be a lifelong source of anguish, also a lifelong source of power.' It is a natural force not peculiar to Andalusians, for I am sure Rimbaud must have had it, though in the photograph of him apparently sulking, by Carjat, he is trying to 'hood' it, much as orientals dim the blaze with the epicanthic fold, or by a *sanpaku* rolling-up of the eyeball. Delahaye writes of Rimbaud that he 'possessed a power, a lightning-flash rapidity of observation that allowed him to penetrate at once the state of mind of whatever individual he came in contact with'. I think this is the real meaning of Rimbaud's sonnet to his arsehole, 'le trou du cul'. The grasping eye. Many of the Romantics had this look, sometimes intimately associated with a thyroid condition – Novalis, Hölderlin, Keats, Shelley.

I was reminded of this curious lavatorial incident when reading Joe's diaries, for in the 28 July 1953 entry we find:

... I enjoy them (public lavatories) for other and more intellectual reasons. I like to see humanity demeaning and humbling itself. I like to think that in the shut-up shit-house boxes respectable people are behaving in a way of which they are slightly ashamed. At Waterloo Station for instance I am often fascinated by the sight of the lines and lines of cubicles all full with the shadows of shitters' coats hanging up against the glass panels from pegs, while some embarrassed young man, who is bursting for a shit, hurries self-consciously up and down the line, with his cricket bag in his hands, trying in vain to get in. Who are occupying all those shit-houses? I think to myself gleefully, and populate them, in my imagination, with all the people I most despise, the eminently respectable and blimpish, the black-coated high-ups, let us say, of the BBC.

Possibly Sir John Reith is shitting there, I think to myself, and Sir Basil Nicolls, and Sir Ian Jacob. I like to think of them all with their black-striped trousers down, sitting with their pale legs apart, having a GOOD SHIT, and I like this because I know that they would not like me to think of it.

Francis King in his Introduction to the diaries points out how two-faced Joe could be, like so many men who lead a double life, or multiple lives. Joe could be perfectly nice to me one moment, then go away and say or write something casually cruel about me – sometimes to Francis himself – or write perfectly libellous accounts of me in his letters and journals. I did not mind this, because I am indifferent to the opinions of others, but also because it was behind my back, not to my face. Yet it meant that I was often secretly frightened of Joe, though of course, as in my dealings with Queenie, whom I hated as well as feared, I never showed it.

I suppose that I am two-faced myself. It is an oriental trait, and I seem to be a born oriental. Because though I loathe and despise dogs, I was able to show affection to Queenie, and indeed I was the only one of Joe's friends she liked. Joe told me the secret of offering the back of my hand for her to sniff as soon as I entered the flat. The first time she licked my hand, I knew I was accepted, by both her and Joe, on a much higher level than had ever been the case before that epoch-making event. Joe also told me one offers the tips of one's fingers to cats, those infinitely more intelligent and subtle creatures.

But Joe lives on! His works, including his diaries, still reprinting, sell well, and he has been translated, most notably into French and Italian. I am always coming across him in continental bookshops. He appears in Aldo Busi's almost unreadable *Vita standard di un venditore provisorio di collant* (made even more unreadable in Raymond Rosenthal's inept English translation). We learn that a complete set of *The Listener* is to be found in the public library in Cremona. I forgive Busi his awful novels, because he translated Joe so well into Italian.

And the other day, going through some of my old friend David Paul's papers (entrusted to me by his wife Angela), I found several scribbles in Joe's unmistakable handwriting on galley proofs for *The Listener*. I was particularly glad to read at the head of David's novels review (20 October 1949): 'Dear Mr Paul, I do thank you for this. How excellent it is – as was, indeed, expected. First rate reviewing – the best I have ever had. Joe A.'

But David turned out to be too good, not for Joe, but for other voices on the editorial staff, and for certain established authors whose new books David dismissed with stinging scorn – always an unforgivable thing in British letters, where, as Joe repeatedly told me and David, 'Dog does not eat dog'. I remember some such author wrote an indignant letter to the editor, complaining about David's acerbic tone, and David struck back with an even more acerbic reply. I can't remember who the author was – no one of any importance, anyhow – but David did no more reviewing for Joe. Publishers, too, were very touchy about David's frankness and critical insights, which were often devastatingly original and witty. Joe never explained to me why he had dropped a reviewer he valued so much, but I sensed a curious uneasiness in him at the time. Intellectually and artistically, David stood head and shoulders above all the hack reviewers of the time, and above some of those whom Joe considered to be the best. The British do not like too much brilliance or too much versatility in their authors: they prefer a familiar humdrum amateurishness, couched in the ineffable tones of middle-class mediocrity. It was America that truly appreciated David, through his extraordinarily witty and perceptive essays in *The New Criterion*, and his translations of Valéry for the Bollingen Foundation. The British, as usual, have failed to spot a genius.

There is something miraculous in finding one's youth preserved in prose like this, in Joe's diaries. How my old self keeps coming back to me through Joe's words! I seem to become once more that outrageous yet abnormally shy and silent creature I was then, entirely without realizing that I could be seen to be outrageous in the eyes of others. I was always aware of being different and persecuted by often unknown forces, private detectives and *agents provocateurs* in Britain, and all through the period covered in Joe's diaries I had one narrow escape after another from the forces of law and order, preserved, I believe, by the angel of essential innocence that always guides and protects me.

I still experience that delicious terror today, if I venture to set foot in Thingland for a day or two, although now I am very careful not to put a foot wrong. All this, and much more, can be found in Joe's deftly written diaries. I cannot wait to read the complete, unexpurgated edition, and look forward to yelling with affectionate laughter at the absurd revelations and witty insinuations of exquisite maliciousness that are to be found in the later volumes. In a true sense, this is Joe's life work: it is one of his best achievements.

I feel sure he must be happy now, in some pagan, golden heaven of beautiful boys and manly young workmen, no longer baffled, bamboozled, bewitched, bothered or bewildered. Bless you always, dear Joe and darling Nancy!

Beyond the Pale
A Retrospective Epilogue

It was when I was in fourth year at my secondary school that I became aware of how different I was from the rest of my class-mates. Until then, though I was never popular, I did not realize how exceptional I was. Lest that sound vainglorious, let me say that I was indeed an exception in many ways. But being different never made me feel 'superior'.

For one thing, I was an only child, thin and pale, and never robust. I suffered from periodic bouts of asthma, a disease that somehow instils quietness and reserve. These qualities come, I think, from one's intense concentration when trying to breathe freely. One keeps absolutely still, in order not to disturb the chance of a fuller breath, to listen internally to the state of one's chest and lungs.

Because of my asthma, I was not good at games. Indeed, I was hopeless: I could not kick or throw a ball straight, or catch one. The rules of cricket and football baffled me. My uselessness and timidity made me shy.

As if all these impediments were not enough to estrange me from the raucous, bullying, sports-mad boys in my class, I loved reading. I read all kinds of books with an insatiable avidity. Poetry was my favourite. There was no one else I knew who could become so 'lost in a book' as I did. I did not expect others to understand this passion. That I was without friends did not bother me. I knew what friendship was through books, but I never expected to encounter it in real life.

In those days, boys were expected to be good at mathematics and science, girls to excel at English and domestic science. But these subjects were total mysteries to me, and the teachers grim and terrifying tyrants. They were all youngish men who played rugby and cricket for the local teams. I saw them as mindless lumps of muscle. When they punished my stupidity, they laid it on strong with the bamboo cane – six on one palm, six on the other – in their mistaken attempts to beat some understanding of their tiresome lessons into my dreamy brain.

What set me really apart from the rest of the boys was that I loved English composition. While the rest of the class groaned at the teacher's announcement of an essay assignment, I felt my heart beating wildly with joy, and I would race home in order to give myself up entirely to an evening's writing. This was the only subject at which I came top of the class until we started learning Latin and French, and then German and Greek. I revelled in those foreign tongues, and I could read them quite fluently long before any of the other boys. I especially enjoyed translation, and my first attempts at Latin verse absorbed and stimulated me so much that for whole hours I would forget my physical weakness, and even ignored attacks of asthma. I spent long hours in the public library reading English and foreign texts that were not on the syllabus, but I never dared admit this to our teachers, for fear of seeming even more unusual. So you see, I really was an outsider, though of course at that age I did not think of myself in those terms.

The end-of-term examinations were always a trial for me. They always brought on asthmatic attacks. I never properly prepared for those intellectual tests: I just hoped for the best, but all my reading stood me in no stead at all when I had to write on some dull 'set book' like *Rob Roy* or *A Tale of Two Cities* which I had just looked at and given up in disgust. At the age of fifteen I was already reading Waugh, Firbank, Wilde, Rupert Brooke, the Sitwells, Wyndham Lewis and the short stories of James Joyce – all authors considered too 'deep' for a fourth-form syllabus.

At examination times, the desks were moved out of the class-rooms and arranged in long rows down the school hall. In order to stop cribbing or cheating, one was placed next to a boy from a different year. On one occasion, I found myself placed next to a much older boy with whom I immediately, blindly, silently fell in love. He tried to engage me in conversation before the examination papers were handed out. But I was so stunned by this sudden access of adoration that I could not speak, could not even look at him. I know he thought me very strange. He kept laughing at his friends in other parts of the hall, pointing at me in a derisive way. But I did not care. Just to sit next to that boy was my first experience of unfulfilled passion, impossible love.

From time to time he would look at what I was writing on my paper, and as he was good at maths he would jog my elbow and point – when the invigilators were not looking – at some elementary mistake I had made. That he was trying to help me filled me with almost unbearable excitement. But I always ignored his hints. I could sense his virile presence so strongly beside me, sometimes I could hardly control my trembling pen. He used to look at me sideways in puzzlement as soon as he had finished his questions – he was always one of the first to finish. But I could never turn my head and look at him. I was afraid that my feelings would appear too openly on a face I never learnt to mask. And when the results of the exams came out, I was as usual not far from the bottom of the class.

In the three or four days following the examinations, we were allowed to do as we pleased while the teachers were marking our papers and adding up our marks. The other boys played cards or board games, or read cheap comics. I alone read books. This was somehow considered subversive. Those days of freedom from teaching and studying were sacred to idleness for the rest of my class. When they saw me 'working' or 'studying' at such times, my class-mates really let me know I was not one of them.

I remember that in the fourth year, after the summer term examinations, I welcomed these free days as precious hours for reading and writing. I had brought from the public library the letters of Rupert Brooke, with whose poems I was already familiar. I was familiar also with that medallion photographic study of his beautiful Grecian head with naked shoulders which was the frontispiece to his poems. I used to moon over it for hours.

I was almost at the bottom of the class, so I had a desk in the front row. During those free days, we were allowed to sit anywhere we liked. So boys would change their seats all the time, joining special friends in a game of cards or moving to a group building a model aeroplane. But I remained in my seat. I do not remember who shared my desk, but certainly he left me alone at it as I read and scribbled in my notebook, where I was writing my first poems under the influence of Swinburne, Roy Campbell and the Sitwells.

Lost as I was in a rapture of reading and writing, I was unaware of what was going on around me. The teachers left us pretty much to our own devices as they went to the staff-room for cups of tea and a smoke, or went round the school collecting the marks of various forms.

Gradually I became aware of a sort of suppressed hilarity. There was an unusual silence in the class-room. Without turning round, I could see, out of the corner of my eye, that all the other boys had moved as far away from me as possible, and had crowded together in the top two rows of desks, leaving at least three rows of empty desks between them and me.

My heart started beating madly. I had been placed beyond the pale. But that was the first time it had been done so deliberately, so cruelly. Now I knew I was not normal. I continued reading, sick at heart. I went on writing in my notebook with trembling hand. I turned pages of my book in a kind of daze, and I could not remember what I had been reading, but I did not turn back to read again those pages that had left no mark. My consciousness was totally occupied by the fact of my separation. I knew I should have to bear it. I somehow suspected all my life would be like this. It was agony. Yet all the while I kept feeling little surges of defiance, of pride, of secret joy. At last I had realized the sort of person I was, and would be all my life, and the prospect filled me with exaltation.